LONDON ART AND ARTISTS GUIDE

Heather Waddell

LONDON ART AND ARTISTS GUIDE

First edition published by ACME Housing Association 1979
Second edition published by Art Guide Publications 1981
Third edition published by Art Guide Publications Ltd 1983
Fourth edition published by Art Guide Publications Ltd 1986
Fifth edition published by Art Guide Publications/A&C Black 1989
Sixth edition published by London Art and Artists Guide 1993
Seventh edition published by London Art and Artists Guide 1997
Eighth edition published by London Art and Artists Guide 2000

Whilst every care has been taken to ensure accuracy throughout this book,
the publishers cannot accept responsibility for any errors that may appear.

BRITISH LIBRARY CATALOGUING IN PUBLICATION DATA
A CIP catalogue record for this book is available from the British Library
ISBN 0 9520004 2 3

Published by London Art and Artists Guide, London
Printed in Slovenia by Gorenjski Tisk
Designed by Waterman Design, Concord, Massachusetts USA

THE LONDON ART WORLD
1979-99

Prue O'Day with sculpture
by Mario Rossi, 1988

David Hockney at Hockney
Paints the stage, 1985

Paul Mattock with Map '96,
1996

To celebrate the 20th anniversary of the London Art and
Artists Guide. The London Art World 1979-99. 90 b/w
photographs by Heather Waddell of artists, dealers, critics,
galleries. studios taken over 20 years and published in the
London Art and Artists Guide and in newspapers, showing
the changing face of the London Contemporary art world.

Introduction by John Russell-Taylor (The Times art critic)

Publication: February 2000
Price: £9.95 UK
       $16.95 USA
       .... Scandinavia

CONTENTS

Please note the major London phone number changes from April 2000: 0171 becomes 020-7, 0181 becomes 020-8. Many mobile numbers change. 0800, 0500 and 0321 become 080, 0645 & 0345 (many travel nos eg BA) become 084, 0990 becomes 087, 0891, 0894, 0897, 0898, 0991 become 090. Contact BT for further details on Freefone.

The Millennium Dome, the Spiral, the Great Court, the ferris wheel, Tate Bankside; 2000 and beyond.

London will be the focus of positive world attention in the year 2000, as the Millennium Dome, the world's largest millennial celebration, opens. Although we read constantly about doom merchants moving to live in remote communities, to avoid the millennium bug, Armageddon and other dire prophecies, it is likely that 2000 will be a year like any other, where goodness prevails. It will however give us a historical perspective, making us aware of past millennia and what might take place in this one. Optimists will enjoy 2000, pessimists no doubt take an opportunity to criticise. Many British citizens in true party spirit will not miss an opportunity to have a party.

So much has been written in Britain about the Millennium Dome near Greenwich, but in other parts of the world it is seen as just one of many world events taking place in 2000. £758 million has been spent on the Dome, causing grumbles and complaints from a conservative British public, but no doubt if the 12 million visitors expected do materialise, the complaints will turn to a guarded enthusiasm, especially from younger people. The Dome is 320 metres and 50 metres high, an impressive Dome sail shape and focuses on the theme of time, containing multi-media and interactive exhibits on the environment, society, culture and future lifestyle.

There are thirteen key areas inside the Dome; the Body Zone includes a couple 170 feet high, with an exhibition centre inside one leg. The Spirit Level explores values, including Christianity and other religions. The Learning Curve focuses on learning as a life-long process, paired with Licensed to Skill, about finding hidden skills to match to a new world of work. Serious Play is an exploration of how leisure can reactivate your life and includes virtual reality 3D objects. The Living Island is a gigantic seaside lido where visitors can protect their day-to-day environment and has games, contests and rides for visitors to try out. Dreamscape a surreal exhibition, invites visitors to "dream, imagine and return refreshed." Atmosphere and Time to Talk are two other sections.

At the heart of the Dome a circular piazza has live performances, with 6 shows a day for 10,000 people at a time. There are also live shows in a concert space in a nearby dome. 20 shops and 30 retail outlets cater for the expected 12 million visitors and a mini hospital for any medical dramas. To reach the Dome, if lucky, the Jubilee Line may have reached the area, but if not, then boats are available from Blackfriars and Waterloo to Greenwich, British Rail to the nearest station and then a shuttle bus. The Dome's future from 2001 is yet to be decided. It could become part of a sports centre.

Apart from the Dome, London will be the focus in the international art world, as two major conferences are taking place for International Art Historians and International Art Critics, in September 2000. The new Tate gallery of Modern Art will hold many of the seminars and discussions, but London galleries and collections will be of major interest too. What they will all want to see is the thriving, dynamic London art world and meet the artists, visit the studios and see why London is a key contemporary and historical art centre. At the V&A museum, The Spiral by Polish-American architect Daniel Libeskind will be underway and completed in 2004. This magnificent geometrical spiral will take its place in world and museum architecture, alongside Frank Gehry's Bilbao Guggenheim, the I.M. Pei Pyramid at the Louvre and Jorn Utzon's Sydney Opera House. The Spiral will provide interactive gallery space, a multi-functional auditorium, a learning laboratory, a new main entrance lobby, an information café and also a new café on the top floor of the spiral, with magnificent views over London. Libeskind himself said, "It's going to be a completely amazing new space, a dramatic building, unlike anything else in the world."

Over at the British Museum the £97 million Great Court opens in autumn 2000. The British Museum was founded in 1753, as the earliest national museum in Britain. The Great Court now creates a national museum for the 21st Century. Now that the British Library, once based at the British Museum, has moved to its own magnificent new building at St Pancras, Sir Norman Foster the architect, has been able to rearrange the space left available. The Reading Room, which now houses the Annenberg information centre and the Paul Hamlyn public reference library, is now at the centre of the courtyard on the main level. The lower level of the Great Court has a Centre for Education and the Sainsbury African Galleries, which include works that were once in the old Museum of Mankind. The mezzanine ellipse floor now houses the Hotung Exhibition gallery and the upper ellipse floor a restaurant and bridge link to the main building and other untouched areas of the British Museum's collection. Once the new Great Court opens, the gallery hours are being extended

Computer-generated view of the Great Court, British Museum.

and a new heritage route will link St Pancras (British Library) with the British Museum in Bloomsbury.

London's riverside will see the geatest revitalisation in the early 21st century. The Millennium Mile on London's South Bank will focus attention on the riverfront between Westminster and London Bridge, covering some 30 projects. Starting at the area between Waterloo and the South Bank Centre the BA Millennium ferris wheel will be opposite the Houses of Parliament from early 2000 for five years. A 500-feet diameter wheel will carry visitors in 60 enclosed passenger capsules, offering spectacular half-hour rides with views as far as Kent and Windsor. The effect should be as dramatic as the Eiffel Tower was on Paris when it first opened. A May 27th-30th, 2000 River Thames pageant will highlight this area, with firework displays and riverside events.

Several new bridges across the Thames will include the Hungerford Bridge providing new footbridges on either side of the railway bridge from Charing Cross to the South Bank Centre. The Norman Foster Millennium Bridge will span the river between St Paul's Cathedral and Bankside, home of the new Tate Gallery of Modern Art and The Globe Theatre. On either side of the bridge there will be huge sculptures by Sir Anthony Caro, devised by Caro and Foster together. The effect should be dramatic, with impressive views from either side.

All along the riverwalk, Millennium Mile, visitors can pass the newly-created Jubilee Gardens, redesigned by Dutch architects West 8 (West 8 is the Dutch meteorological code for a gale warning), so expect something different! The National Theatre at South Bank is undergoing improvements and the Oxo Tower wharf is now a centre for contemporary applied arts and design, a thriving community of small creative outlets, also restaurants and cafés. Further along Gabriel's Wharf is a pleasant open-air shopping and restaurant area, free from traffic and cool in summer from the river breeze.

Further downriver between Blackfriars bridge (scene of the gruesome Italian banker Roberto Calvi's murder), and Southwark bridge, is the area known as Bankside. In the 21st century Bankside becomes a major new arts area in London, when the new Tate Gallery of Modern Art opens in May 2000. Tate Bankside will be not only a major British museum, but a world arts centre. Swiss architects Herzog and de Meuron have successfully created a modern art gallery out of what was originally a Power station,designed by Sir Giles Gilbert Scott.

The Tate Gallery of Modern Art takes over where the National Gallery of Modern Art leaves off at the end of the 19th century. The Tate Bankside becomes the National Gallery of Modern Art

Deatho Knocko 1982, Gilbert and George (Janet Woolfson de Botton gift), Tate Gallery of Modern Art.

starting at the 20th century and is recognised as one of the world's most important 20th century international art collections. Key 20th century movements cover Surrealism, Abstract Expressionism, Pop Art, Minimal and Conceptual art can all be seen here, as well as the Janet Woolfson de Botton collection.Contemporary British artists will be seen both here and at the newly named Tate Gallery of British Art at Millbank. The Turner Prize, in November annually, the most prestigious British contemporary art prize, will still be held at Millbank, as it is British art. Tate Bankside focuses on international 20th century fine art but also architecture design, film and decorative arts in certain displays. The new galleries are organised chronologically in three large suites of galleries, but there are also large and small-scale special, temporary exhibitions. Major loan exhibitions of work by a single artist, or major touring "blockbuster" exhibitions from the USA and Europe will now be able to come to Britain, as the Tate Bankside now has a separate series of galleries for such events. The effect will be much like the opening of the Musée d'Orsay, once a station,in Paris.

The new Bankside area already includes the magnificent Shakespearean Globe Theatre, which holds regular performances of all his plays and has a café, shop, restaurant and exhibition space in the basement. Obviously as Bankside expands, the Tate will be like a magnet for new art galleries and art-related shops. At present galleries include Bankside in Hopton Street, Purdy & Hicks, Tom Blau Gallery, Marcus Campbell Art Books in Holland Street and the nearby new Jerwood Space. The recent Jerwood Foundation opened this beautiful 3-gallery space, with 5 rehearsal rooms for theatre and dance groups and an outside sculpture space, also Café 171, in 1998. The £30,000 Jerwood Painting Prize is held here annually, with an exhibition of shortlisted artists and the Jerwood Foundation has funded many other prizes for fashion, crafts, design and literature as well as individual galleries in museums. The ICA (Institute of Contemporary Arts) is planning to move to Bankside from its current home in the Mall SW1. Hopefully Bankside will not become a commercial mess, like the area near the Centre Pompidou, Beaubourg, in Paris. Artists such as Gillian Wearing (Turner prizewinner '97) already live in the Bankside area, but like other local artists, she is wary of too much gentrification, with fashionable shops and restaurants already moving in before 2000. Whatever happens to Bankside, it is a welcome breath of fresh air to the London arts scene for a new century, a new millennium.

Paintings from the Jerwood Prize at Jerwood Space, SE1.

Dome visitor centre and information: 0181 (020-8 from mid 2000) 305 3456. Internet: www.mx2000.co.uk.

The V&A Museum spiral: 0171 (020-7 from mid 2000) 938 8441.

The British Museum Great Court: 0171 (020-7 from mid 2000) 636 1555.

The British Library, St Pancras. 0171 (020-7 from mid 2000) 412 7332. Internet: www.bl.uk.

Tate Gallery of Modern Art, Bankside SE1. 0171 (020-7 from mid 2000) 887 8000 (central Tate no. This may change for Bankside)

Jerwood Space, SE1. 0171 (020-7 from mid 2000) 654 0171. www.jerwoodspace.co.uk.

Marcus Campbell Art Books, 43 Holland St, SE1. 0171 (020-7 from mid 2000) 261 0111.

Bankside galleries, Bankside, Purdy & Hicks, Tom Blau (see Contemporary galleries section).

Introduction

It will be interesting to see if the Millennium is a cut-off point for current art trends in the international mainstream, or whether the boom in YBAs (Young British Artists) continues. Certainly Anthony d'Offay Galleries may well continue to flourish and expand, as they did in 97/98 with contemporary artists, 1980s painters and 20th century masters. Past employees have moved on to set up their own galleries, learning from Anthony d'Offay's successful example. Similarly at Waddington Galleries past employees have learned from Leslie Waddington's vast experience in art dealing and coping with the recession.

Richard Green, in the Old Masters and Impressionist market,with three flourishing galleries in the Bond Street area, made £44 million in sales in 96/97 and Simon Dickinson, also in this market, £35.3 million, compared to Anthony d'Offay's profits of £16.7 million, but figures in the run up to 2000 will show if the successful contemporary art dealers could ever match Old Masters sales?

Battles over droit de suite (tax on the resale of art, which gives a royalty to the artist for up to 70 years after death), have threatened the UK art market. The European Union tried to harmonise this area to make it payable in advance by the vendor, on paintings worth £800 or more! The main beneficiaries are the heirs of Picasso and Matisse, who will continue to benefit into the mid 21st century. Many British artists will welcome this change as a recent Arts Council survey found that 37% of artists earn less than £5000 a year. Droit de suite does not exist in New York, consequently making it attractive to vendors to sell there instead of London. 5% VAT is also to be imposed on art sent into the European Union for sale, starting in June '99, creating a Eurotax, which is disastrous for London or any other European city. The UK art market represents £2.2 billion, which makes it clear how great the damage could be! These were the melodramas of pre-millennium London and hotly debated at Parliament.

While researching briefly for a Channel 4 arts series in '99, I discovered that in the gap between the 7th and 8th editions of this guide, that some 90 new contemporary art galleries had opened in London, with about 20 closing and several merging. In 2000 it is the 20th anniversary of this guide, which started as a humble little book of 60 pages in late1979, selling at £1.50. I worked then at ACME Gallery and Housing Association for artists in Covent Garden, alongside David Panton, Jonathan Harvey, Richard Layzell, Roger Kite, Sarah Greengrass and Richard Deacon, administering the International Visual Artists Exchange Programme, setting up branches in Europe, Canada America, Australia and New Zealand. At that time ACME Gallery was the avant garde gallery in London, showing Helen Chadwick, John Bellany, Bert Irvin, Gary Wragg, Jill and Bruce Lacey and various performance artists such as Stuart Brisley. In the early '80s galleries started such as Hester van Royen (now a director at Waddington's), Barry Barker (now a Lisson gallery director), Anthony Stokes, Robert Self and most were in the lively Covent Garden area (pre commercial hype). None of these galleries exist now, except the Paton gallery, which survived Covent Garden and moved next to Flowers East in the east end, but Marlborough, Waddingtons, d'Offay, Gimpel Fils, Annely Juda and Mayor still do and continue to flourish.

Turner prize shortlisted artist '91, Fiona Rae, Tate Gallery Millbank.

With the boom in house buying by a young generation of new house buyers in the 80s Thatcher era, more people wanted to buy original art and more art critics and arts writers started to write about the burgeoning art scene in London, and new papers such as the Independent (founded late 80s) and The European (founded1990) gave visual arts and photography more coverage. At that time there were 15 contemporary art galleries in the Portobello Road area, now there are three. The Times, Guardian, Telegraph and Observer followed their example of extensive arts coverage, shortly afterwards. At that time I wrote on art freelance for The Independent ('88-'89), The Glasgow Herald (London art critic '80-'84), as staff on The European (Arts Events editor, covering 40 European cities '89-'91), as London correspondent for Vie des Arts ('79-'89), as well as a 7-page feature on the thriving London art scene, (when Neo-Expressionist figurative painting was all the rage), for Artnews USA, also reviews for European and British art magazines such as Artline. Everyone in America and Europe wanted to know about the Scottish painters such as Peter Howson, Steven Campbell, Adrian Wiszniewski, Ken Currie and English painters Ken Kiff, Henry Kondracki, Graham Crowley, Jonathan Waller, Christopher Le Brun, Eileen Cooper and others, part of the Neo Expressionist euphoria in the '80s; started in Italy with paintings by Clemente, Chia and Cucchi, fêted as the International Transavantgarde and which then spread to the rest of Europe and America.

In the '90s, in particular in the last five years, contemporary art reviews news and features began to appear almost daily, after the arrival of Damien Hirst, Tracey Emin and the YBAs and advertising dream stories, such as the black sheep episode at the Serpentine gallery and subsequent hilarious court case. Reporters began to write about art, with scant information, but obviously loved roaming into new territory. Art became fashionable, as Hirst made rock videos with Britpop friends and rock musicians bought contemporary art. "Cool Britannia" as fêted by Newsweek (USA), and Le Monde (Paris), brought renewed euphoric interest in London, much as there had been in the '60s. At the same time more and more contemporary galleries opened all over London, fired by the press interest. When Charles Saatchi appeared at a contemporary art gallery, it would set off a buying spree from others, just as sighting Bob and Sue Summers, the American art collectors of British contemporary art, would do the same in the Portobello Road area in the '80s. When Saatchi sold off 10% of his art collection in 1998 the art world waited with bated breath. A Lucian Freud painting sold for

£2 million, making the reclusive British painter a major international late 20th century artist, after shows in America and London. In 1999 Charles Saatchi donated 100 works by 64 artists to the Arts Council collection; mostly YBAs such as Abigail Lane, Claude Heath, Kerry Stewart and Melanie Manchot, the photographer. The Saatchi influence is here to stay.

Where do we go from here one wonders? Will the bubble burst or will London continue to rise as a world art centre, with the new Tate Gallery of Modern Art and Bankside arts area expanding? Certainly the London art world is much more

Stephen Friedman with sculpture by Vong Phaophanit, at his gallery.

international than it was 20 years ago and the opportunities for artists to exhibit and reach a wider public are far greater now than ever before. Sometimes though, the hype of young artists is ridiculous, choosing to ignore some exceptionally talented mid-career and older artists. Perhaps it is time for galleries to stop being so obsessive with young and "new faces" and redis-cover work by some of the more mature artists, who had the misfortune to be in their twenties in the 1950s-70s, when there were fewer commercial galleries and arts sponsorship was minuscule compared to 2000.

In the last few years and in future, Hoxton, Bankside and Spitalfields will continue to attract galleries, artists and certainly recently these districts have more of an art buzz and atmosphere than in Cork Street. Artists studios still predominate in the east end, where rents are lower and studio groups have multiplied, making access to them through events such as the Whitechapel Open (every two years 2000/2002) possible for the general art buying public. The Windmill street party for Rebecca Hossack, Curwen, New Academy and other Fitzrovia galleries in September and the annual November weekend for Cork Street galleries, both encourage new art buyers to congregate on a welcoming open-gallery basis. The London Art Fair in January made £6.5 million worth of sales for galleries exhibiting in '98 and much more in '99, showing just how much art buying for contemporary art has increased. Similarly the 20th Century Art Fair in September and the Art on Paper Fair in February annually have seen huge increases in revenue.

Corporate sponsorship has increased enormously in the last ten years and organisations such as Hambros, Bank of Scotland, Flemings, Crédit Suisse, Bank of England, all collect art for corporate collections, which are then exhibited in their offices for employees to enjoy. Sponsorship is vital to many exhibitions and the main museum and gallery shows that we enjoy in London at the Royal Academy, Tate, National and V&A, to name a few, would not be possible without large financial sponsorship. The sponsorship works both ways, as many new collectors are employees from these companies, who become interested in contemporary art and start buying as they realise what a pleasure it can be following an artist's career; without the sponsorship we would be deprived in London of some of the major shows in recent years such as Cézanne (Tate '95), Jackson Pollock (Tate '99), Art in Africa ('95), Monet in the 20th century (RA '99), William Morris and American Photography (V&A '96 and '97), Picasso's photographs (Barbican '99) and many more. Comparing London with Paris we are extremely fortunate to have such a wide range of major exhibitions from overseas, whereas Paris has the chance to see major shows by the great French artists such as Cézanne, Matisse, Corot and Manet. Many of the major shows tour internationally, or if you miss them in one city, you can follow them to Paris, New York, Washington DC, London or Amsterdam. Sometimes London misses out, as in the case of the major Matisse show, but the new Bankside Tate building from 2000 will enable very large shows to come to London in the 21st century and beyond, such as Picasso-Matisse in 2002.

The year 2000 will be a busy one for the art world in London. Not only will the Tate gallery open its new Tate Gallery of Modern Art Bankside, the British Museum Great Court will soon open and not long after the V&A Museum Daniel Libeskind futuristic spiral, but there will also be international congresses for both the International Association of Art Critics and the International Association of Art Historians. London will be welcoming key art critics, art dealers, art historians and artists from across the world. It seems that London will continue to be the centre of the contemporary art world in 2000, as the rest of Europe still suffers from internal nationalist problems and America suffers from financial problems, Presidential scandal and government cutbacks. Although there have been many changes in the London art world, somehow London seems to have a very solid base to survive ups and downs, for which we should be grateful. The creation of the National lottery has also brought untold wealth, allowing money to be allocated towards new buildings such as The Great Court and the Spiral. There is much to be thankful for in Britain.

I have included a new article about the Dome, spiral, Great Court and Tate Bankside at the beginning, as the year 2000 is such a historical and monumental turning point in history, for the world as well as the art world. There are also interviews with artists Christopher Le Brun and Charlotte Verity, art dealer Guy Beddington, Lars Nittve the Tate Gallery of Modern Art Director and photography dealer Helena Kovac, of Focus gallery. Feedback showed that they were helpful to readers. I have tried to vary the people interviewed to offer different experiences of the London art world. I have always loved London and hope that this book helps you, the reader, enjoy the city too. There is always something new to discover, or someone new to meet in this endlessly fascinating, civilised and yet dynamic buzzing city. City life is not always easy, but somehow Londoners' enthusiasm for life is infectious.

As it is the 20th anniversary of this guide I would like to thank

Madeleine Strindberg, winner of the '98 Jerwood painting prize.

my family in Scotland; my mother most of all, who helped through some horrendous experiences, Bill and Brenda Martin and the rest of the Martins on the Black Isle, my aunt Fiona Buchanan, my cousins Jane, Charles, Oliver, Suzannah and Kate Royds at West end Farm in Surrey, my sister Sheila and all my closest friends and their children, in and around London. Thank you everyone for putting up with all the hair-raising snakes and ladders in my life. I was obviously not meant to lead a quiet life! Maybe the 21st century will be more peaceful and stable. It has certainly not been dull for me!

Heather Waddell

London Art Galleries

Contemporary Art

Cork Street is still an important contemporary art area in London, but has seen changes in the last five years. Additions in recent years include most recently **Robert Sandelson, Helly Nahmad, Asprey Jacques** and earlier **Art First**, **Entwistle** and **Alan Cristea** (who took over Waddington Graphics). **Boukamel** gallery brings international artists from France, Germany and Italy to a British public. Art First has some excellent

Allen Jones in front of Back Flip, Chelsea Harbour.

colourful, figurative artists, such as Barbara Rae. Theo Waddington has taken over one of his brother Leslie's galleries. **Waddington Galleries'** stable of artists has not changed dramatically, but has the exceptional painter Fiona Rae and personally I enjoy Mimmo Paladino's work. Other Cork Street galleries include the **Piccadilly Gallery**, a very English gallery, **Victoria Miro** a very avant-garde, **Browse and Derby**, **Redfern**, **Mayor**, **Stoppenbach** and **Delestre**, **Mercury** and the **Atrium Arts bookshop**. **Bernard Jacobson's gallery** is in Clifford Street, also **Asprey Jacques**.

The Benjamin Rhodes and Gillian Jason partnership ended in 1999, and **Gillian Jason** is now based in N.1 and **Benjamin Rhodes** opens a new gallery in Autumn 1999. **Stephen Friedman**, in Old Burlington Street shows work by lively contemporary conceptual and Minimal artists, such as Vong Phaophanit, who was shortlisted for the Turner Prize, also Kerry Stewart.

Old Bond Street and New Bond Street

At the Green Park end in Albemarle street **Marlborough Galleries**, one of London's established and international galleries with branches in New York, Tokyo and Madrid has exhibitions of note, with artists such as Bill Jacklin, Christopher Le Brun, Stephen Conroy, Paula Rego, Sarah Raphael and work from the estate of Barbara Hepworth. **Agnew's** is another established family-run business with historical and contemporary art on show.

Sotheby's auction house is in Bond Street and dominates the galleries in the area. Auctions are held daily and pictures and objets d'art can be viewed daily, before the auction. Sales at Sotheby's are often a barometer for the fluctuating art market. When Saatchi sells part of his contemporary art collection the rest of the contemporary art world waits with bated breath. How he must laugh!

Bruton Street, an offshoot from Bond Street, has several galleries showing historical work, such as the well-known **Lefevre gallery** where French artists predominate. **Berkeley Square Gallery** shows contemporary paintings and prints. The **Gimpel Fils Gallery** is in Davies Street and the Gimpel family has been dealing in art for centuries. Recent exhibitions have included the colourful abstract Bert Irvin and Alan Davie shows. At the top end of Bond street, nearer to Oxford Street, is Dering Street, where the **Anthony d'Offay galleries** hold court. Three gallery spaces show works by international established names such as Warhol, Kiefer, Baselitz and Clemente and young British artists such as Rachel Whiteread. This is an important gallery for anyone at all interested in international mainstream contemporary art developments, rather than local trends. **Annely Juda** is in the same cul-de-sac in a magnificent light, airy space and **Anthony Reynolds gallery** for avant-garde conceptual work and installation.

Chelsea

Chelsea used to be the artist area in London in the 17th-19th centuries and still houses the odd famous, more successful artist. The **Chelsea Arts Club** on Old Church Street continues to provide a meeting place for artists, actors, lawyers and media people interested in the arts. It makes a marked contrast to the Dover Street W.1. Arts club, where businessmen predominate and there is not a bohemian in sight! There has been a recent scandal at the latter with paintings disappearing and

Waddington Galleries, Cork Street.

reappearing at auction. Most of today's artists live in the east end rather than Chelsea, which is now one of London's wealthiest areas.

Green and Stone of Chelsea sell a good selection of artists' materials, art magazines and frames. Artists often work in the shop, giving it a friendly atmosphere.

East end and the City

In contrast with Chelsea, the East end is a changing area with the Docklands developments bringing newspapers, once based in Fleet Street, to Canary Wharf. Wapping was for a time an area full of artists' studios and still has some, but only for successful artists, also design and photography studios; designers can afford to pay the spiralling rents. Docklands development still helps artists to show work in the area, which livens up another concrete business area with City banks and their conventionally -dressed employees. The Docklands light railway feels on occasions like a train to Futureworld! The riverside wine bars and restaurants are pleasant though on a hot summer's evening.

The Whitechapel Gallery dominates the east end art scene with well-lit galleries and international shows. The Whitechapel Open, every two years (last one '98) allows the public to see work by east end professional artists, of whom there are many thousands. Studios and galleries throughout the east end are open in a well-publicised opportunity to see what is going on in the east end art scene. **Flowers East** is the contemporary art venue of note in the commercial east end art scene and Matthew and Angela Flowers have brought interesting new artists to the fore, as well as providing shows such as the annual Abstract art exhibitions every summer. **The Paton Gallery** is in the Flowers East complex at 282 Richmond Road, run by the effervescent Graham Paton.

Interim Art in Beck Road is run by Maureen Paley, a dynamic American, who helps artists show work that is not perhaps so viable financially. She is well-respected internationally. **Matt's gallery**, **Chisenhale Art**, **Lamont Gallery**, **The Showroom**, are all East end galleries worth mentioning. Time Out weekly and The Independent and The Times on Tuesday list current shows there.

The City

Francis Graham-Dixon has moved to N.16., but exhibits at Art '99 and the 20th Century Art Fair at the RCA annually. The **Barbican Arts Centre** in Silk Street in the City has a variety of art venues. The level 3 galleries have major photographic and painting shows and the Concourse gallery is often used by artists' groups such as the London Group and Printmakers or by galleries wishing to reach a wider public. The other areas at the Barbican have craft and art shows, often smaller or more intimate. The fountains and lake outside the centre are attractive and peaceful after the City pollution and noise and the cafés and restaurants at the centre provide a welcome breathing space for visitors.

Knightsbridge and Belgravia

Motcomb Street is another area with many galleries, tucked behind Knightsbridge shops. On Brompton Road the **Crane Kalman** gallery is run by the Kalman family, showing 20th century British artists and contemporary artists Jenny Franklin and Jonathan Huxley. Robert Sandelson has moved to Cork Street, but J**ames Colman Fine Art** is now at **Montpelier Sandelson**.

Portobello / Notting Hill Gate

At one point in the late '80s this area was throbbing with contemporary art galleries, but most have now closed, except **East West gallery** which thrives and shows work by British and international artists from Argentina and Eastern Europe. The **Special Photographers Company** on Kensington Park Road has also survived, but they also act as photographers' agents. Catherine Turner and Chris Kewbank are both aware of international photography trends and exhibitions reflect this insight.

Westbourne Grove, towards Queensway, has now become another small art area. **England & Co** has been there for some time and Jane England's Art Boxes show has become legendary every summer. She tends to show artists from the '50s and '60s as well as some contemporary art. Jenny Todd's **Todd Gallery**, on Needham Road shows avant-garde contemporary artists.

Charlotte Street/Bloomsbury

On Windmill Street the **Rebecca Hossack** gallery shows lively work by British and Australian Aboriginal artists. As Rebecca is now the Australian Cultural Attaché, the gallery has been left in the hands of a competent manager. **Curwen gallery** also has paintings on show nearby. The Windmill street art party is a good opportunity to see work by many artists at all the local galleries.

Rest of London

It is impossible to cover all of London, but some areas that do fall into categories are St James's, where many galleries specialise in Old Master paintings and antiques. Christies auction

David Solomon and Jill Morgan of East West Gallery.

house is in this area, in King street. Fischer Fine art has gone but Mathiesen Fine Art, Spink & Son, Bourne Fine Art and Whitford Fine Art remain. It makes an interesting comparison to look at works that in their day were seen as avant-garde, but are now established Old Masters. The **White Cube Gallery**, where Damien Hirst the "enfant terrible" of the '90s art world, shows, is also in St James's. Jay Jopling also shows Tracey Emin, Sam Taylor-Wood and other YBAs shown at the RA "Sensation" exhibition in '97.

In Covent Garden the **Photographers Gallery** is in Great Newport Street with several galleries for contemporary and historical photos and an excellent photography bookshop and print room with advice for buying photographs.

Further out of the centre of London the **Camden Arts Centre** near Hampstead has regular exhibitions and travelling major contemporary shows. In Hampstead itself the **Locus gallery** on Heath street shows sculpture, **Gallery K** work by Greek origin artists and **Duncan Miller Fine Art** paintings by established Scottish artists.

The **Saatchi collection** in Boundary Road, NW8, a private museum of contemporary art, but open to the public, covers the Saatchi collection of Minimal art, neo-expressionism, Pop art and New Neurotic Realism. Recent exhibitions have included all the latest British and American conceptual and Minimal art "hot" artists. Damien Hirst is one of many Saatchi protégés. The **Boundary gallery** run by Agi Katz has a fine collection of works by Jewish artists such as Jacob Kramer, Josef Herman and many younger contemporary non-Jewish artists.

There are many new galleries — 51 in the last year to be precise — (90 since the last edition) such as **Lotta Hammer**, **Wigmore Fine Art**, **Peter Gwyther**, **Emily Tsingou**, **507**, **Hackelbury** and **Focus** (both photography galleries), **Lothbury gallery**, **Robert Prime**, **Rocket**, **London Projects**, **Robert Sandelson** and many others. Hoxton and Spitalfields have both attracted new galleries, alongside lively bars and restaurants. Many dealers are also choosing to deal from home such as Prue O'Day, Danielle Arnaud, Jibby Beane, Mary Jane Alderen (Nylon) and others.

The full adresses of all the galleries mentioned above are listed alphabetically under the appropriate sections. Art maps are at the front and back of the guide. Enjoy the rich variety of art that London has to offer!

Heather Waddell

Interview with Lars Nittve, Director of the Tate Gallery of Modern Art, Bankside

HW: You have been involved with three major museums in Scandinavia; Director of the Louisiana Museum, near Copenhagen, '95-'98, founding director of the Rooseum Center for Contemporary Art in Malmö, '90-'95, senior curator at the Moderna Museet, Stockholm, '86-'89, as well as being senior art critic at Svenska Dagbladet and writing for Artforum. How different is your current position as Director of the Tate Gallery of Modern Art from previous positions?

LN: The main difference is to do with the scale of the project and the fact that it is a new museum in a major world capital. Another aspect of Tate Bankside is that it is one of four Tate Galleries (St Ives, Liverpool, Bankside and Millbank) and so we are a new museum under an old name, as part of the Tate Galleries.

HW: What do you see as the Tate Bankside's most important contribution to international art in the early 21st century?

LN: We are Britain's first major Museum of Modern Art; that in itself is an important thing. It's a new and different version of a MOMA, reflecting the fact that it is opening in the 21st century. Tate Gallery of Modern Art will alter how we see early 20th century art and see it in a contemporary perspective, to try to mirror contemporary art in a historical light. We have no hierarchy between contemporary and historical works and we also try to have a contemporary Gallery of Modern Art perspective on everything.

HW: Have you taken most of the major decisions about the organisation of the collection at Bankside or is this done with a team of advisors together? How much say do the curators have?

LN: We have already taken most of the decisions but will continue the work over the summer. It's led by the curators; Iwona Blazwick (Head of Exhibitions and Display) and Programme Curator Frances Morris. It is done in collaboration with curators of the existing Tate at Millbank. All four Tates will share resources (finances and personnel) and assets (the collection). We collaborate between curators at all four galleries.

HW: Do you think that the interaction with the local Southwark

Lars Nittve, Director of the Tate Gallery of Modern Art at Bankside.

community is important? Have you met many of the local people yet?

LN: Yes, I've met some locals. We have already started a series of events with the community at Southwark and Southwark Council is investing a lot of time and money in northern Southwark. I think that the interaction is extremely important and one of the keys to success for the gallery. I am aware that we are a public gallery and here for the public as well as the art. It is not enough to just sit and wait; we have to tell the community that we are here and here for them. If we need to break down barriers,we should try to do that. Bankside Browser, a new local open exhibition for amateur and professional artists is being held at the nearby St Christopher's House on Zoar Street in April and May '99 for the first time. For a year we have had pre-opening programmes with schools and local organisations, including "The Wedding Project" at Borough Market, which Anna Best conceived with Tate Bankside. One local couple even allowed their actual wedding to be part of the project. We have also had film projections onto the building in autumn '98 and '99.

It's important that we don't repeat the Centre Pompidou, Beaubourg, experience in Paris. What I would like is that if you arrive as a visitor, you should feel that this is a British and local experience, local to this particular area. George Cochrane works with the community as Bankside Development Officer. He seems to know everyone in Southwark and is a key figure to this local development. After the Millennium Bridge to St Paul's and the City is completed in mid April 2000, we will have two communities on our doorstep, Southwark and also the City; two completely different areas.

HW: Which 20th century and contemporary artists interest you the most?

LN: That is almost impossible to answer; it changes every week. Artists' bodies of work that really interest me are ones that challenge me and make me curious, that stimulate me. Art is about being challenged and not just accepting prejudices.

HW: Do you collect art yourself and if so, by which artists?

LN: I do own art pieces and mainly by artists that are friends and that I have worked with. Some are international and others are Scandinavian. I have worked a lot with non-Scandinavian artists and the works reflect that.

HW: Since you arrived in London last year,what have you particularly enjoyed about the contemporary art scene here?

LN: I know it fairly well. Copenhagen is much smaller and so I enjoy London's wealth of galleries and museums. In particular I really enjoy the vibrant new, young scene in Hoxton and East London and developing art areas.

HW: How does the contemporary art scene in London differ from Scandinavia? Do you find people here very ignorant about Scandinavian contemporary and 20th century artists?

LN: The London art scene is very different to Scandinavia, which is very diverse, covering the five main cities of Stockholm, Copenhagen, Oslo and Helsinki. They all have different histories. The scale is also totally different as in London the commercial art scene, the number of art schools, students and artists is much larger. It is very competitive here. Los Angeles is perhaps comparable, with some good art schools, but London is unique.

Yes, people are ignorant about Scandinavian art here, but Scandinavians are also ignorant about British art, except for Francis Bacon, David Hockney, Richard Hamilton and a few more.

HW: What are you looking forward to once the Tate Bankside opens in May 2000?

LN: I'm looking forward to seeing how the public makes use of the building, the museum and to see how it works, what needs changing if necessary and to see how it works with the local community.

HW: How do you think that Tate Bankside will compare with the other great international Modern Art museums?

LN: One of the main things is the building. It will be a memorable experience for visitors, but also the best base for the international collection. The qualities of the space and the architecture will make it unique. It is a great architectural scheme and has been a wonderful project from the beginning. It is natural to compare Tate Bankside to New York and Paris. There are already future projects that we will work on together. Major blockbuster exhibitons can now come to London. **Picasso-Matisse** is starting here in **2002** and will then move to Paris and New York. This gives an idea of the level we are working on, but I would also like to see the Tate Bankside compared with Kunsthalles in Basel and Zurich also, as we can work on a smaller scale too.

HW: Is there anything else about Tate Bankside that you think might interest readers.

LN: It might be interesting to know that the decision to start the project was taken after a Gallup poll in '93, asking artists what type of space they had most enjoyed their experience of art in. Top of the list was converted industrial buildings, then came historical Beaux Arts buildings with skylights and bottom of the list was newly-designed museums of modern art. This gave a good idea of what we should look for to create and rethink the idea of the Tate Gallery of 20th century international art. We are also fortunate that Herzog and de Meuron is one of the finest architectural practices in the world and has made a fine conversion of the old power station. Tate Bankside will encourage diversity and hopes to reach several audiences on several levels. We don't want a distinction between historical and contemporary. We want to expand the field in terms of technique and acknowledge that some artists work between media. Architecture, design, photography, film, video and live art will all be shown beside painting and sculpture in many instances and in appropriate displays.

Christopher Le Brun in his studio.

Interview
with Artist, Christopher Le Brun

HW: Can you fill me in briefly about the art schools that you studied at?

CLeB: I went to the Slade straight from school and then to Chelsea for my postgraduate degree.

HW: How did you first start showing your painting at Nigel Greenwood's gallery? How long did you show there and was it a happy relationship?

CLeB: Nigel Greenwood saw my work at the John Moores in Liverpool in 1978 where I had won a prize. He took a painting to his gallery, which he sold almost immediately. I showed there until 1992. It was a very good relationship: he has a good eye and was brave enough to be critical, which for a young artist experiencing success for the first time is invaluable.

HW: From Nigel Greenwood you progressed to showing at Marlborough Fine Art. How did that occur? How does the relationship work, as one of their stable of artists and how often do you show in London and abroad?

CLeB: Nigel Greenwood closed in 1992 and I moved to Marlborough then. Since the early 1980s I had been showing with several galleries, notably Laage Salomon in Paris (in fact my first one-man show of painting) and Sperone Westwater in New York, where I had as many shows as in London. There is one exhibition about every three years now in London, but more abroad in between.

HW: Historically, which artists have interested you and why?

CLeB: The grandest of the grand of course. The English and the French Romantics and The Venetians. I think a natural predisposition to certain atmospheres or colour-space harmonies will find wonderful things across the whole field of painting. I have always been able to enjoy both historical and recent painting equally. As you can see I'm reluctant to name particular artists — the beauties of the Masters are self-evident and as you progress in experience one is bound to seek out the rarer corners of Art to improve one's eye.

HW: Your work, which was greatly celebrated internationally from the 1980s onwards, has developed in a very confident way, the colours more vibrant. The recent paintings seem to radiate confidence and happiness.Is this correct or do you still feel that you are searching and developing new themes and ideas tentatively?

CLeB: I am always searching and trying to realise new themes; confidence is never unthinking, it is always attended by self-criticism, but I don't think that I would use the word "tentative".

HW: Who are your favourite authors, musicians and what other non-artist influences are important to you?

CLeB: I read very widely — literature, history, poetry and philosophy. I hope you'll excuse me again not giving a list, but it's true that in music classical music of the 20th century has been particularly important in helping my thinkng about painting.

HW: Recently you seem to have turned more to sculpture and printmaking as well as painting. Has this always been the case or do you find sculpture more appropriate at times?

CLeB: I have been making prints for about ten years now and it has become an essential part of my work. I enjoy the collaboration with the printers, the chance to travel and work away from the studio and the fresh discoveries I can make. Many of my ideas originate from printntmaking. Recently I've taken the same approach with sculpture with, I hope, similar results.

HW: What plans do you have for the future? Are there any particular shows planned internationally for the next century, say in Japan, Australia or America?

CLeB: I'm collaborating on a book on my work written by Bryan Robertson, to be published by Booth-Clibborn Editions in Autumn 1999. There are also shows planned for Paris, Milan and Siena.

HW: You were elected RA a few years ago. What are the benefits of this and what do you think that you can contribute to the Royal Academy?

CLeB: The Academy is an extraordinary independent institution, where artists from different generations can meet.

Recent members include Tony Cragg, Richard Deacon and David Mach. It's in another period of rapid change and increase in influence, that will see it having a much more central role for the good of painting and sculpture in our time. I'd be happy to contribute in any way that I can.

Christopher Le Brun's work can be seen at Marlborough Fine Art, 6 Albemarle Street, London W.1. Telephone 0171 (020-7 from 4/2000) 629 5161. A book on his work by Bryan Robertson, published by Booth-Clibborn Editions is planned.

Guy Beddington, art dealer.

Interview
with Art Dealer, Guy Beddington

HW: How long have you been selling 19th century and early 20th century paintings? How did you start as an art dealer, what was your background in art?

GB: I have always had a love of art, as members of my family have for generations been artists, collectors or dealers. I studied History of Art at University and, in 1982, tired of working in Life and Pensions, I began to scour the auction rooms and galleries for stock for my first exhibition.

HW: What were the first paintings and drawings that you sold and to whom?

GB: Although I was already enthralled by the Mediterranean region, my first, and a number of subsequent exhibitions comprised an eclectic mix of traditional 19th century, mostly British, landscapes, marines, wild life, sporting and a small number of figurative works. The first purchasers were, in equal part, collectors, young couples keen to decorate their homes and dealers, who saw value in my initial pricing system!

HW: Is there a specific kind of painting or artist that interests you?

GB: It is worth stressing that a mediocre work by a famous artist will always merit a mediocre price. Primarily we look for images, often unsigned and unattributable, mostly Mediterranean in subject or inspiration, which are either fluently painted or topo-graphically well-drawn within the unforgiving medium of water-colour, or, in terms of later oils or pastels ones that contain passion and skill in their form or execution. 100 years ago, a relatively small number of artists earned their living on the Côte d'Azur, selling their paintings directly from their studios, to the English visitors of the time. They are keenly sought after as also are, of course, the more important works by the Impressionists and the Post-Impressionists and Fauves, who were drawn from the sombre North of France to this region by the almost unimagined drama to be made of pured rugged landscapes.

HW: In the summer you used to exhibit and sell paintings in the south of France there as a family most of the year. What kind of people do you sell to? Are they mainly French or European or Brits living abroad?

GB: We exhibit at a number of different venues down here and sell to all of these. English School works sometimes go to French buyers and French pictures, bought in the UK, are often sold back to English clients. Visiting Americans form a significant part of our clientele.

HW: Was it difficult establishing yourself in both London and in the south of France? Obviously it is an enjoyable lifestyle selling in both, but is it easier selling in London or in France?

GB: As a sole trader, to be in two places at once requires an exceptional wife and compliant colleagues in the trade. London was and is a very large pond brimming with fish, sometimes spoiled for choice, whereas in the South of France interested people are prepared to travel great distances to view an exhibition, or attend a concert. Business is conducted in a rather more relaxed fashion down here; I cannot say however that it is necessarily any easier than elsewhere.

HW: Which artists are particularly popular and why?

GB: I have great respect for the natives of Provence, and for the pride they hold in their heritage, so, if one must choose I would go for the short-lived but brilliant lawyer-turned-artist Paul Guigou; for the Roux family of marine watercolourists in Marseille and for relevant works by Cross, Montézin and Valtat, whose prices are rising sharply. Those apart, it goes almost without saying that attractive works by any artist, that are relevant to a certain area, will always find buyers, the more so as that region becomes progressively defaced by urbanisation and tourism.

HW: Do you ever exhibit at Art Fairs and if so which ones? I think that you used to exhibit at the World of Watercolours and Drawings, or the 20th Century Art Fair? Did you find Art Fairs useful?

GB: Yes, at the World of Watercolours and, inter alia, Yacht shows. Like Olympia and Grosvenor House, such Fairs are important proving grounds for your stock and, beyond the sales that are necessary to cover the high costs of exhibiting there, these Fairs provide excellent contacts with potential future clients.The Internet cannot,as yet,replace the personal contact that they offer.

Guy Beddington Fine Art is at 55 Ladbroke Road, London W11. Telephone 0171 (020-7 from 4/2000) 229 4913. In France at Le Mas du Murier, Quartier les Etangs, Route de Seillans, 83830 Bargemon,Var.Telephone/Fax (From the UK 0033) 4 94 76 72 80.

Charlotte Verity in her studio.

Interview
with Artist, Charlotte Verity

HW: Where did you grow up and what was your childhood like? Were there any artists in your family?

CV: In England. I was brought up in the country. My father being in the RAF meant that we travelled too, including two and a half years in Cyprus and Turkey. My father was an amateur artist and we used to paint together on our summer holidays.

HW: You were a student at the Slade and very obviously influenced by some of your tutors. Would you agree and if so which tutors had the greatest influence?

CV: I was at the Slade between '73-'77. Initially we were given tutors at random and I had Noel Foster who was helpful throughout, but after a while the life studios seemed very quiet and appealing and consequently Patrick George and Euan Uglow became important influences. Visits from artists were very stimulating; Bernard Cohen, Lucien Freud, Michael Andrews, Prunella Clough were just a few. I feel privileged to have been there while Professor William Coldstream ran the school and was lucky enough that Lawrence Gowing was giving regular art history lectures.

HW: You've had a break from exhibiting while you brought up your family. Was this difficult for you to do and do you find it difficult dividing time between your family and working in your studio?

CV: I did work fairly consistently while the first two children were young. It was not a complete break. I had my last show in 1990, just before my third child was born. With the three children being young and demanding I found that I was not working well and thought it best to stop. It was not an easy decision. More recently I've had a pattern of working and manage to work intensely but for relatively short periods.

HW: The paintings in this exhibition at Browse and Darby gallery in Cork Street seem very peaceful, delicate, serene and yet strong. Are you a peaceful person?

CV: I can't answer that one.

HW: Which artists have influenced you internationally and is 20th century English art important to you? If so, which period in particular and which artists?

CV: Yes, of course, 20th century British art is very important to me. I'm very curious about art and the older I become the more I

appreciate how much other artists have achieved. Living in London I have seen astonishing exhibitions over the last twenty years or so.

HW: Describe your current work for readers and artists who are not familiar with it. What are you mainly concerned with?

CV: I am very concerned with looking at things and how they appear. I try to make good, strong paintings, with nothing that is superfluous. This may sound obvious but in order for this to happen I have to have what I can only describe as a visual idea. This may stem from a number of different experiences. What I choose to paint has an element of the random, but the placing of things in both the work and the set-up is not random at all.

HW: Has your work changed greatly since you showed with Anne Berthoud in the 1980s?

CV: I cannot see a radical change, but naturally my experience of the last ten years is reflected in the work. I am conscious however of a growing interest in a certain kind of figurativeness. Painting the rose has to do with this. It has almost the complexity of painting the figure, a central issue.

HW: Who buys your work? Is it bought by overseas as well as British collectors? Have you shown abroad and if not where would you like to exhibit internationally?

CV: Yes, I would like to show internationally. I have work in collections in the States and have shown in Los Angeles and Berlin, where we lived between 1987-89. When I was there I realised how little I knew about German art. The contemporary art world was lively at that time and we met Baselitz, Koberling, Lupertz and others. My work seemed foreign to them and I realised how English it appeared, even though we shared a type of northen sensibility. It was a revelation to see the importance that they gave to a kind of strength and toughness.

HW: Is there anything else that you think might interest readers?

CV: When I left college I looked, and still do, to see how women artists managed looking after their children, combining painting and family life; Barbara Hepworth, Mary Potter and more recent female artists.

Charlotte Verity's work can be seen at Browse and Darby Gallery, 19 Cork Street, London W1. Telephone 0171 (020-7 from mid 2000) 734 7984.

Collecting Photographs

Sotheby's and Christies, the top auction houses, are now holding major sales of 20th century photographs, both in London and New York. Previously they concentrated mainly on 19th century photographs, but with prints by Edward Weston reaching $77,000 and the late Robert Mapplethorpe $33,000 at a New York Sotheby's auction on October 17th, 1990, 20th century photography is becoming more important than it was five years ago. In the May '98 sales at Sotheby's London Eugene Atget photographs were sold for £10-31,000.

In 1985 I had to sell six black and white photographs by Barbara Morgan the photographer, best known for her images of Martha Graham, the dancer, as in "Letter to the World". The photographs were in lieu of payment owed by the Morgan family in America, which distributed the international Art Guide series that I published in the1980s. Sotheby's London office at that time showed little interest in 20th century photography, so the prints were sold in New York for $1000 and the New York Art Guide author then received the sum for royalties due to her from USA sales. At that same sale a Man Ray photo was estimated at $1000-$2000, whereas in 1990 £4000 ($8000) would be the lowest price and probably far higher. An Henri Cartier-Bresson at that sale was estimated at $1000 and would now fetch about 6 or 8 times more (90) and in 2000 probably 10 times or more. Edward Weston nudes in 1985 were estimated at $1000-$2000, but in the 1990 New York Sotheby's sale, an Edward Weston print reached a staggering $77,000! It does of course depend on the quality of each print. In '98 at Sotheby's London a David Bailey fetched £1092 but in general it is the famous names such as Weston, Adam, Mapplethorpe, Cartier-Bresson, Lartigue that attract the large sums.

When buying photographs, either for interest or investment, there are many important factors to be taken into consideration, such as whether the photographer printed the print himself, whether it has been signed and the condition of the print. It is also important to know if the print was done at the time the photograph was taken or whether it was printed later. The National Portrait Gallery in London insists that photographers sell prints on fibre-based paper which lasts longer. For example, Imogen Cunningham early prints in platinum are more valuable than silver prints from the same negative, but printed later. The collector also needs to know the number of the edition, although unlike with etchings or graphics this does not necessarily affect the price. Ansel Adam's famous image "Moonrise, Hernandez, Mexico" has some 900 prints and all are still fetching large prices.

Collecting is an enjoyable pastime and can open a new world of contacts. The main factor when buying photographs is that "they are accessible to most income brackets", says Zelda Cheatle of the **Zelda Cheatle** photography **gallery** in Mount Street, London. She sells work by British photographers from £200 upwards, as well as photographs by international names. £200 would buy a Fay Godwin atmospheric landscape of say Cornwall or Devon, whereas a Mari Mahr surreal composition would cost £500 or more. As with most galleries, such as The **Photographers Gallery** where Zelda once worked, or The **Special Photographers Company** near Portobello Market, or **Focus Gallery** in Museum Street WC1, or **Michael Hoppen** at Jubilee Place, Chelsea SW3, once you have been put on the mailing list, you will receive invitations to shows. Gradually you will be able to build on knowledge about what you might like and be able financially to buy.

The variety of photographs on display in most capital cities such as London, Paris, New York, Cologne, Frankfurt, Madrid or Rome, is enormous. There are always stock prints by the big international names such as Brassai who specialised in Parisian low-life and café scenes, whose prints sell for several thousand pounds now. Robert Doisneau's image of a Parisian couple kissing is well-known internationally, not least due to the court case about the couple who claimed to have modelled for it, (they lost), would cost about £700 now, whereas a Cartier-Bresson French scene would cost about £1500 or more. Sebastiao Salgado, a Magnum photographer took some breathtaking photographs of the Sierra Pelada mine in Brazil, photos almost mediaeval in composition and content, might be about £1000. Bravo or Imogen Cunningham prints of exquisite still-lives would be nearer £2000 now. Various exhibitions of her work in 1991 meant a rise in prices. In general much photography was under-priced for a long time and now that New York and London have both got many established photography dealers and buyers, the market is rising. Many of these galleries have exhibitions of work by contemporary photographers and prices are very accessible, especially compared to painting or sculpture.

In cities such as London, Paris and New York there are also key museums that exhibit photo collections. It is essential to visit

La Hija de los Danzntes, Mañuel Alvarez Bravo (Zelda Cheatle Gallery).

several to see the kind of work that has been produced and merits attention. In New York, The **International Photography Center** holds major shows and has an excellent bookshop, also the **Museum of Modern Art** collection where spectacular views of the city can be seen by the great American names such as Paul Strand, Berenice Abbott, Steichen, Stieglitz, as well as contemporary names. London has the **Photographers Gallery** and **The Canon Photography Gallery at the V&A Museum** which opened in 1998 and has had many notable exhibitions of 19th and 20th century photographs from the collection. The **National Portrait Gallery** has photo-portraits of famous British people. In Paris the **Centre National de la Photographie** and the **Bibliothèque National**, also the **Centre Georges Pompidou** has photo displays and collections. **Agathe Gaillard**, **Zabriskie** and the **Comptoir de la Photographie** are known Paris photography galleries and in November each second year there is a Mois de la photo. In Spain the **Centro de Arte Reina Sofía** in Madrid, the Kunsthalle in Hamburg and the **Stedelijk** in Amsterdam all hold regular photography exhibitions.

Once you have bought photographs, it is important to know how to look after them. It is unwise to hang framed prints above central heating, but on the other hand they do need to be kept in a warm, moist atmosphere. Museums aim at 65 Fahrenheit and 40% humidity but in general it is wise to avoid excesses of heat or cold. Most galleries will advise on mounting, framing and care of photographs if you are at all uncertain.

Whether you enjoy taking photographs or acquiring images by other photographers, a world of pleasure awaits. At galleries you will meet other collectors and the photographers themselves: eventually you will see your personal taste in photographs emerging. The important advice that the great American collector Lee D. Witkin gave was to, "follow your instincts when you collect; collect for pleasure and life-enrichment."

See the photography galleries section for addresses of all London photography galleries.

Interview
with Photography Dealer, Helena Kovac

HW: When did your gallery first open?

HK: At the beginning of December1998. Dorothy Bohm and I are both Directors.

HW: You ran a photography gallery in the early 1980s in central London. What is the difference between then and now? Were you dealing in photography in between?

HK: The difference is the awareness of photography commercially. Between 1980 and 1983 Contrasts Gallery was the only privately-owned photography gallery in London. After that I moved out of gallerism and worked for major American corporations, still involved with the visual arts, but in an executive position. In '92 I ran an American stock library for six and a half years.

HW: Which photographers do you represent and what is the gallery specifically interested in?

HK: We have an eclectic taste in photography; Jonathan Bayer, Ian Berry, Erwin Blumenfeld, Dorothy Bohm, David Buckland, Bryn Campbell, Priscilla Carrasco, Cozette de Charmoy, Gautier Deblonde, Franco Fontana, Joan Fontecuberta, Georg Gerster, Fay Godwin, Sam Haskins, David Hurn, Caroline Hyman, Barbara Lloyd, Marketa Luskacova, Olivia Parker, Enzo Ragazzini, George Rodger and Magnum photographers.

HW: What price do you start selling contemporary prints at and what is the maximum?

HK: Small contemporary black and white prints start at £100 up to £7/£8,000, for Erwin Blumenfeld.

HW: Do you sell vintage prints by say Kertész, Cartier Bresson, Brassai, Weston, Man Ray and others? If so, what is the price range?

Dubo, Dubon, Dubonnet, 1934, André Kértesz (Focus Gallery).

HK: We have Bill Brandt, Kertész, Man Ray, Ida Kar, Tim Gidal (the father of photojournalism) and others. We also specialise in out-of-print and rare photographic books, also 19th century photographs.

HW: Do you think that the gallery location near the British Museum is useful? Was the space a gallery before you opened in '98?

HK: It's very useful and I call it an "intelligent" street. You get print and book collectors, overseas visitors and regular visitors to Museum Street in particular. It was an empty and vandalized shell when we took it over and before that a silversmith's.

HW: What is the gallery policy for contemporary professional photographers applying for shows?

HK: Diversity and fascination for fine photography. We invite photographers to show. We do prefer people to make an appointment and discuss their work and not turning up with portfolios.

HW: What do you think is the current standing of photography and how do you see the next 50 years developing? Is London an important centre or is New York more important?

HK: New York is the centre and the leader of the photography world. In France and Germany there is government sponsorship. London has always been second to New York. There is a young generation of professionals aware of photography through books, visits to New York and through graphics. Young professionals are embracing photography in general and awareness of photography as a creative, collectable investment medium is here to stay. However we still have a lot of hard work in front of us and I hope that Focus contributes to creating a solid staying market for photography in the UK.

HW: What are your future plans?

HK: We try with each exhibition to be as versatile as possible. We have our stable of photographers, 10 to begin with and now over 20. The present exhibition is Young Meteors of British Photojournalism between 1957-65. The next one is Cozette de Charmoy, a London-based photographer currently living in France. We have George Rodger, a relatively unknown Gautier

Deblonde in connection with a book "Artists" from Tate Publishing, then a still-life photographer and a show of photographs of London in the summer of '99. From September we show Sam Haskins, Caroline Hyman, Ian Berry. We always try to have two exhibitions; one in the main gallery upstairs and one in the little gallery downstairs. Downstairs we show 19th century and collectors' photographs.

Focus Gallery is at 43 Museum Street, London WC1. Telephone 0171 (020-7 from 4/2000) 242 7191. Fax (7) 242 7127.

Museums

London is well-endowed with museums and there are some 150 in the area. I have only listed about half of these, many with particular reference to their art collections. Remember to ring first to check opening hours especially on holidays. Some museums charge entrance fees.

PLEASE NOTE NEW LONDON TELEPHONE NUMBERS FROM APRIL 2000. 0171 becomes 020-7 and 0181 becomes 020-8, from mid 2000.

Apsley House, No. 1 London, Hyde Park corner, London W.1. Telephone 0171 (0207 from 4/2000) 499 5676. Open Tuesday-Sunday 11-5. Admission £3./£1.50 concessions.
Re-opened to the public in 1995 this magnificent home of the Duke of Wellington houses Velázquez's "The Waterseller of Seville", works by Goya, Rubens, Caravaggio, Brueghel, Steen, De Hooch, Wilkie and Lawrence. Although the colours in some rooms question the word "taste", the opulent impression serves as a backdrop to memories of Waterloo and the Duke's great victory. The house was built by Robert Adam between 1771 and 1778 for Baron Apsley and has been home to the Dukes of Wellington since 1817. Well worth a visit. Underground Hyde Park Corner.

The Hotung Gallery of Oriental Antiquities, British Museum.

Bethnal Green Museum of Childhood, Cambridge Heath Road, London E.2. Telephone 0171 980 3204. Recorded information 0171 (0207 from 4/2000) 980 2415. Open Monday-Thursday 10-6, Saturday 10-6, Sunday 2.30-6.
Good collection of toys, children's games, dolls. Part of the V&A museum. 17th-century dolls' houses, children's clothing and artefacts. Special activities for children, often at holiday time. Underground Bethnal Green.

British Museum, Great Russell Street, London WC1. Telephone 0171 (0207 from 4/2000) 636 1555. Open Monday-Saturday 10-5, Sunday 2.30-6. Extended opening hours from 2000.
In autumn 2000 the museum's inner courtyard becomes the Great Court, a large square covered by a magnificent glass roof. Designed by Norman Foster and Partners, the Great court houses a Centre for Education, galleries and temporary exhibition space, alongside improved facilities such as a terrace restaurant and easier access. The Reading Room, which is now a central part of the Great Court, now houses a new public reference library. 6.1 million people visit the British Museum annually, making the new additions very welcome. The cost of the project — a mere £97 million, but money well spent.
  One of the largest museums in the world, built in 1823-27. It is best to visit one section at a time, as you could easily spend a week in this museum alone. Wander through Greek pottery, Egyptian remains, past the famous Elgin Marbles brought from Greece in 1802, Bronze Age tombs, Indian paintings and exquisite manuscripts, Tibetan amulets, the Hotung gallery of Antiquities and the recent Mexican gallery. The Museum of Mankind moved back to the BM. Underground Tottenham Court Road.

British Museum (Museum of Mankind), This is now back at the British Museum in Bloomsbury.

British Museum (Natural History), Cromwell Road, South Kensington, London SW7. Telephone 0171 (0207 from 4/2000) 938 9123. Open Monday-Saturday 10-6, Sunday 11-6.
Magnificent building next to the V&A museum and Geology museum. Best known for its lively displays and dinosaurs. Displays show the history of the world with mammals, fossils, plants and animals. Ideal museum to take children to. The new Earth Galleries are of great interest at the moment. Underground South Kensington.

British Library, 96 Euston Road, St Pancras, London NW1 2DB. Telephone 0171 (0207 from 4/2000) 412 7332. The main building is open Monday, Wednesday, Thursday and Friday 9.30-6, Tuesday 9.30-8, Saturday 9.30-5, Sunday 11-5. The new British Library buildings opened at St Pancras at a cost of many millions more than expected, but the building, designed by Professor Sir Colin St John Wilson, is more attractive than had been predicted. There are 11 reading rooms, 3 exhibition galleries, a bookshop, a fully equipped conference centre with 255-seat auditoium and restaurants. In the piazza and building there are sculptures by Eduardo Paolozzi, R.B.Kitaj and Antony Gormley. The British Library is the national library of the United Kingdom, one of the world's greatest libraries. There are some 12 million books here, including The King's Library (donated by George IV in 1823), Rare Books, music and manuscripts, books on display in exhibitions in the John Ritblat Gallery, (Magna Carta, The Gutenberg Bible, Shakespeare's first Folio (1623), works by many famous writers, composers and artists, and the Lindisfarne Gospels), The Pearson Gallery of Living Words, The Workshop of Words, Sounds and Images tracing the story of communication through the ages and a permanent exhibition of philately. There are seats for 1200 readers and excellent Online Public access and atomated book request system.

The galleries are open to view manuscripts on Monday, Wednesday, Thursday and Friday 9.30-6, Tuesday 9.30-8, Saturday 9.30-5, Sunday 11-5. There are also talks by living contemporary writers, making this magnificent new building very welcome to London contemporary life. A café, restaurant and coffee shop in the Piazza are also worth visiting for views of the King's Library. Underground Euston.

Buckingham Palace, State Rooms, Buckingham Palace, London SW1. Telephone 0171 (0207 from 4/2000) 321 2233. These magnificent State Rooms are open to the general public between August and October (check dates each year as they may change). Although some of the rooms are over-the-top in richly-coloured excessive taste, the paintings are worth visiting. On the one hand you have paintings by Winterhalter of Victoria and Albert and their children and grandchildren and on the other great masterpieces by Rembrandt and Dutch, British and Flemish Masters. The White Drawing room is particularly attractive and the downstairs rooms have interesting collections of porcelain and china and views of the garden. Underground Victoria.

Carlyle's House, 24 Cheyne Row, Chelsea, London SW3. Telephone 0171 (0207 from 4/2000) 352 7087. Open Wednesday-Sunday 11-5 (April-October). Entrance fee £2.50. Thomas Carlyle, the writer, lived in this 18th-century Chelsea house for many years. Maintained by the National Trust with many nteresting items on display. Carlyle was friendly with Dickens, Thackeray, Browning and Tennyson and they all visited him here from time to time. Underground Sloane Square and then buses 11, 19 or 22.

Portrait of Agathe Bas, Rembrandt (Buckingham Palace).

Commonwealth Institute, Kensington High Street, London W.8. Telephone 0171 (0207 from 4/2000) 603 4535. Recorded information 0171 602 3257. Open Monday-Saturday 10-5.30, Sunday 2-5.
This institute houses the history, geography and general development of Commonwealth countries. At present the main galleries are closed for complete renovation until 2002. The new galleries will have virtual reality and internet facilities. At present the reference library and temporary exhibition spaces are open. Contract Nicola Harold about how to apply for shows. Regular exhibitions of work by contemporary Commonwealth artists. Ideal gallery for children. Information centre, cinema (free films), art gallery, library and excellent shop, also a restaurant (both closed until 2002). Underground High Street Kensington.

Courtauld Institute Galleries, Somerset House, The Strand, London WC2. Telephone 0171 (0207 from 4/2000) 873 2526. Groups 0171(0207 from 4/2000) 873 2549. Open Monday-Saturday 10-6. Sunday 2-6. This is one of London's most rewarding museums with a permanent collection consisting of several collections given to the University of London. Apart from the Italian Pre-Renaissance paintings the Impressionist and Post-Impressionist paintings alone are magnificent; 3 Monets, 4 Degas, 6 Seurat, Manet's "Bar at the Folies-Bergère", 9 Cézanne, Gauguin, 2 Van Gogh, Lautrec and 3 Manets. This is a unique and important art collection and very central to visit. There are also temporary exhibitions. The Courtauld Institute for postgraduate studies in fine art is next door. The print and study room is open to the public. Underground Temple or 15, 23 buses.

Cricket Memorial Gallery, Lords Cricket Ground, St John's Wood, London NW8. Telephone 0171 (0207 from 4/2000) 289 1611. Open match days only 10.30-5. Ground admission and entrance fees.
The history of cricket. Next to the famous Lords cricket ground. A must for cricket enthusiasts. Underground St John's Wood.

Cutty Sark, Greenwich Pier, London SE10. Telephone 0181 (0208 from 4/2000) 853 3589. Open Monday-Saturday 10-5, Sunday 12-5. Admission £3 or more.
One of the most famous clipper ships. Exhibition on board of how the sailors lived on board ship in those days. A trip to the Cutty Sark and the National Maritime Museum can be done on the same day by taking the boat from Westminster Pier or Charing Cross to Greenwich, downriver. I'd also recommend a visit to the Royal Observatory and to Queen Anne's House, which is far more attractive than Buckingham Palace. On the way down the River Thames you will pass "Oliver Twist" warehouses, newly-converted loft properties and the Docklands development at Canary Wharf. BR Greenwich or take the boat from Westminster pier or Charing Cross Pier.

The Design Museum, Butler's Wharf, Shad Thames, London SE1 2YD. Telephone 0181 (0208 from 4/2000) 403 6933. Entrance fee £4.75, £3.50 students. Information 0171 (0207 from 4/2000).
The Design museum examines the role of design in our lives and allows the visitor to look at mass-produced products and see why they have been designed in a particular way. Regular exhibitions of new and old designs. There are guided tours, a library, a well-stocked shop and a famous Riverside café/bar. Membership scheme often includes visits to designer workshops and special access to events and activities. Individuals £22, special £10, Dual £38, group £150-£500, corporate

£1000-£4000. School and college visits are welcomed. Technology and Design are important parts of the National Curriculum in British schools now. Underground Tower Hill and walk over Tower bridge. Boats by river.

Dickens House Museum, 48 Doughty Street, London WC1. Telephone 0171 (020-7 from 4/2000) 405 2127. Open Monday-Friday 9.45-5.30, Saturday 10-5.30. Admission fee.
Charles Dickens rented this house between April 1837-December 1839. He wrote the Pickwick Papers, Oliver Twist and Nicholas Nickleby while living here as well as some journalism. Portraits, letters, illustrations and household items from that era. In the dining room you can see the quill that he used to write The Mysteries of Edwin Drood with. The study has a painting called "Dickens Dream" by R.W.Buss and the table where Dickens wrote his last words. The Georgian terraced house was opened as a museum in 1925 by the Dickens Fellowship. Underground Holborn.

Dulwich College Art Gallery, College Road, London SE21. Telephone 0181 (0208 from 4/2000) 693 5254. Admission, but free on Fridays. Check for opening hours.
Dulwich in South London is an attractive area with old historical houses. The gallery was designed by Sir John Soane (his museum at Lincoln's Inn Field may also be of interest) in 1811. Works by Rembrandt, Van Dyck, Rubens, Reynolds and the Italian Masters. It was the first public gallery in London. There are many excellent temporary exhibitions during the year. There are

Courtauld Institute Galleries.

also open-air public sculpture exhibitions by established British contemporary artists. British Rail West Dulwich.

Chelsea Royal Hospital Museum, Royal Hospital Road, London SW3. Telephone 0171 (0207 from 4/2000) 730 0161. Open Monday-Saturday 10-12, 2-6, Sunday 2-6.
Home of the famous Chelsea Pensioners, some whom you can occasionally see walking slowly in their heavy, red uniforms along the King's Road. Founded by Charles II. Wren building, with additions by Adam and John Soane. Wren's chapel is worth a visit. Underground Sloane Square.

Estorick Collection of Modern Italian Art, 39A Canonbury Square, London N1 2AN. Telephone 0171 (0207 from 4/2000) 704 9522. Open Wednesday-Saturday 11-6, Sunday 12-5. Entrance fee.
Works from the collection of Modern Italian art created by Eric and Salomé Estorick. Magnificent opportunity to see paintings by the early 20th century avant-garde Futurist painters including Balla, Boccioni, Carra, Severini and Russolo. Paintings by de Chirico, Modigliani, Sironi and Campigli are also on show. There is also a library of 2000 books, open by appointment. The bookshop is run by Zwemmers. Café for weary visitors. Underground Highbury and Islington.

The Fan Museum,12 Croom Hill, Greenwich, London SE10. Telephone 0181 (0208 from 4/2000) 858 7829. Ring for opening hours.
A collection of fans through the ages, with occasional temporary exhibitions. Ideal to combine this with a visit to Greenwich's Cutty Sark or the National Maritime Museum. British Rail Greenwich or boat by the River Thames from Westminster pier.

Faraday Museum, The Royal Institute, 21 Albemarle Street, London W.1. Telephone 0171 (0207 from 4/2000) 409 2992. Open Tuesday and Thursday 1-4. Entrance fee.
Michael Farady the great discoverer of electromagnetism worked here and the great Electrical Machine built in 1803 is on display. Underground Green Park.

Fenton House, Hampstead Grove, London NW3. Telephone 0171 (0207 from 4/2000) 435 3471. Open April-October Saturday and Sunday 11-5.30, Monday-Wednesday 1-7. Closed except weekends in December, January and February. Entrance fee.
This is a wonderful house to visit, high up above Hampstead village, with views over London. It is maintained by the National Trust and houses the Binning collection of porcelain and furniture and the Benton Fletcher collection of keyboard instruments. Some musical instruments from the 16th and 18th

centuries are still used by music students. The paintings in the house are by Dürer, Constable, Lawrence, Daubigny and William Nicholson. There are open-air theatre and concert performances in the summer, in the garden. I'd recommend a visit if you want to escape central London pollution and noise. Underground Hampstead.

Florence Nightingale Museum, 2 Lambeth Palace Road (St Thomas's hospital), London SE1 7EW. Telephone 0171 (0207 from 4/2000) 620 0374. Open Tuesday-Sunday 10-4. Entrance fee.
Well-known to British schoolchildren as the "lady with the lamp" during the Crimean war. In fact this episode was only a two-year period in her 90-year life. The history of this remarkable woman and her nursing life. Opposite the Houses of Parliament on the other side of the Thames. Underground Westminster and walk over the bridge.

Foundling Hospital (Coram Foundation), 40 Brunswick Square, London WC1. Telephone 0171 (0207 from 4/2000) 278 2424. Open Monday-Friday 10-4. Entrance fee.
Founded in 1739 by Captain Coram for the care of destitute children. Hogarth painted the Captain's portrait and persuaded artists to give works of art for sale. The Foundling's Court Room, with a series of paintings, by Hogarth, about children being rescued,is on view by appointment at the Coram Foundation. The paintings include "The March to Finchley". Paintings by Gainsborough, Reynolds, Raphael, Millais, also Captain Coram's portrait. Underground Russell Square.

Northampton Lodge, home of the Estorick Collection.

Freud Museum, 20 Maresfield Gardens, London NW3 5SX. Telephone 0171 (0207 from 4/2000). Open Wednesday-Sunday 12-5. Entrance fee.

Once the home of Sigmund Freud and his family, after escaping the Nazis in 1938. The library is the focus of the museum, where the founder of psychoanalysis centred his discoveries and research. 18th and 19th century Austrian furniture and Biedermeier chests. Underground Finchley Road.

The Geffrye Museum, Kingsland Road, London E.2. Telephone 0181 (0208 from 4/2000) 739 9893. Open Tuesday-Saturday 10-5, Sunday 2 -5.

It is worth making a special visit to this museum, set next to peaceful East London almshouses, dating from 1715. The museum specialises in furniture and furnishings and various rooms have been re-constructed to create the exact era. The chapel is also worth visiting. There are various children's activities and special courses and lectures throughout the year. Underground Liverpool Street. Buses 22, 67, 48, 149 and 243.

Geological Museum, Exhibition Road, South Kensington, London SW7. Telephone 0171 (0207 from 4/2000) 589 3444. Open Monday-Saturday 10-6, Sunday 2.30-6.

There are various displays to help visitors understand the Story of the Earth and the various rocks and minerals that make the earth so rich with colour and wealth. A piece of moon rock is on display. Special activities for children and temporary exhibitions throughout the year. Undergound South Kensington.

Gilbert Collection, Telephone 0171 (0207 from 4/2000) 240 5782. This magnificent gift to the nation should be on permanent display at Somerset House by 2000. Somerset House, designed by George III's architect Sir William Chambers (1723-1796) is being restored. The Gilbert Collection will be housed in the South Building of the Great Court. Silver items include a silver-gilt Elizabethan cup given by the Duke of Wellington as a christening gift in1824. Underground Temple.

Gunnersbury Park Museum, Pope's Lane, London W.3. Telephone 0181 (0208 from 4/2000) 992 1612. April-September open Monday-Friday 1-5, Saturday and Sunday 2-6. October-March daily 2-6.

Once the home of part of the famous Rothschild family. Magnificent setting overlooking parkland, with a small classical temple. Various coaches and a Hansom cab are on display and local history items. Underground Acton Town.

Goldsmiths Hall, Foster Lane, London EC2. Telephone 0171 (0207 from 4/2000) 606 8971. Ring the gallery for details and an appointment to see the collection. Largest collection of modern silver in the country. There are also temporary exhibitions of work by contemporary silversmiths. Underground St Paul's.

Gordon Medical Museum, St Thomas Street, London SE1. Telephone 0171 (0207 from 4/2000) 407 7600. By application to the curator.
Mainly used by medical students. Amazing collection of specimens of rare deformities and diseases. Not for the squeamish. Underground Waterloo.

Hogarth's House, Hogarth Lane, Chiswick, London W.4. Telephone 0181 (0208 from 4/2000) 994 6757. Open April-September, Monday-Saturday 11-6, Sunday 2-6. October-March, Monday-Saturday,(except Tuesday) 11-4.
Hogarth, the famous English painter's country house in Chiswick, now sadly next to a thundering motorway. Drawings, prints and other items related to Hogarth's life are on display. Underground Hammersmith and bus 290.

Hampton Court Palace, Hampton Court, Surrey. Telephone 0181 (0208 from 4/2000) 977 9441. Opening hours vary according to the time of the year.
Italian masterpieces including Tintoretto and Titian. After the devastating fire, the Palace has been restored by contemporary craftsmen and women. Worth visiting to see what a magnificent job they have done. Famous in English history in the times of Henry VIII. Magnificent gardens and a maze to get lost in. Situated next to the River Thames. Ideal for family visits. Take the boat from Westminster pier for the most picturesque way to see the Thames. British Rail Hampton court.

Heinz Gallery, 21 Portman Square, London W.1. Telephone 0171 (0207 from 4/2000) 580 5533 ext 230. Open Monday-Friday 11-5 (8 Thursday), Saturday 10-1.
Displays of material from the collection of some 200,000 architectural drawings owned by the Royal Institute of British Architects. Designed by John Adam. Changing exhibitions throughout the year. Underground Marble Arch.

Horniman Museum, London Road, Forest Hill, London SE23. Telephone 0181 (0208 from 4/2000) 699 1872. Open Monday-Saturday 10.30-6, Sunday 2-6.
Museum of Ethnography covering arts, crafts and religions worldwide. Collection of items relating to all these fields such as tools, dance masks and various musical instruments. Library, aquarium and a fascinating building. British Rail Forest Hill.

Imperial War Museum, Lambeth Road, London SE1. Telephone 0181 (0208 from 4/2000) 600 140. Enquiries 0171 (0207 from 4/2000) 416 5000. Admission £4.70. Children

£2.35. Open daily 10-6.

Museum recording visually the British Commonwealth forces in two world wars. Weapons, photographs, paintings by war artists such as Nash, J.D.Fergusson, Spencer, and more recently Peter Howson in Bosnia and Linda Kitson in the Falklands. The building was once "Bedlam", the famous Bethlehem hospital for the insane. Ideal gallery to take children to to show them the horrors of war and the misery that it brings with it. Major redevelopments open in 2000 to house exhibitions about the Holocaust and Total War. Also new conference and teaching facilities. Also a cinema and gallery talks. Underground Lambeth North and Elephant and Castle.

Jewish Museum, (Camden) Albert St, NW1. (7) 284 1997. Also The Jewish Museum Finchley East end Rd N.3. (8) 349 1143. Two specialist museums with displays about all matters relating to the Jewish faith and way of life. Underground Camden and Finchley Central.

Kenwood House, Hampstead Lane, London NW3. Telephone 0171 (007 from 4/2000) 348 1286. Open daily 10-7. Closes at 5 in October, February and March; at 4 in November-January.

A beautiful setting, perhaps the best in London, looking down onto the city of London over rolling acres of trees and lush green fields. Robert Adam designed the house and the Iveagh bequest collection of paintings, furniture and other works of art, is one of London's most enjoyable. Superb Adam library and drawing room. Paintings from English, Dutch and Flemish schools of art. Vermeer's "Guitar Player", Rembrandt's self-portrait, Gainsborough portraits, Van Dyck, Frans Hals, Romney and Boucher are all on display in this magnificent country house. Kenwood is the setting for large open-air classical concerts in the summer. Best time to visit Kenwood House is on a Saturday or Sunday, when you can combine it with a visit to the Spaniards Inn, up the road, where Dick Turpin the highwayman is sup-posed to have stayed. Good restaurant and café by the old stables. Underground Archway then bus 210 or Golders Green and bus 210.

Doctor Johnson's House, 17 Gough Square, London EC4. Telephone 0171 (0207 from 4/2000) 353 3745. Open May-September, Monday-Saturday 11-5.30. October-April, 11-5. Reductions for students and children.

A Queen Anne house quite near Fleet Street. First edition of his Dictionary on show. Doctor Johnson was a well-known literary figure in the 18th century. He was famed for saying "If a man is tired of London, he is tired of life." Underground Blackfriars.

Keats House, Keats Grove, Hampstead, London NW3. Telephone 0171 (0207 from 4/2000) 435 2062. Open Monday-

Saturday 10-6, Sunday 2-5. Free entrance to the house.
The famous English poet lived here for two years in this attractive Hampstead setting. The house has memorabilia connected with Keat's life, including love letters to Fanny Brawne and various manuscripts. The garden is covered in exotic flowers in the summer and it is here that Keats wrote "Ode to a Nightingale". Combine a visit to Keats house with a tour of literary Hampstead to see where DH Lawrence lived. Underground Belsize Park or 24 bus to South End Green from Oxford Street or Trafalgar Square.

Keats House and garden.

Leighton House, 12 Holland Park Road, London W.14. Telephone 0171 (0207 from 4/2000) 602 3316. Open Monday-Saturday 11-5. Entrance free.
A beautiful Victorian house with a very exotic interior, home of Lord Leighton the painter and one-time President of the Royal Academy. Persian 15th and 16th century tiles in a cool Arabic room with fountain. The upstairs rooms have a display of Lord Leighton's drawings and Pre-Raphaelite paintings by Burne-Jones, also exquisite De Morgan tiles. Lord Leighton's large Victorian sculptures can be seen in the rambling garden outside. Worth a visit to sample the kind of Victorian idealism of the period. A Leighton exhibition was slammed by the critics for the excesses and idealism of the period and it is true that his paintings are rather overdone. Whatever you feel about his paintings the house is worth a visit. There are also many temporary exhibitions throughout the year. Underground High Street Kensington.

London Transport Museum, Covent Garden, London WC2. Telephone 0171 (0207 from 4/2000) 379 6344. Open daily 10-6. Entrance fee.

The museum houses London Transport buses and trams, across the last two centuries of the city's transport system. Magnificent buildings next to the market, with spacious rooms and high ceilings. The shop sells books and London Transport posters. Underground Covent Garden.

Museum of Moving Image, South Bank Arts Centre, Waterloo, London SE1 8XT. Telephone 0171 (0207 from 4/2000) 401 2636. Open daily 10-6. Admission charges.
The Museum of Moving Image is in the South Bank complex, next to the NFT. It is an ideal museum to take children to, as they can have a wonderful day exploring the world of film and can even animate cartoons, read the news and audition for Hollywood. Any film buff will find it hard to leave. The entire museum is well-planned, with many attractions for all ages and explains how early films were made, with clips from early and recent films. You will need at least two hours for a visit, if not longer. Underground Waterloo or sometimes the riverbus, if operating along the Thames. Planned closure August '99.

Museum of London, London Wall, London EC2. Telephone 0171 (0207 from 4/2000) 600 3699 ext 240. Open Monday-Saturday 10-5.50, Sunday 12-5.50.
Here you can see the history of London developing through the ages. Conveniently set near the ruins of the original Roman London Wall. Various displays show pottery, tools, costumes, room settings and reconstruction of shops. The magnificent Lord Mayor's coach is on display here and is used annually in

The Adoration of the Shepherds, Luca Signorelli (National Gallery).

November for the Lord Mayor's procession through the City of London. Also regular exhibitions of contemporary photography and exhibitions related to London life. The Roman London gallery opened in recent years. Museum on the Move, the Museum in Docklands mobile exhibition trailer to convey the history of the Docklands to local schools and communities. The Museum in Docklands has a visitors' centre at the Royal Victorian Dock to receive coach parties. This project reaffirms London as an important maritime, industrial and commercial centre. The museum site is yet to be chosen but the collection is growing. Underground for Museum of London Barbican, Moorgate.

National Army Museum, Royal Hospital Road, Chelsea, London SW3. Telephone 0171 (0207 from 4/2000) 730 1717. Open Monday-Saturday 10-5.30, Sunday 2-5.30.
History of the British army from 1485 to the outbreak of the First World War. Displays of weapons, documents and battle plans. The art gallery has paintings by Lawrence, Reynolds, Gainsborough and Romney among others. Underground Sloane Square.

National Gallery, Trafalgar Square, London WC2. Telephone 0171 (0207 from 4/2000) 747 2885. Open Monday-Saturday 10-6, Wednesday until 9, Sunday 10-6. Exhibitions in the Sainsbury wing open until 10pm on Wednesdays, also the Brasserie and shop. Excellent brasserie with Paula Rego murals. Prêt a Manger café in the main building basement has the best cappuccino in London. Plenty of space for group visits in the café. Friendly staff.
With the exchange of paintings between the Tate and the National Gallery, the National has inherited 50 19th century paintings, while 14 early 20th century paintings have gone to the Tate. The arrivals at the National include more paintings by Monet, Pissarro, Degas, Seurat, Gauguin, Cézanne and Van Gogh. A magnificent collection of paintings through the ages, ranging from early Italian paintings in the Sainsbury Wing, the Spanish School, Flemish to Impressionist and Post-Impressionist paintings in the main building. Particularly worth mentioning are Rousseau's Tiger, Van Eyck's Arnolfini Marriage, Botticelli's Mars and Venus, Monet's Lilies and Vermeer's Woman standing at a Verginal. The North Galleries have been re-designd in a Franco-British venture with support from Yves Saint Laurent among others. The French collection paintings are dominated by Claude Lorrain and Nicolas Poussin, but paintings in the Dutch collection include several by Cuyp. The Rembrandt room is also worth visiting and Uccello's spectacular Rout of San Romano, which is near many other Italian masterpieces in the Sainsbury Wing. This wing also has major exhibitions every month or two in the basement, often with videos on show about the painter or period. The bookshop is much larger now and has an excellent selection of

art books, as well as cards and posters; well-informed staff are very helpful. **Exhibitions include Rembrandt by himself until September 5th '99**. Underground Charing Cross.

Hendricjke Stoffels, Rembrandt, Rembrandt by Himself exhibition at the National Gallery until September, then at the Mauritshuis, The Hague until January 2000.

National Portrait Gallery, St Martin's Place, Trafalgar Square, London WC2. Telephone 0171 (0207 from 4/2000) 306 0055. Open Monday-Saturday 10-5.45, Sunday 12-5.45. Excellent new bookshop and café.

A historical collection of portraits of famous British men and women. Although many of the portraits are by famous painters such as Holbein, Hogarth, Lely, Romney, Van Dyck and Reynolds, they have often been chosen for their subject matter rather than the painting's merits, so are not necessarily the best examples of the painter's work. There are magnificent portraits showing the splendour of the 16th-19th centuries, but some of the most interesting portraits are downstairs of more recent writers, scholars and 20th century celebrities. These galleries are also more lively, with temporary exhibitions often on display, highlighting certain periods of the 20th century. There are many other major exhibitions in the gallery over the year, including prize awards of both painting and photography. In the opening of the new millennium there will be a new entrance hall, galleries, rooftop café and lecture theatre, in the new extension between the National and the National Portrait Gallery. **Exhibitions '99-2001 include Faces of the Century, Jan 3rd, 2000; Lord Snowdon retrospective in 2000 and Painting the Century, mid Oct 2000-2001, followed by Restoration Beauties.** Underground Charing Cross.

National Maritime Museum, Romney Road, Greenwich, London SE10. Telephone 0181 (0208 from 4/2000) 858 4422. Open Monday-Sunday 10-5. Entrance fee.

Multi-million pound renovations have now provided new galleries, including "The Future of the Seas" exhibition, monitoring ecology. The museum is set in the picturesque area of Greenwich and has on permanent display models of ships, nautical instruments, relics and a fine selection of marine paintings by artists such as Turner, Gainsborough, Reynolds, Romney and Lely. The library and print room are full of maritime historical information for students and enthusiasts. The Queen's House was built by Inigo Jones for James VI of Scotland and 1 of England's wife, Queen Anne of Denmark. This is a far more beautiful palace than the current royal residence. Period music is also sometimes played in summer.

The Royal Observatory contains astronomical instruments and is near the Maritime Museum. It was built by Sir Christopher Wren in 1676. This is where Greenwich Meantime starts. The Dome can be seen from here. British Rail Maze Hill or boat from Westminster Pier in the summer months.

National Museum of Labour History, Limehouse Town Hall, Commercial Road, London E.1. Telephone 0181 (0208 from 4/2000) 515 3229. Open Tuesday-Friday 9.30-5.

The history of the development of the Labour movement in Britain. The Tolpuddle Martyrs, the Peterloo massacre, the foundation of the Fabian Society, the General Strike, the foundation of the Trades Union Congress (TUC) and the foundation of the first Labour Government, are all related in various displays. Underground Aldgate East then bus 5, 15, 23, 40. British Rail Stepney East.

National Postal Museum, London Chief Office, King Edward Street, London EC1. Telephone 0171 (0207 from 4/2000) 432 3851. Open Monday-Thursday 10-4.30.

Extensive collection of postage stamps in this museum, mostly from the Reginald Phillips collection of 19th century stamps. The Post Office's own collection of every stamp issue since 1840 is also here. Reference library for philatelists. Underground St Pauls.

Orleans House Gallery, Riverside, Twickenham. Telephone 0181 (0208 from 4/2000) 892 0221. Open Tuesday-Saturday 1-5.30, Sunday 2-5.30.
Various loan exhibitions are held here every year. The famous Octagon was designed by James Gibb in 1720. Orleans House was partially demolished in 1926. Louis Phillippe the French King lived here between 1815 and 1817. Underground Richmond or British Rail St Margarets.

Passmore Edwards Museum, Romford Road, Stratford, London E15. Telephone 0181 (0208 from 4/2000) 519 4296. Open Monday-Friday 10-6 (Thursday -8), Saturday 10-1, 2-5.
A local museum specialising in the history of Essex, with archaeology, geology and local history. Bow porcelain was produced locally. Maritime history shows that Ilford was once a port instead of being inland as it is now. Underground Stratford.

Percival David Foundation, 53 Gordon Square, London WC1. Telephone 0171 (0207 from 4/2000) 387 3909. Open Monday 2-5, Tuesday-Friday 10.30-5, Saturday 10.30-1.
Chinese porcelain from the Sung to Ch'ing Dynasties. Exquisite shapes and colours and a must for any ceramics or porcelain collectors. A specialist collection. Underground Russell Square.

Pollocks Toy Museum, 1 Scala Street, London W.1. Telephone 0171(0207 from 4/2000) 636 3452. Open Monday-Saturday 10-5. Entrance fee. Children free on Saturdays. Under-18s 75p.
This museum is a real delight for parents and children. Collection of toys, dolls' houses, puppets, games and reconstructions of Victorian nurseries. Benjamin Pollock was a publisher of toy theatres, hence the museum's name. It is an Educational Charitable Trust. There is an excellent toy shop for presents for children. Next to the Cyberia Internet café (ideal for fathers or older children) Underground Goodge Street.

Public Records Office Museum, Chancery Lane, London WC2. Telephone 0171 (0207 from 4/2000) 405 0741. Open Monday-Friday 1-4.
The nation's archives are held here. Signatures of English Royalty through the ages and also of Guy Fawkes and Shakespeare among others. The Domesday Book is here and visitors can look at a copy, made for reference. Wealth of interesting documents for interested historians. Underground Aldwych, Chancery Lane.

The Queens Gallery, Buckingham Palace Road, London SW1. Telephone 0171 (0207 from 4/2000) 839 1377. Open Tuesday-Saturday 11-5, Sunday 1-5.
The gallery is closed until 2002 the Queen's Golden Jubilee. £15 million is being spent on extending the gallery to include a lecture theatre, a micro-gallery with electronic access to 500,000

Bridget Riley by Jorge Lewinski (National Portrait Gallery).

works and a coffee shop. There will also be a new elegant entrance and new gallery space. Situated at the back of Buckingham Palace, it was once the Palace Chapel Royal collection of paintings, with an especially good selection of Italian masters. Regular exhibitions of the Royal collection so that the public can see the wide range of work owned by the Royal family. Underground Victoria.

Rangers House, Chesterfield Walk, Blackheath, London SE10. Telephhone 0181 (0208 from 4/2000) 348 1286/8530035. Open daily 10-5.
Built by Snape in 1694 and enlarged in 1749. Houses the Suffolk Collection of Jacobean and Stuart portraits, with a heavy

65

emphasis on the costumes of the period. Set near Greenwich Park with views across the River Thames. Underground New Cross, then bus 53.

Royal Academy, Burlington House, Piccadilly, London W1. Telephone 0171 (0207 from 4/2000) 300 8000. Open daily 10-6. Entrance fee for temporary exhibitions.
The Royal Academy is the oldest society in Britain, founded 1768, and is devoted to the fine arts. It is famous for its annual Summer Exhibition of some1000 paintings, drawings, prints and sculpture. It holds a variety of major exhibitions throughout the year, some major world exhibitions touring the major art capitals, such as Monet in the 20th century (99) and Van Dyck (99). Apart from the vast galleries downstairs, the Sackler galleries upstairs have been added in recent years to show smaller exhibitions in a light airy venue. There is a good shop selling art books, cards, posters, t-shirts and jewellery or objets d'art related to specific shows. The restaurant in the basement is excellent and gives you a chance to look at some of the RA's permanent collection of paintings on the stairs. Friends of the RA can gain discounts and receive the RA magazine. Better management has led to a more modern 21st century approach at the RA recently. **Exhibitions include: Van Dyck 11th September-10th December '99, John Soane Sept-Dec '99, Corot to Matisse 20th- November 20th-February 2000.** Underground Piccadilly or Green Park.

Royal Air Force Museum, Hendon, London NW9. Telephone 0181 (0208 from 4/2000) 205 2266. Open Monday-Saturday 10-6, Sunday 2-6.
Built on the site of Hendon aerodrome, this museum relates the history of the Royal Air Force. Exhibits show how far we have come from the days of the fragile airplanes that tempted to cross the Atlantic. Engines, weapons, uniforms, models are all on display for enthusiasts. Underground Colindale.

Science Museum, Exhibition Road, South Kensington, London SW7. Telephone 0171 (0207 from 4/2000) 938 8000. Open Monday-Sunday 10-5.50. Entrance fee, but free after 4.30pm.
The Science Museum displays how science relates to industry and to our everyday life, showing a variety of trains, underground carriages, planes, boats, engines and all sorts of machinery. A moon buggy is also on display, relating to the Apollo 10 space capsule and man's historic landing on the moon. Ideal gallery for children, with special children's activities and exhibits. Underground South Kensington.

Sir John Soane's Museum, 13 Lincoln's Inn Field, London WC2. Telephone 0171 (0207 from 4/2000) 405 2107. Open Tuesday-Saturday 10-5.

As you will probably have already noted, Sir John Soane, the architect, designed quite a number of London's buildings. The collection of Sir John's artefacts range from paintings by Turner, Reynolds and the famous Hogarth Rake's Progress series, to Roman remains and furniture from the last few centuries. The house is a joy to visit. There are also 20,000 architectural drawings in the collection. Underground Holborn.

South London Art Gallery, Peckham Road, Camberwell, London SE5. Telephone 0181 (0208 from 4/2000) 703 6210. Open Monday-Saturday 10-6, Sunday 3-6.
Variety of exhibitions held here during the year. Opened in 1891 and was apparently the first London gallery to be opened to the public on Sundays. See press for details of exhibitions. Underground Oval.

Tate Gallery of British Art, (from 2001 the Tate gallery will only show British Art from 1500 to the present day, including the Turner Bequest. The Tate Gallery of Modern Art (opening May

Monna Vanna, Dante Gabriel Rossetti (Tate Gallery of British Art).

2000) will concentrate on international art since 1900, starting from where the National Gallery in Trafalgar Square ends. Until then visit the Tate Gallery Millbank, London SW1. Telephone 0171 (0207 from 4/2000) 887 8000 (24-hour information.) Open daily10-6.

There are two main collections in the Tate gallery; the British collection and the Modern collection (the international collection of paintings and sculpture throughout the 20th century). The national collection holds a wealth of paintings by Turner, Gainsborough, Constable, Blake and many Pre-Raphaelite paintings. The Modern Collection (which moves to the Tate Gallery of Modern Art in early 2000) shows sculpture by Rodin, Degas, Moore, Giacometti and Epstein and the painting collection Impressionist, Post-Impressionist, Expressionist, Futurist, Fauvist and more recent movements since the 1960s. The movements show how 20th century art has moved from figurative to abstract, back to figurative and now conceptual and Minimal art. Exhibits such as the latter move to Bankside in 2000. The Tate Café designed by John Miller and the Tate Espresso Bar have been added to cope with the Tate gallery's increased number of visitors. The restaurant has Rex Whistler murals. There are free films and lectures. Friends of the Tate membership includes invitations to major shows and the Tate magazine (excellent value). The Clore Gallery displays the Turner Bequest in a separate building. The Tate Gallery Liverpool and the Tate St Ives are affiliated. A must for anyone interested in Modern or contemporary art. Excellent bookshop with friendly staff. Underground Pimlico or 88 bus from Oxford Circus or Trafalgar Square.

Tate Gallery of Modern Art, Bankside, Sumner Street, London SE1. Telephone (020-7) 401 7302 (visitor centre until it opens in May 2000) or 887 8000 (central Tate number). Open daily 10-6. (see Contemporary art galleries section for more details)

Designed by Herzog and de Meuron, the Swiss architects, the new Tate Gallery of Modern Art will regenerate this riverside part of the Borough of Southwark. A new pedestrian bridge designed by Sir Norman Foster and Sir Anthony Caro also opens to link the City and Southwark. There are seven levels; three for galleries and varying kinds of space for display. There are also educational facilities, a shop, café, auditorium, film and seminar room. All international art from 1900 transferred from Millbank making the Tate Bankside a major world modern art museum. The Janet Wolfson de Botton Gift of 60 works by 29 artists joins the Tate Modern collection, including works by Clemente, Sherman, Warhol, Samaras, Andre and Gilbert and George. Underground Jubilee Line (due to open 2000).

Theatre Museum, 1E Tavistock Street, London WC2E 7PA. Telephone 0171 (0207 from 4/2000) 836 7891. Public entrance in

Russell Street. Open Tuesday-Sunday 11-7. Closed Monday. Café and box office open 11-8, Sunday 11-7. Entrance fee. Friends of the V&A free and children under 5. School parties also free.

With the transformation of Covent Garden's Flower Market the V&A's Theatre Museum was installed in this busy tourist area. Starting with a gift in1924 of Mrs Gabrielle Enthoven's collection of theatrical memorabilia, adding collections of the British Theatre museum and the proposed Museum of the Performing Arts, the final result became this fine museum in Covent Garden. There are two temporary galleries in honour of Sir John Gielgud and Sir Henry Irving. At the entrance the angel from the Gaiety Theatre at the Aldwych greets you. The lower foyer holds the painting collection, an Edwardian re-creation which acts as a foyer to the adjacent platform theatre, or performances and lunchtime lectures. There is also a café, shop, research facilities, studio theatre and rooms can be hired for receptions and conferences. (0171 (0207 from 4/2000) 938 8366). Underground Covent Garden.

Victoria and Albert Museum, Cromwell Road, South Kensington, London SW7. Telephone 0171 (0207 from 4/2000) 938 8441. Recorded information (7) 938 8349. Open daily 10-5.45, Wednesdays late 6.30-9.30. Entrance fee but well worth it! Free after 4.30pm.

The £75 million Daniel Libeskind futuristic spiral was agreed by Kensington and Chelsea council in late 1998 and will be ready early in the millennium. In 2001 the renovated British galleries will re-open, after a £31 million facelift. The recent Canon Photography Gallery is also very welcome. It includes early and recent photography in colour and b/w.

A magnificent collection of decorative arts, including 7 acres to roam and admire jewellery, costumes, textiles, porcelain,

Srinagar, Kashmir, Henri Cartier-Bresson (Canon Photography Gallery, V&A).

armour, furniture, carpets, embroidery, musical instruments and much more. Interesting collection of prints and paintings by Constable, also the famous Raphael Cartoons, English miniatures, Eastern art ranging from India to the art of Islam. The costume collection is fairly unique, ranging from Edward VII's hunting clothes to fashionable 1920s, 30s dresses by Schiaparelli, 50s by Chanel, 60s and 70s by Biba and Mary Quant and other interesting private gifts.

Students of fashion and design can arrange to see specific items on request. The Henry Cole Wing houses the Frank Lloyd Wright room and the 20th-century galleries. The main wing has the Nehru Gallery of Indian art, the Samsung gallery of Korean art and other privately donated collections. The V&A enters the 21st-century with a new building the futuristic spiral designed by Daniel Liebeskind. A dramatic cube design will change the genteel area of South Kensington by 2004 and add a bit of pzazz to the V&A, which at times seems like a fairytale princess, asleep for a hundred years; charming but in need of some additional space to breath.

The National Art Library, V&A Picture library and Print Room are all important services on offer to the public as well as lectures and courses. There is also now a research and conservation of art centre at the museum.

In 1998 the Canon Photography gallery opened and the Ironwork galleries, also the Raphael gallery and the Tsui gallery of Chinese Art. The Silver Galleries open in 2000, The British Galleries in 2001 and the Spiral in 2004. All the more reason to visit this wonderful museum again and again. The restaurant is excellent and spacious and the shop has a selection of books, postcards, objets d'art and craft, also good children's toys.

Exhibitions include: The Grand Design until January 2000; Art Nouveau April-July 30th 2000; Brand New Oct 2000-Jan 2001; The Victorians October 2001-January 2002. Underground South Kensington.

Wallace Collection, Manchester Square, London W.1. Telephone 0171 (0207 from 4/2000) 935 0687. Open Monday-Saturday 10-5, Sunday 2-5.

The house was built for the Duke of Manchester in 1776-88 and is set in a fine square behind Oxford Street. It is near Selfridges store and offers a peaceful break from busy Oxford Street for visitors. The collection includes French 18th century paintings by Fragonard, Watteau and Boucher, also Dutch paintings by Rembrandt, Van Dyck and Frans Hals' Laughing Cavalier. The clocks are exquisite and the furniture reflects the splendid lifestyle in which the owners must once have lived. The decorative arts include porcelian, French furniture, clocks, bronze sculpture, snuff-boxes, majolica, enamels, glass and silver. The house itself gives one an idea of what life must have been like in this 18th-century townhouse. Underground Bond Street.

Painting by Pieter de Hooch at the Wallace Collection.

Wellcome Historical Medical Museum, 183 Euston Road London NW1. Telephone 0171 (0207 from 4/2000) 611 8582. Open to the public, admission free. Part of the Wellcome Trust. Open Monday, Wednesday, Friday 9.45-5.15; Tuesday and Thursday 9.45-7.15. Saturday 9.45-1. Closed Bank Holidays. Wide-ranging reference library of books, manuscripts, archives, paintings, prints from 1100BC to the present day, international in scope. In an elegant 1930s neoclassical building near Euston. Computer catalogue, videodisc and illustrated publications available. Useful resources for artists. Temporary exhibitions in History of Medicine Gallery. Underground Euston

Wesley's House, City Road, London EC1. Telephone 0171 (0207 from 4/2000) 253 2262. Open Monday-Saturday 10-1, 2-4. Entrance fee.

The home of the famous Methodist preacher John Wesley from 1779-91. The chapel next door and the graveyard are also worth visiting and the famous Bunhill Fields across the road where many famous London writers are buried; William Blake the artist was also buried here. Underground Old Street.

Westminster Treasures, Broad Sanctuary, London SW1. Telephone 0171 (0207 from 4/2000) 222 5152. Open Monday-Saturday 10.30-4.30. Sunday (April-September) 10.30-4.30.
900 years of Abbey history are related in various plans, documents and costumes. Wax funeral effigies of various Kings and Queens and other famous historical figures such as Nelson. Combine a visit to the Abbey itself with the museum. Underground Westminster.

William Morris Gallery, Lloyd Park, Walthamstow, London E17. Telephone 0181 (0208 from 4/2000) 527 3782. Open Monday-Saturday 10-5 (on Tusday and Thursday April-September), first Sunday of each month open 10-12 and 2-5.
William Morris, the Victorian artist/craftsman and writer lived here from 1848-56. Some of the many exquisite Morris designs can be seen here, also tiles and furniture. Work by contemporary Pre-Raphaelites such as Burne-Jones and Ford Madox-Brown can be seen. Worth visiting, especially after the V&A major exhibition in 1996. Underground Walthamstow Central.

Wimbledon Tennis Museum, The All-England Lawn Tennis Club, Church Road, Wimbledon, London SW19. Telephone 0181 (0208 from 4/2000) 946 6131. Open Tuesday-Saturday 11-5, Sunday 2-5. Special opening times during Wimbledon fortnight (end June, beginning July).
The development of lawn tennis with various items relating to the game; racquets, tennis fashion, atmosphere, films, documents about tennis photographs. Underground Southfields.

Whitechapel Art Gallery, Whitechapel High Street, London E.1. Telephone 0171 (0207 from 4/2000) 377 0107. Open Tuesday-Sunday 11-5, Wednesday-8. Closed Monday.
Many artists live in the east end, so this gallery has a wide range of historical and contemporary exhibitions. The Whitechapel Open is held every two years (last one 1998) with affiliated studio and east end gallery shows. The East end houses some 20,000 artists! Good bookshop run by Zwemmers and a café. Underground Aldgate East.

Self portrait at 34, Rembrandt by Himself, National Gallery until September 5th '99 and then at The Mauritshuis, The Hague until January 2000.

Many other museums have not been listed as they are either too specialised or just outside London. These include:

Battle of Britain

HMS Belfast

Bruce Castle Museum

Chartered Insurance Institute Museum

Down House (home of Charles Darwin) Kent

Kew Bridge Engines

Kingsbury Watermill Museum

Martinware Pottery Collection, Southall

Mosquito Aircraft Museum, Herts

Old Operating Theatre

Rotunda Museum

St Albans City Museum

Verulamium Museum

Vestry House Museum

Syon Park, Brentford

Ham House, Surrey

Osterley Park, Middlesex

Livesey Museum, London SE15

Marble Hill House, Twickenham

Museum of Fulham Palace

Spencer House (Tel 499 8620)

London Canal Museum

Yet to open:

Dalí Museum

Museum of Women's Art

Art Galleries
Old Masters & Early 20th-century Art

This section is mainly for collectors, overseas dealers and people interested in prints, Old Master paintings and sculpture. Although many of these galleries vary in size and the kind of work they deal in, if you are interested in one particular area of art this list should help save time. See interview with Guy Beddington, a 19th and early 20th century art dealer.

Many of these galleries are situated in St James's, London SW1, near Bond Street and Sotheby's and Christies auction rooms. The latter are worth visiting if at all interested in buying or selling art or just viewing to compare prices. Ring the galleries to check on opening hours if not listed.

St James's area is nearest to Green Park tube. Motcomb Street is near Knightsbridge. The Portobello Road area galleries, mainly Ledbury Road, are near Notting Hill Gate tube and walk down the hill towards Portobello Road. Many of these galleries do restoration work and framing.

Refer to main newspapers or Galleries magazine for exhibition listings.

PLEASE NOTE NEW LONDON TELEPHONE NUMBERS FROM APRIL 2000. 0171 becomes 020-7 and 0181 becomes 020-08.

Abbot and Holder, 30 Museum Street, London WC1A1LH. Telephone 0171 (0207 from 4/2000) 637 3981. Open Monday-Saturday 9.30-6, Thursday -7.
Stock of over 1000 pictures always on view. 19th and 20th century art. Underground Tottenham Court Road.

Ackermann and Johnson, 27 Lowndes Street, London SW1. Telephone 0171 (0207 from 4/2000) 235 6464. Open Monday-Friday 9-5, Saturday 10-12.
Sporting paintings. 18th-20th century British oil paintings and watercolours. Underground Knightsbridge.

Agnews, 43 Old Bond Street and 3 Albemarle Street, London W.1. Telephone 0171 (0207 from 4/2000) 629 6176. Open Monday-Friday 9.30-5.30, Thursday -6.30.
18th and 19th century prints and Old Master paintings, also contemporary established British painters such as Bernard Dunstan. Underground Green Park.

Anthony Mould, 173 New Bond Street, London W.1. Telephone 0171 (0207 from 4/2000) 491 4627. Open Monday-Friday 9.30-6.
English portraits. Underground Bond Street.

Archeus Fine Art, 1st floor, 65 New Bond Street, London W.1. Telephone 0171 (0207 from 4/2000) 499 9755. By appointment. 19th and 20th century paintings, prints and sculpture. Underground Green Park.

Attwell Galleries, 124 Lower Richmond Road, Putney, London SW15. Telephone 0171 (0207 from 4/2000) 785 9559. Open Tuesday-Saturday 10-5.30.
19th and early 20th-century British and Italian oil and water-colour paintings. Restoration, conservation, framing and gilding.

Axia, 21 Ledbury Road, London W11 2AQ. Telephone 0171 (0207 from 4/2000) 727 9724. Open Monday-Friday 10.30-6.
East Christian and Islamic art. Underground Notting Hill Gate and walk down the hill.

Barnsbury Gallery, 24 Thornhill Road, London N1 1HW. Telephone 0171 (0207 from 4/2000) 607 7121. Open Tuesday-Saturday 12-6.
Prints, maps, children's games and ephemera. Peepshows, panoramas and optical toys. Lassalle framing.

Baumkotter Gallery, 63A Kensington Church Street, London W.8. Telephone 0171 (0207 from 4/2000) 937 5171. Open Monday-Friday 9.30-6.
17th-19th-century oil paintings. Restoration work available. Underground High Street Kensington.

Beaufort Gallery, 313 Kings Road, London SW3. Telephone 0171 (0207 from 4/2000) 351 2077. Open Monday-Saturday 10-6.
19th and 20th-century English watercolours and drawings. Also limited edition prints.

Belgrave Gallery, 53 Englands Lane, London NW3. Telephone 0171 (0207 from 4/2000) 722 5150. Open Monday-Friday 10-6. British Post-Impressionists and Moderns. 20th-century paintings, watercolours, prints and sculpture. Underground Belsize Park.

The Bloomsbury Workshop Ltd, 12 Galen Place, London WC1. Telephone 0171 (0207 from 4/2000) 405 0632. Open Tuesday-Friday 9.30-5.

Bloomsbury Group and Modern British. Paintings, drawings, prints, especially by Vanessa Bell and Duncan Grant. Also a stock of Bloomsbury Group books (first editions, secondhand and new). Underground Tottenham Court Road.

Bonhams, Auctioneers and Valuers since 1793. Montpelier Galleries, Montpelier Street, London SW7. Telephone 0171 (0207 from 4/2000) 584 9161/4577. Open Monday-Friday 9-5.30. Underground Knightsbridge.

Burlington Gallery, 10 Burlington Gardens, London W.1. Telephone 0171 (0207 from 4/2000) 734 9984. Open Monday-Friday 9.30-5.30.

Richard III at the National Portrait Gallery.

Specialises in early 19th and early 20th-century oil paintings and watercolours. Underground Green Park.

Caelt Gallery, 182 Westbourne Grove, London W.11. Telephone 0171 (0207 from4/2000) 229 9309.
Victorian paintings, landscape, marine, Arab horses and animals. Underground Notting Hill Gate and walk down the hill.

Christies, 8 King Street, St James's, London SW1. Telephone 0171 (0207 from 4/2000) 839 9060. Open Monday-Friday 9-4.45. Auctions and viewing daily of; books, carpets, clocks, watches, porcelain, pictures, prints, sculpture, silver, stamps, wines etc. Free valuations of any work of art given on the premises. Underground Green Park.

Chris Beetles, 8 & 10 Ryder Street, St James's London SW1. Telephone 0171 (0207 from 4/2000) 839 7551. Open daily 10-5.30. England's largest stock of 19th and 20th-century British oils. Underground Green Park.

Christopher Mendez, 58 Jermyn Street, London SW1. Telephone 0171 (0207 from 4/2000) 491 0015. Open Monday-Friday 10-5.30.
16th-18th-century Old Master prints. Underground Green Park.

Colin Denny, 18 Cale Street, Chelsea Green, London SW3. Telephone 0171 (0207 fom 4/2000) 584 0240. Open Monday-Saturday 9-6.
19th and 20th-century marine paintings, watercolours and prints, plus restoration and framing. Underground Sloane Square.

P&D Colnaghi Ltd, 14 Old Bond Street, London W.1. Telephone 0171 (0207 from 4/2000) 491 7408. Open Monday-Friday 9.30-6. Old Master paintings, prints and drawings, also watercolours. Oriental department. 14th-19th-century art. Supplies many of the world's major museums. 200 years old. Underground Green Park.

Collins and Hastie, 5 Park Walk, London SW10. Telephone 0171 (0207 from 4/2000) 351 4292.
19th-century British paintings. Specialises in animal and sporting subjects.Underground Fulham Broadway.

Connaught and Brown, 2 Albemarle Street, London W.1. Telephone 0171 (0207 from 4/2000) 408 0362. Open Monday-Friday 10-6, Saturday 10-12.30.
European Post-Impressionist, Modern British and contemporary

paintings, drawings, watercolours and sculpture. Underground Green Park.

Connoisseur Gallery, 14 Holland Street, London W.8. Telephone 017(0207 from 4/2000) 937 0788. Open Monday-Saturday 10-6.
Orientalism. Specialists in old books, maps, prints, paintings and works of art of the Middle East. Very large collection of the prints of David Roberts, RA. Underground High St Kensington.

Cooper Fine Art, 768 Fulham Road, London SW6. Telephone 0171 (0207 from 4/2000) 731 3421.
Watercolours and oil paintings 1850-1930. Underground Fulham Broadway.

Cox and Company, 37 Duke Street, St James's London SW1. Telephone 0171 (0207 from 4/2000) 930 1987. Open Monday-Friday 10-5.30, Saturday by appointment.
19th and 20th-century paintings, watercolours and prints. Engslish sporting and landscape paintings. Underground Green Park.

Cyril Humphris, 8 Pembroke Walk, London W.8. Telephone 0171 (0207 from 4/2000) 629 6240.
Renaissance and Baroque sculpture and paintings. Underground High Street Kensington.

David Carritt Ltd, 15 Duke Street, London SW1. Telephone 0171 (0207 from 4/2000) 930 8733. Open Monday-Friday 9.30-5.30.
Old Masters, 19th-century and contemporary paintings. Underground Green Park.

David James Gallery, 8 Halkin Arcade, Motcomb Street, London SW1. Telephone 0171 (0207 from 4/2000) 235 5552. Open Monday-Friday 11.30-6, Saturday 11.30-2.30.
Fine Victorian watercolours. Marine, landscapes and figurative work. Sidney Cooper, Charles Dixon, Charles Taylor, Sylvester Stannard and John Henry Mole. Underground Knightsbridge.

Daniel Katz Ltd, 59 Jermyn Street, London SW1. Telephone 0171 (0207 from 4/2000) 493 0688. Open Monday-Friday 9-5.30. European sculpture and works of art. Renaissance, 17th &18th-century Old Master paintings. Underground Piccadilly.

Durini Gallery, 150 Walton Street, London SW3. Telephone 0171 (0207 from 4/2000) 581 1237. Open Monday-Friday 10-6, Saturday 10-5.

19th and 20th-century Spanish, Italian, French and Latin American oil paintings and sculpture. Underground Knightsbridge.

Didier Aaron, 21 Ryder Street, London SW1. Telephone 0171 (0207 from 4/2000) 839 4716.
18th century French furniture, paintings. Old Master paintings and drawings. Underground Green Park.

Douwes Fine Art, 38 Duke Street, St James's London SW1. Telephone 0171 (0207 from 4/2000) 839 5795. Open Monday-Friday 9.30-5.30. Also in Amsterdam at 46 Rokin.
17th-century Dutch, Flemish and 19th-century French and Dutch paintings, drawings, prints and watercolours. Underground Green Park.

Duncan Miller Fine Art, 17 Flask Walk, London NW3. Telephone 0171 (0207 from 4/2000) 435 5462.
Selection of British traditional and Impressionist paintings. Specialists in Scottish Colourist paintings and contemporary art now also. Underground Hampstead.

Duncan Campbell Fine Art, 15 Thackeray Street, Kensington Square, London W.8. Telephone 0171 (0207 from 4/2000) 937 8665. Open Tuesday-Friday 11-6, Saturday 10-5.
19th and 20th-century paintings and watercolours. Duncan Grant, Cornelius Kuypers, Clement Quinton, Paul Mathieu, José de Zomora. Underground High Street Kensington.

Eaton Gallery, 34 Duke Street, St James's London SW1. Telephone 0171 (0207 from 4/2000) 930 5950. Open Monday-

Duncan Miller Fine Art, Hampstead.

Saturday 10-5.30 and by appointment.
19th-century British and European paintings. Underground Green Park.

Editions Graphiques, 3 Clifford Street, London W.1. Telephone 0171 (0207 from 4/2000) 734 3944. Open Monday-Friday 10-6, Saturday 10-1.
Art Deco, Art Nouveau fin de siècle prints, posters and paintings 1880-today. Underground Bond Street.

Eskenazi, 10 Clifford Street, London W.1. Telephone 0171 (0207 from 4/2000) 493 5464. Open Monday-Friday 9.30-6.
Chinese and Japanese art. Underground Green Park or Bond Street.

Faustus Fine Art, 32 Duke Street, St James's London SW1. Telephone 0171 (0207 from 4/2000) 930 1864. Open Monday-Friday 9.30-5.30.
European prints and ancient art. Underground Green Park.

Fine Art Society, 148 Bond Street, London W.1. Telephone 0171 (0207 from 4/2000) 629 5116. Open Monday-Friday 9.30-5.30, Saturday 10-1.
19th and 20th-century British art. Emphasis also on Scottish paintings. Underground Bond Street.

Fleur de Lys Gallery, 227A Westbourne Grove, London W.11. Telephone 0171 (0207 from 4/2000) 727 8595. Open Monday-Saturday 10.30-5.
Decorative 19th century oil paintings. English, Dutch and European. Private, export and trade. Also English watercolours. Underground Notting Hill Gate and walk down the hill.

Frost and Reed Ltd, 2 King Street, London SW1. Telephone 0171 (0207 from 4/2000) 839 4645. Open Monday-Friday 9-5.30. 19th and 20th-century English and French paintings. Underground Bond Street.

Galerie Besson, 15 Royal Arcade, 28 Old Bond Street, London W.1. Telephone 0171 (0207 from 4/2000) 491 1706. Open Tuesday-Friday 10-5.30.
Modern pottery and Lucie Rie the great 20th-century potter. Underground Bond Street.

Gallery 19, 19 Kensington Court Place, London W.8. Telephone 0171 (0207 from 4/2000) 937 7222. Open Sunday-Saturday 10-6.
Original art and prints of Kensington. Underground Notting Hill Gate.

Galerie Moderne Le Style Lalique, 10 Halkin Arcade, Motcomb Street, London SW1. Telephone 0171 (0207 from 4/2000) 245 6907. Open Monday-Friday 10-6, Saturday by appointment.
Specialists in pre-war René Lalique glass, including vases, scent bottles, tableware, lighting fixtures, designs, car mascots, jewellery and sculpture. Underground Knightsbridge.

Gallery 25, 4 Halkin Arcade, Motcomb Street, London SW1. Telephone 0171 (0207 from 4/2000) 235 5178. Open Monday-Friday 9.30-5.30.
Decorative arts 1890-1930. Paintings, bronze, silver, Bugatti, good Art Deco furniture and furnishings. Underground Knightsbridge.

Gavin Graham Gallery, 47 Ledbury Road, London W.11. Telephone 0171 (0207 from 4/2000) 229 4848. Open Monday-Friday 10-6, Saturday 10-4.
17th-19th-century English and European oil paintings. Underground Notting Hill Gate and walk down the hill.

Green and Stone of Chelsea, 259 Kings Road, London SW3. Telephone 0171 (0207 from 4/2000) 352 6521. Open Monday-Saturday 9-5.30.
19th century watercolours and drawings. Also fine art materials for sale. Underground Sloane Square and bus.

The Greenwich Gallery, 9 Nevada Street, Greenwich. Telephone 0181 (0208 from 4/2000) 305 1666. Open Monday-Saturday 10-5.30.
18th and 19th-century watercolurs and paintings. Also deals in Modern British paintings. Oppsoite the Greenwich Theatre. British Rail Greenwich.

Grosvenor Gallery, 18 Albemarle Street, London W.1. Telephone 0171 (0207 from 4/2000) 629 0891. Open Monday-Friday 10-5.
Publishes works by Gerald Scarfe. Watercolours, sculpture from Art Nouveau to 20th-century Masters. World representatives of Erté. Underground Bond Street.

Hancock Gallery, 184 Westbourne Grove, London W.11. Telephone 0171 (0207 from 4/2000) 229 7827. Open Monday-Friday 10-6, Saturday 10-5.
Fine and decorative arts. 19th and 20th-century paintings. Underground Notting Hill Gate and walk down the hill.

Harari & Johns Ltd, 12 Duke Street, St James's, London SW1. Telephone 0171 (0207 from 4/2000) 839 7671. Open Monday-

Friday 9.30-5.30.
Old Master paintings. Underground Green Park.

Hazlitt Gooden and Fox, 38 Bury Street, St James's, London SW1. Telephone 0171 (0207 from 4/2000) 930 6422/6821.
French and English 19th-century paintings and drawings. Underground Green Park.

Hollywood Road Gallery, 12 Hollywood Road, London SW10. Telephone 0171 (0207 from 4/2000) 351 1973. Open Monday-Friday 11-7.30, Saturday 11-3.
Late 19th-century English and French oils and watercolours. Good stock of original gilt and rosewood frames. Underground Fulham Broadway.

Iona Antiques, PO Box 285, London W.8 6HZ. Telephone 0171 (0207 from 4/2000) 602 1193. By appointment only.
Largest selection of primitive 19th-century animal paintings in England.

Japanese Gallery, 66 D Kensington Church Street, London W.8. Telephone 0171 (0207 from 4/2000) 229 2934. Also at Camden Passage, London N.1. Open Monday-Saturday 10-6.
Japanese prints; Utamaro, Hiroshige, Toyokuni, Kunyoshi. Prints at reasonable prices from £10-£3000. Underground High Street Kensington.

Silver tigress, Roman Britain galleries, British Museum.

John Campbell Picture Frames, 164 Walton Street, London SW3. Telephone 0171 (0207 from 4/2000) 584 9268. Open Monday-Friday 9.30-5.30, Saturday 9.30-1.
Post-Impressionist and Modern British oils and watercolours. Also a large selection of sporting prints. Trade and retail master framers; hand-finished, custom-made frames, restoration and gilding. Expert restoration of oils and watercolours. Underground South Kensington.

John Mitchell & Son, 160 New Bond Street, London W.1. Telephone 0171 (0207 from 4/2000) 493 7567. Open Monday-Friday 11-5.30.
Old Masters, 17th-century Dutch and Flemish, 18th-century English watercolours and paintings and French 19th-century. Underground Bond Street.

Johnny Van Haeften Gallery, 13 Duke Street, London SW1. Telephone 0171 (0207 from 4/2000) 930 3062. Open Monday-Friday 10-5.30 or by appointment.
Dutch and Flemish 17th-century Old Master paintings. Underground Green Park.

The Kilim Warehouse Ltd., 28A Pickets Street, London SW12 8QB. Telephone 0171 (0207 from 4/2000) 675 3122. Open Monday-Saturday 10-4, other times by appointment.
Old, decorative and antique kilims from Asia Minor and beyond. New kilims handwoven in the Anatolian villages using classical designs.

Kufa Gallery, Westbourne Hall, 26 Westbourne Grove, London W.2. Telephone 0171 (0207 from 4/2000) 229 1928. Open Tuesday-Saturday 10-5.
Middle-Eastern arts; architecture, viusla arts, music and literature with changing traditional and contemporary art exhibitions. Underground Queensway.

Lefevre Gallery, 30 Bruton Street, London W.1. Telephone 0171 (0207 from 4/2000) 493 2107. Open Monday-Friday 10-5, Saturday 10-1.
Edward Burra and L.S.Lowry. 19th and 20th-century major European masters. Contemporary British artists. Underground Bond Street.

Spink Leger, 13 Old Bond Street, London W.1. Telephone 0171 (0207 from 4/2000) 629 3538/9. Open Monday-Friday 9.30-5.30. Saturday by appointment.
English 18th and 19th-century paintings, early English watercolours and Old Masters. Underground Green Park.

Llewellyn Alexander (Fine Paintings) Ltd., 124-126 The Cut, Waterloo, London SE1. Telephone 0171 (0207 from 4/2000) 620 1322. Open Monday-Friday 10-7.30, Saturday 2-7.30. Director; Gillian Llewellyn Lloyd. British and early 20th-century, also contemporary British figurative and landscape painters. They also hold the annual alternative RA summer show exhibition. Underground Waterloo. Opposite the Old Vic Theatre.

Loggia Gallery, 15 Buckingham Gate, London SW1. Telephone 0171 (0207 from 4/2000) 828 5963. Open Monday-Friday 6-8, Saturday and Sunday 2-6. Temporary exhibitions held by the Free painters and sculptors.

Lucy B Campbell, 123 Kensington Church Street, London W.8. Telephone 0171 (0207 from 4/2000) 727 2205. Watercolours, 17th-19th-century prints. Underground Notting I Iill Gate.

Lumley Cazalet, 33 Davies Street, London W.1. Telephone 0171 (0207 from 4/2000) 491 4767 / 499 5058. Open Monday-Friday 10-6. Late 19th and 20th-century European masters. Chagall, Picasso, French 19th-century prints. Printmakers can show portfolios. Underground Bond Street.

The Maas Gallery, 15A Clifford Street, London W.1. Telephone 0171 (0207 from 4/2000) 734 2302/3272. Open Monday-Friday 10-5. 1800-1920 English paintings. Victorian artists and Pre-Raphaelites. Underground Green Park.

MacConnal-Mason and Son Ltd, 14 Duke Street, St James's, London SW1. Telephone 0171 (0207 from 4/2000) 839 7693/4. Open Monday-Friday 9.30-5.30, Saturday (Burlington) 9.30-1. 19th-century European paintings and contemporary British. Underground Green Park.

Manya Igel Fine Arts, 21-22 Peters Court, Porchester Road, London W.2. Telephone 0171 (0207 from 4/2000) 229 1669/8429. By appointment only. 19th and 20th-century British oils and watercolours.

Maria Andipa's Icon Gallery, 162 Walton Street, London SW3. Telephone 0171 (0207 from 4/2000) 589 2371. Open Monday-Friday 10.30-6. Greek, Russian, Serbian icons and Romanian 14th-19th century icons. 18th-century furniture. Underground Knightsbridge.

Marina Henderson Gallery, 11 Langton Street, London SW10. Telephone 0171 (0207 from 4/2000) 352 1667. Open Tuesday-Saturday 11-6.
Theatrical and architectural designs from 1800.

The Mark Gallery, 9 Porchester Place, London W.2. Telephone 0171 (0207 from 4/2000) 262 4906. Open Monday-Friday 10-1 and 2-6, Saturday 11-1.
Russian icons from the 16th-19th-century. Contemporary prints. Dalí, Chagall, Ecole de Paris prints. Underground Marble Arch.

Martyn Gregory, 34 Bury Street, St James's London SW1. Telephone 0171 (0207 from 4/2000) 839 3731. Open Monday-Friday 10-6.
Early English watercolours. Far East and Chinese paintings. Underground Green Park.

Mathaf Gallery, 24 Motcomb Street, London SW1. Telephone 0171 (0207 from 4/2000) 235 0010. Open Monday-Friday 9.30-5.30.
Oriental paintings from the Middle East. Underground Knightsbridge.

Matthiesen Fine Art Ltd., 7-8 Masons Yard, Duke Street, London SW1. Telephone 0171 (0207 from 4/2000) 930 2437. Open Monday-Friday 10-6.
Late 19th and 20th-century prints and paintings. Italian, Spanish and French 13th-15th century paintings. Underground Green Park.

Medici Galleries, 7 Grafton Street, Bond Street, London W.1. Telephone 0171 (0207 from 4/2000) 629 5675 and 26 Thurloe Street South Kensington. Telephone 0171 (0207 from 4/2000) 589 1363. Open Monday-Friday 10-5.30. Saturday 10-6 (Thurloe St). British contemporary artists at Grafton Street. Fine art publishers. Prints, old postcards and cards. Underground Bond Street and South Kensington.

Michael Simpson Ltd., 11 Savile Row, London W.1. Telephone 0171 (0207 from 4/2000) 437 5414. Open Monday-Friday 9.30-5.30.
Old Master paintings, drawings and prints. English watercolours and paintings. Underground Green Park.

Milne and Moller, 35 Colville Terrace, London W.11. Telephone 0171 (0207 from 4/2000) 727 1679. Open Saturday 10-4, otherwise by appointment.
19th and 20th-century British and continental watercolours.

Morton and Morris, 32 Bury Street, St James's, London SW1. Telephone 0171 (0207 from 4/2000) 930 2825/6422. Open Monday-Friday 10-5.30.
English 17th, 18th and early 19th-century paintings and water-colours. Underground Green Park.

Noortman, 40-41 Old Bond Street, London W.1. Telephone 0171 (0207 from 4/2000) 491 7284. Open Monday-Friday 9.30-5.30.
Old Masters and 19th-century French Impressionists and Barbizon school. Underground Green Park.

Old London Galleries, 4 Royal Opera Arcade, Pall Mall, London SW1. Telephone 0171 (0207 from 4/2000) 930 7679. Open Monday-Friday 10.30-5, Saturday 11.30-2.30.
Antique decorative prints 17th-19th-century. London views, fishing, sporting and other subjects. Underground Piccadilly.

Oliver Swann Galleries, 170 Walton Street, London SW3. Telephone 0171 (0207 from 4/2000) 581 4229 / 584 8684.
Marine paintings, oil paintings, watercolours, prints of marine, coastal yachting and battleship subjects. Underground South Kensington.

Omell, 46 Albemarle Street, London W.1. Telephone 0171 (0207 from 4/2000) 499 3685. Open Monday -Friday 9.30-5.30. 18th and 19th-century European and British oil paintings. Underground Green Park.

NR Omell, 6 Duke Street, St James's, London SW1. Telephone 0171 (0207 from 4/2000) 839 6223. 18th and 19th-century paintings. Underground Green Park.

O'Shea Gallery, 120A Mount Street, London W.1. Telephone 0171 (0207 from 4/2000) 629 1116. Open Monday-Friday 9.30-6, Saturday 9.30-1.
Antiquarian maps, prints and atlases. Specialist dealers in 15th-19th-century maps, topographical, illustrated books. Framing and restoration. Underground Bond Street.

Parker Gallery, 28 Pimlico Road, London SW1. Telephone 0171 (0207 from 4/2000) 730 6768. Open Monday-Friday 9.30-5.30.
Marine, military, sporting, topographical subjects. A large selection of 18th and 19th-century prints and oil paintings, some map and ship models. Underground Sloane Square.

Paul Mason Gallery, 149 Sloane Street, London SW1. Telephone 0171 (0207 from 4/2000) 730 3683. Open Monday-Friday 9-6.30, Wednesday 9-7, Saturday 9-1.

Specialist dealer in 18th and 19th-century marine, sporting and decorative paintings and prints. Restoration, conservation and framing. Underground Sloane Square.

Pawsey and Payne Ltd., 90 Jermyn Street, London SW1. Telephone 0171 (0207 from 4/2000) 930 4221. Open Monday-Friday 9-5.30.
18th and 19th-century sporting paintings. Watercolours, prints and engravings. Underground Green Park.

Peter Nahum Ltd., (at the Leicester Galleries) 5 Ryder Street, London SW1. Telephone 0171 (0207 from 4/2000) 930 6059. 18th-20th-century paintings, drawings and sculpture. Underground Green Park.

Phillips Fine Art Auctioneers, 101 New Bond Street, London W.1. Telephone 0171 (0207 from 4/2000) 629 6602. Open Monday-Friday 8.30-5, Saturday 8.30-12.
Auctions and viewings held daily of paintings, prints, English and European, works of art, miniatures, Art Nouveau and Art Deco, collectors' items. Underground Bond Street.

Phillips, 10 Salem Road, London W.2. Telephone 0171 (0207 from 4/2000) 229 9090.
Textiles, clothes, memorabilia at reasonable prices. Underground Queensway/Bayswater.

Piano Nobile Fine Paintings, 26 Richmond Hill, Richmond. Telephone 0181 (0208 from 4/2000) 940 2435. Open Tuesday-Saturday 10-6.
Impressionist and Post-Impressionist British and continental oil paintings. Underground Richmond.

Piano Nobile, 129 Portland Road, London W.11. Telephone 0171 (0207 from 4/2000) 229 1099.
20th-century British paintings at the Holland Park branch. Underground Holland Park.

Polak Gallery, 21 King Street, St James's, London SW1. Telephone 0171 (0207 from 4/2000) 839 2871. Open Monday-Saturday 9.30-5.30. 19th century English and European paintings and early English watercolours. Marine paintings. Underground Green Park.

Portland Gallery, 9 Bury Street, St James's, London SW1. Telephone 0171 (0207 from 4/2000) 321 0422.
Scottish paintings 1880 to today. Underground Green Park.

Pruskin Gallery, 73 Kensington Church Street, London W.8. Telephone 0171 (0207 from 4/2000) 937 1994 / 3761285. Open Tuesday-Saturday 10-6 and by appointment.
Art Nouveau, Art Deco, post-war decorative arts. Underground High Street Kensington.

Pyms Gallery, 9 Mount Street, London W.1. Telephone 0171 (0207 from 4/2000) 629 2020. Open Monday-Friday 10-6.
British paintings and watercolours 1590-1930. Underground Bond Street.

Rafael Valls Gallery, 11 Duke Street, St James's, London SW1. Telephone 0171 (0207 from 4/2000) 930 1144. Open Monday-Friday 10-6, Saturday by appointment.
Old Master paintings. 18th and 19th-century paintings. Dutch, Flemish and Spanish schools. Underground Green Park.

Rafael Valls (Contemporary), 6 Ryder Street, St James's, London SW1. Telephone 0171 (0207 from 4/2000) 930 0029. Gallery also for hire.

RMB Art, Stand 9, Alfie's Antique Market, 13-25 Church Street, London NW8. Telephone 0171 (0207 from 4/2000) 724 3437. Open Tuesday-Saturday 10.30-6.
18th-20th-century watercolours and drawings, also Modern British and contemporary art. Interest-free credit scheme.

Richard Green, 39 Dover Street, London W.1. Telephone 0171 (0207 from 4/2000) 499 4738. Also 147 New Bond Street, 493 3939 and 33 New Bond Street, 499 5553. Open Monday-Friday 9.30-6, Saturday 10-12.30.
Fine Old Master paintings (33 New Bond Street) Impressionist, Post-Impressionist and Modern British, Sporting and Marine paintings (147 New Bond St). Victorian and European paintings (Dover Street). An important, major gallery in London. Underground Green Park.

Robert Douwma Ltd., 173 New Bond Street, London W.1. Telephone 0171 (0207 from 4/2000) 495 4001. Open Monday-Friday 10-5.30.
15th-20th-century original prints, especially Stanley Hayter and Atelier 17. Underground Green Park.

Royal Exchange Gallery, 14 Royal Exchange, London EC3. Telephone 0171 (0207 from 4/2000) 283 4400. Open Monday-Friday 10.30-5.15.
19th and early 20th-century watercolours and paintings.

Roy Miles Fine Paintings Ltd., 29 Bruton Street, London W.1.
Telephone 0171 (0207 from 4/2000) 495 4747.
Major British paintings 1750-1950. Also Russian art specialists with many exhibitions of work by contemporary Russian artists.
Underground Green Park / Bond Street.

Sara Davenport Fine Paintings, 206 Walton Street, London

Choson Dynasty painting, Arts of Korea, British Museum.

SW3. Telephone 0171 (0207 from 4/2000) 225 2223/4. Open Monday-Friday 10-6, Saturday 11-4.
18th and 19th-century dog paintings. Oils and watercolours. Prices from £200-£40,000. Underground South Kensington.

The Schuster Gallery, 14 Maddox Street, London W.1. Telephone 0171 (0207 from 4/2000) 491 2208. Open Monday-Friday 10-5.30, Saturday 10-1.
David Roberts, antique prints of Egypt and the Holy Land.

Sladmore Gallery, 32 Bruton Place, London W.1. Telephone 0171 (0207 from 4/2000) 499 0365. Open Monday-Friday 10-6, Saturday 10-1.
Sporting paintings and prints. 19th and 20th-century sculpture. Underground Bond Street.

Sotheby's, 34-35 New Bond Street, London W.1. Telephone 0171(0207 from 4/2000) 493 8080. Open Monday-Friday 9-4.30.
Auctions held daily of antiquities, Asian art, paintings, drawings, watercolours, prints, Chinese, Japanese and Islamic works of art, 20th-century decorative arts, photographs, portrait miniatures, icons and Russian works of art, tribal art. Free advice and valuations given on the premises. Underground Bond Street/Green Park.

Spink & Sons Ltd., 5/7 King Street, St James's, London SW1. Telephone 0171 (0207 from 4/2000) 930 7888. Open Monday-Friday 9-5.30, Tuesday 9-7.30.
Largest art company in the world. English paintings and drawings of all periods. Oriental art, furniture and other objets d'art. Underground Green Park.

Stern Art Dealers, 46 Ledbury Road, London W.11. Telephone 0171 (0207 from 4/2000) 229 6187. Open Monday-Saturday 10-6.
19th-century English and European oil paintings. Underground Notting Hill Gate and walk down the hill.

Tadema Gallery, 10 Charlton Place, Camden Passage, London N.1. Telephone 0171 (0207 from 4/2000) 359 1055. Open Wednesday, Friday, Saturday 10-5 or by appointment.
Decorative art of the 20th-century, including Modern British and continental paintings and sculpture.

The Taylor Gallery, 1 Bolney Gate, London SW7. Telephone 0171 (0207 from 4/2000) 581 0253. Open Monday-Friday 10-5.30.
Specialists in English, Irish and American 19th and 20th-century paintings. Sir William Orpen, Sir Alfred Munnings,

Stanhope Forbes, Roderic O'Connor, Jack B. Yeats.

20th Century Gallery, 821 Fulham Road, London SW6. Telephone 0171 (0207 from 4/2000) 731 5888. Open Tuesday-Friday 10-6, Saturday 10-1.
Post-Impressionist and Modern British oils and watercolours. Underground Parsons Green.

Temple Gallery, 6 Clarendon Cross, London W.11. Telephone 0171 (0207 from 4/2000) 727 3809. Open Monday-Friday 10-5. Russian, Byzantine and Greek icons. Underground Holland Park.

Thompsons Gallery, 18 Dover Street, London W.1. Telephone 0171 (0207 from 4/2000) 629 6878. Open Tuesday-Friday 10-6, Saturday 12-5.
19th and 20th-century paintings and sculpture. Underground Green Park.

The Totteridge Gallery, 61 Totteridge Lane, London N.20. Telephone 0181 (0208 from 4/2000) 446 7896. Open Monday-Saturday 10.30-7.
Continental British 19th and 20th-century paintings and water-colours. Russell Flint prints also on sale. Underground Totteridge and Whetstone.

Tryon and Swann Gallery, 23-24 Cork Street, London W.1. Telephone 0171 (0207 from 4/2000) 734 6961. Open Monday-Friday 9.30-5.30.
Sporting and natural history paintings, prints and sculpture. Underground Green Park.

Verner Amell, 4 Ryder Street, St James's, London SW1. Telephone 0171 (0207 from 4/2000) 925 2759. Open Monday-Friday 10-5.30.
Old Master paintings. Underground Green Park.

Walpole Gallery, 38 Dover Street, London W.1. Telephone 0171 (0207 from 4/2000) 499 6626.
Old Masters gallery with splendid interior. Underground Green Park.

Waterhouse & Dodd, 110 New Bond Street, London SW1. Telephone 0171 (0207 from 4/2000) 491 9293.
British and European paintings and watercolours 1850-1930. Includes paintings by Bastien-Lepage,Mucha, Edward Lear and others. Underground Bond Street.

Waterman Fine Art, 74A Jermyn Street, London SW1. Telephone 0171 (0207 from 4/2000) 839 5203. Open Monday-Friday 9-6, Saturday 10-4.
Modern British paintings. Underground Piccadilly.

Whitford Fine Art, 6 Duke Street, St James's, London SW1. Telephone 0171 (0207 from 4/2000) 930 9332.
20th-century European paintings. Underground Green Park.

Wildenstein, 48 St James's Place, London SW1. Telephone 0171 (0207 from 4/2000) 629 0602. Open Monday-Friday 10-5.30. Specialises in French 19th and 20th-century paintings. Underground Bond Street.

William Beadleston, 13 Mason's Yard, St James's, London SW1. Telephone 0171 (0207 from 4/2000) 321 0495. Open Monday-Friday 10-5.
Impressionist and early 20th-century art. Underground Green Park.

William Weston Gallery, 7 Royal Arrcade, Albemarle Street, London W.1. Telephone 0171 (0207 from 4/2000) 493 0722. Open Monday-Friday 9.30-5, Saturday 10.30-1.
Etchings and lithographs from the 19th and 20th-century. Monthly catalogue available on subscription. Undergound Green Park.

Witch Ball, 2 Cecil Court, Charing Cross Road, London WC2. Telephone 0171 (0207 from 4/2000) 836 2922.
17th-19th-century engravings. Specialises in theatre, ballet and opera. Underground Charing Cross.

Woollahra Trading Company, 6 Bury Street, St James's, London SW1. Telephone 0171 (0207 from 4/2000) 839 9252. Also at 160 Queen Street, Woollahra, Sydney, Australia.
17th and 18th-century oil paintings and porcelain. Underground Green Park.

Sculpture by Niki de St Phalle at Chelsea Harbour.

Galleries showing
20th Century & Contemporary Art

There are commercial galleries all over London, but some areas have attracted a large number of galleries such as Cork Street, behind Bond Street, London W1, Dering Street, Charlotte Street, where a variety of commercial galleries and restaurants exist side by side. Whereas Cork Street tends to exhibit established artists and 20th-century Master prints and paintings, areas such as the East end, where there are now many alternative galleries, show cutting-edge and new art, often installations, conceptual, Minimal or even outrageous.Damien Hirst's work, once seen as shocking, is now establishment and shown at the White Cube Gallery. All things are possible in London these days and that is what makes it so exciting for overseas visitors and art enthusiasts. London has always been unconventional, eccentric and at the cutting edge of international art.

The list below includes contemporary art galleries alphabetically and gallery-policy for artist-applications has been included as often as possible. Some galleries treat artists well and return work, others are notorious, so be prepared. It is best to visit the space first and essential to enclose a stamped addressed envelope when sending details and slides. Always check with the gallery first, before sending details blind. Be business-like. For art buyers, do read the interviews at the front, to gain some idea about first-time buying, or how to avoid making mistakes. Many galleries do sell work at the low end of the market as well as the top end. The interview with Helena Kovac, photography dealer, will give an insight into buying photographs.

It is interesting to note that all London contemporary galleries were sent a questionnaire for this edition and nearly half replied: the better known galleries and some of the smaller ones went out of their way to supply information. As the information is published free, this is somewhat surprising. Small galleries please note, as the book is bought by art collectors and visitors, as well as by artists and the general art public.

The art maps are at the front and the back of the guide.

PLEASE NOTE NEW LONDON TELEPHONE NUMBERS FROM APRIL 2000. 0171 becomes 020-7 and 0181 becomes 020-8. i.e. 7+no or 8+no.

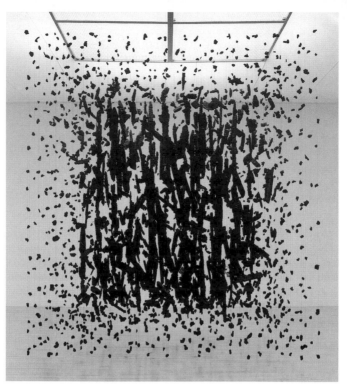

Mass, '97, Cornelia Parker (Turner prize shortlisted artist 1997).

Accademia Italiana, (now known as The European Academy for the Arts) 8 Grosvenor Place, London SW1. Telephone 0171 (020-7 from 4/2000) 235 0303. Open Monday-Saturday 10-6. 13,000 Square metres of gallery space for hire for exhibitions, receptions and special events. A major Italian art centre in London with important exhibitions throughout the year, as well as showing work by contemporary artists linked with Italy. The Accademia has joined with the European Academy for the Arts and is now based in an1868 French-Renaissance style building on 5 spacious floors. Also a lecture theatre, Café Europa, Galleria bookshop and Accademia club, restaurant and Friends membership. Underground Hyde Park Corner.

Africa Centre, 38 King Street, London WC2. Telephone 0171 (020-7 from 4/2000) 836 1973. Open Monday-Friday 10-5.30, Saturday 11-4.
Exhibitions either by African artists or with themes related to Africa. Underground Covent Garden.

The Agency, 35-40 Charlotte Road, London EC2A 3DH. Telephone 0171 (020-7 from 4/2000) 613 2080. Open Tuesday-Friday 11-6, Saturday 11-4, or by appointment.
A gallery interested in current trends in conceptual sculpture and installations. A programme of solo shows in a private space. Contact Bea de Souza and David Selden. Underground Old Street/Liverpool Street.

Agnew's, 43 Old Bond Street, London W.1. Telephone 0171 (020-7 from 4/2000) 629 6176. Fax 629 4359. Open Monday-Friday 9.30-5.30, Thursday until 6.30. Directors; Julian Agnew, Richard and Christopher Kingzett, Andrew Wyld, Mark Robertson, Gabriel M. Naughton.
Selection of 20th century British paintings, drawings, watercolours and prints by contemporary traditional artists such as Bernard Dunstan, John Wonnacott, Stephan Finer and Andrew Gadd. Also sells Old Master drawings. Established top London gallery. No applications considered. Underground Green Park.

Air Gallery, 32 Dover Street, London W.1. Telephone 0171 (020-7 from 4/2000) 409 1544. Open Thursday-Saturday 10-6. Originally Davies and Tooth who have taken over this central gallery space. Contemporary art including paintings and drawings. They sell to corporate clients. Underground Green Park.

Alan Cristea Gallery, 31 Cork Street, London W.1X 2NU. Telephone 0171 (020-7 from 4/2000) 439 1866. Fax 734 1549. Open Monday-Friday 10-5.30, Saturday 10-1.
Director: Alan Cristea. Alan Cristea purchased Waddington Graphics and the Alan Cristea gallery continues to publish prints by international artists, as well as deal in Master graphics and contemporary prints; Roy Lichtenstein, Mimmo Paladino, Howard Hodgkin, Jim Dine, Patrick Caulfield, Antoni Tapies, Joe Tilson, Mick Moon, David Hockney, Braque, Picasso, Matisse. The gallery holds excellent print shows, including an annual Matisse show, which is well worth visiting, Underground Bond Street/Green Park.

Alberti Gallery, 114 Albert Street, Camden Town, London NW1. Telephone 0171(020-7 from 4/2000) 485 8976. Open by appointment.
Contemporary Russian paintings from Moscow and St Petersburg. Underground Camden Town.

Alternative Art Galleries, 47A Brushfield Street, Spitalfields, London E1 6AA. Telephone 0171 (020-7 from 4/2000) 375 0441. Fax 375 0484. Director: Maggie Pinhorn. This organisation arranges a variety of exhibitions, with support from London companies, at venues around London. Artists can apply for exhibitions but ring first to check details. Ideal organisation for first-time exhibitors and artists recently out of art school. Artists invigilate their own shows, but they select the artists. Open 10-5 on Sundays, April-December each year. Up to 25 artists shown each week. Artists must apply with completed application form and slides/photos of their work. Alternative Arts selects each artist from their own 3-sided unit for exhibitions. Spitalfields has become quite an artists' area with studios and galleries near the old market.

The Alton Gallery, 2A Suffolk Road, Barnes, London SW139TH. Telephone 0181(020-8 from 4/2000) 748 0606.
Work by established young painters. 20th-century British art. British Rail Barnes.

Memories of Landscape, Tim Harrisson
(New Art Centre Roche Sculpture Park, Wiltshire).

Anderson O'Day Graphics, 5 St Quintin Avenue, London W.10. Telephone 0171 (020-7 from 4/2000) 969 8085. Open by appointment only. Directors: Don Anderson and Prue O'Day. Applications considered all year round. Prints only. Publish and deal in prints by Norman Ackroyd, Mandy Bonell, Michael Carlo, Yvonne Cole, Delia Delderfield, Brendan Neiland, Donald Wilkinson and others. Prue O'Day also curates contemporary cutting-edge shows in London, with some of her old gallery artists from Anderson O'Day Fine Art.

Andrew Mummery, 33 Great Sutton Street, London EC1V ODX. Telephone 0171 (020-7 from 4/2000) 251 6265. Open Tuesday-Saturday 11-6. Director: Andrew Mummery.
Andrew Mummery had a good training working for the European Raab Gallery, before setting up on his own. Contemporary artists, including painting and sculpture, usually fairly cutting-edge. Underground Farringdon.

Anna Bornholt Gallery, 3-5 Weighhouse Street, London W.1. Telephone 0171 (020-7 from 4/2000) 499 6114. Open Monday-Friday 9.30-6, Saturday by appointment. Director: Anna Bornholt. Contemporary paper works, paintings, prints. Artists include Christopher Bledowski, Anita Ford, Mark Firth, Jane Paulton and others. Also a consultancy for corporations. Underground Bond Street.

Anne Berthoud, 4A Stanley Crescent, London W.11.2NB. Telephone 0171 (020-7 from 4/2000) 229 8400. Fax 0171 (020-7 from 4/2000) 221 8185.
Anne Berthoud runs what she calls a "flying gallery", showing her artists regularly at different spaces. Artists include Stephen Buckley, Simon Lewty, Alison Turnbull, Michael Upton, Noel Forster and Robert Mason. She can be contacted by appointment.

Annely Juda Fine Art, 23 Dering Street, London W.1. Telephone 0171 (020-7 from 4/2000) 629 7578. Fax (7) 491 2139. Open Monday-Friday 10-6, Saturday 10-1.
Directors: Annely and David Juda, Ian Barker. Professional artists may apply, but the gallery is fully committed for many years. Roger Ackling, Anthony Caro, Alan Charlton, Prunella Clough, Hamish Fulton, Yuko Shiraishi, Russian Constructivism, Christo, Eduardo Chillida, Al Held, David Hockney, Leon Kossoff, Edwina Leapman, Alan Green, David Nash, Alan Reynolds and other British and international established artists. Annely Juda is a very charming and well-respected "grande dame" of the British art world. Staff are extremely courteous at this gallery. Underground Bond Street.

Anthony d'Offay, 9, 21 and 23 Dering Street, London W.1. Telephone 0171 (020-7 from 4/2000) 499 4100. Fax (7) 493 4443. Open Monday-Friday 10-5.30, Saturday 10-1.
This is a major London international contemporary art gallery with important exhibitions by Warhol, Clemente, Kiefer and Baselitz. 20th-century British art. Artists include: Carl Andre, Georg Baselitz, Joseph Beuys, Christian Boltanski, Francesco Clemente, Gilbert & George, Richard Hamilton, Howard Hodgkin, Jasper Johns, Ellsworth Kelly, Anselm Kiefer, Yves Klein, Willem de Kooning, Jeff Koons, Jannis Kounellis, Roy Lichtenstein, Richard Long, Bruce McLean, Mario Merz, Mucha, Nauman, Orozco, Polke, Richter, Ruscha, Kiki Smith, Turrell, Cy Twombly, Bill Viola, Andy Warhol, Boyd Webb, Weiner and Rachel Whiteread. Artists are welcome to submit slides or other material to the gallery but they cannot give interviews.
Underground Bond Street.

Anthony Reynolds, 5 Dering Street, London W.1. Telephone 0171 (020-7 from 4/2000) 491 0621. Open Tuesday-Sunday 11-6. Director: Anthony Reynolds. Small gallery space on two floors with exciting work by some of the best contemporary artists, especially recent conceptual and Minimal art. Underground Bond Street.

Anthony Wilkinson Gallery, 242 Cambridge Heath Road, London E2 9DA. Telephone 0181 (020-8 from mid 2000) 980 2662. Fax 980 0028.
Contemporary art; Glen Baxter, Simon Callery, Edward Chell, Nicky Hirst, Dhruva Mistry, Mike Silva, Bob and Roberta Smith, Jessica Voorsanger.

The Approach, 1st floor, 47 Approach Rd, Bethnal Green, London E2 9LY. Telephone/fax 0181 (020-8 from 4/2000) 983 3878. Open Thursday-Sunday 12-6.
Cutting edge art.

Architectural Association, 34 Bedford Square, London WC1. Telephone 0171 (020-7 from 4/2000) 636 0974. Open Monday-Friday 10-7, Saturday 10-1.30.
Art and architectural exhibitions. Large gallery space. Bookshop and café. Underground Russell Square.

Argile Gallery, 7 Blenheim Crescent, London W.11. Telephone 0171 (020-7 from 4/2000) 792 0888. Open Tuesday-Friday 3-6, Saturday 11-6.
Friendly small gallery showing small works by a variety of contemporary artists. They also run art courses. In the heart of the

Portobello Road market area, opposite East West gallery. Underground Notting Hill Gate and walk down the hill or Ladbroke Grove.

Art First, 1st floor, 9 Cork Street, London W1X 1PP. Telephone 0171 (020-7 from 4/2000) 734 0386. Open Monday-Wednesday, Friday 10-6, Thursday 10-8, Saturday 11-2.
Directors: Geoffrey Bertram and Clare Stracey. A very friendly gallery with a range of gallery artists, both painters and sculptors covering Britain. Scottish artists include: Wilhelmina Barns-Graham, Will Maclean and Barbara Rae. Other artists include Lino Mannocci, Clement McAleer, Eileen Cooper, Simon Lewty, Margaret Hunter. Prices accessible for buyers. Underground Bond Street/Green Park.

Art for Offices, 15 Dock Street, London E.1. Telephone 0171 (020-7 from 4/2000) 481 1337. Open Monday-Friday by appointment.
Andrew Hutchinson and Peter Harris. Artists can submit 35mm colour slides of work and if suitable these will be shown to architects, designers and business clients. Underground Whitechapel.

Art House, 213 South Lambeth Road, London SW8. Telephone 0171 (020-7 from 4/2000) 735 2192.
Monika Kinley runs the Outsider Archive based on the Outsiders exhibition, 1979, at the Hayward Gallery. Many interesting, unusual artists. By appointment only.

Artmonsky Arts, 108A Boundary Road, London NW8. Telephone 0171 (020-7 from mid 2000) 604 3990. Open Tuesday-Saturday 11-6, Sunday 1-6.
Variety of contemporary art shows including landscapes by contemporary artists. Underground Swiss Cottage.

Artists Register, 110 Kingsgate Road, London NW6. Telephone 0171 (020-7 from 4/2000) 328 7878. Open Thursday-Sunday 2-6.
Gallery within a studio context. Contact Stephen Williams. A selection panel meets every three months. Applications open to artists at any time of the year. Gallery walls 20 x 8 and 60 x 10. Contemporary artists. See Kingsgate Workshops also.

Arts Club, 40 Dover Street, London W.1. Telephone 0171 (020-7 from 4/2000) 499 8581. Open Monday-Friday 10-1, 3-6 for exhibition visitors. A private club that holds regular exhibitions mainly for members. Underground Green Park.

Art Space Gallery, 84 St Peter's Street, London N.1. Telephone 0171 (020-7 from 4/2000) 359 7002. Open Tuesday-Saturday 11-7 and by appointment.
Contemporary British art. Director: Michael Richardson. Artists include; Ray Atkins, George Rowlett, Anthony Whishaw, Kevin O'Brien, Nigel Massey, John Kiki. Underground Angel.

Artworks Space, 2 Sycamore Street, London EC1. Telephone 0171 (020-7 from 4/2000) 253 7394.
Barbican arts group shows work here, with sponsorship from major corporations. Gallery within a studio space for artists.

Asprey Jacques, 4 Clifford Street, London W.1. Telephone 01717 (020-7 from 4/2000) 287 7675. Fax 287 7574. Open Tuesday-Friday 10-6, Saturday 11-5. Directors: Charles Asprey and Alison Jacques. Contemporary British and European contemporary art, including cutting-edge. Underground Green Park/Bond Street.

Association Gallery, 81 Leonard Street, London EC2. Telephone 0171 (020-7 from 4/2000) 608 1441. Open usual gallery hours 9.30-6, Saturday 12-4.
A central photography gallery with a wide range of exhibitions of work on various themes or by groups of photographers. Underground Old Street.

Atlantis Gallery, 146 Brick Lane, London E.1. Telephone 0171 (020-7 from mid 2000) 887 4852. Open Monday-Sunday 11-7.
Gallery in an art materials supplier setting in the heart of Brick Lane in the east end. Variety of shows here, often by local professional artists. Many visitors due to the materials sales venue. Underground Aldgate East.

Atlas Gallery, 55-57 Tabernacle Street, London EC2. Open Monday-Friday 10-6, Saturday 12-5.
Has shown 19th century photography by world travellers.

Austin Desmond Fine Art, 15A Bloomsbury Square, London WC1. Telephone 0171 (020-7 from 4/2000) 242 4443. Open Monday-Friday 10.30-6.30.
Director: John Austin. This gallery is in a charming cul-de-sac, Pied Bull Yard (between Bury Street and Bloomsbury Street) with friendly local wine bar and other shops, near the British Museum. The gallery concentrates on dealing in contemporary artists and Modern British and Irish art. Worth a visit. Underground Holborn.

Bankside Gallery, 48 Hopton Street, Blackfriars, London SE1. Telephone 0171 (020-7 from 4/2000) 928 7521. Fax 928 2820. Open Tuesday-Saturday 1-5, Sunday occasionally 2-6. Watercolours and prints. Home of the Royal Watercolour Society, Royal Society of Painter-Printmakers and the RWS Art Club. Mostly members only, exhibiting in regular exhibitions. Ideal place for conventional first-time buyers. Now in the heart of Bankside, near the Tate Gallery of Modern Art. Underground Blackfriars and walk over the bridge.

Viaduct with rainbow, Peter Archer (Austin Desmond Fine Art).

Barbican Centre, Silk Street, London EC2. Telephone 0171 (020-7 from 4/2000) 638 4141 (admin) 0171 (020-7 from 4/2000) 638 8891 (reservations and enquiries), 24-hour information 0171 382 7272. Barbican Art Gallery Telephone 0171 (020-7 from 4/2000) 638 4141 ext 306/346. Open Monday, Thurs-Sat 10-6.45, Tuesday 10-5.45, Wed 10-7.45. Sunday and Bank holidays 12-6. Admission fee. Reduced admission fee after 5pm. Barbican Card Membership means a 20% discount off full price tickets.

Art gallery curator: John Hoole. The arts centre has been much in the news over the years but now has John Tusa as its director who has provided stability to the centre. Opened in 1982 the centre houses the London Symphony Orchestra, Royal

Shakespeare Company, Barbican Library, three cinemas, one major gallery on two levels, several exhibition spaces (Concourse gallery and there are smaller ones), The café, restaurant and coffee bar, a conservatory, conference centre and thousands of metres of corridor space to get lost in! There are many surprises including beautiful woodwork in the auditorium, a series of murals by Gillian Wise-Ciobotaru with mirrors and in pastel colours, on your way down to the cinemas. I have to admit to having rather a soft-spot for the centre, despite the crazy yellow lines to lead you to it. The fountains and lake are very relaxing after polluted, busy city streets and you can sit outside in summer and drink cappuccino and enjoy the peace and quiet.

The gallery on level 3 has major exhibitions of historical interest, of photography or contemporary art. The Concourse gallery is often hired by galleries and artist-groups for large exhibitions and to reach a wider public. The space can be rented. Contact 0171 (020-7 from 4/2000) 638 4141 ext 303 for details about the Concourse gallery or the foyer space. Exhibitors have to pay for any expenses and security costs. Excellent bookshops run by Zwemmers. Underground Barbican/Moorgate/Liverpool Street.

BAC, Lavender Hill, London SW11. Telephone 0171 (020-7 from 4/2000) 223 6557/9. Open Wednesday-Friday 5-9, Saturday/Sunday 11-9.
Applications open to all artists and artists are often asked to show work to the Director. Run by an independent trust. Classes in drawing, pottery, photography. Theatre, cinema and café. The Battersea Art Fair is held here annually. British Rail Clapham Junction or 49 bus from South Kensington.

Barrett Marsden Gallery, 17-18 Great Sutton Street, London EC1V ODN. Telephone 717(020-7 from 4/2000) 336 6396. Fax 336 6391. Directors: Juliana Barrett, Tatjana Marsden, Nelson Woo. Open Tuesday-Friday 11-6, Saturday 11-4.
Contemporary ceramics, glass, metal, wood and furniture. Artists include: Gordon Baldwin, Alison Britton, Caroline Broadhead, Ken Eastman, Bryan Illsley, Maria van Kesteren, Robert Marsden, Steven Newell, Sara Radstone, Michael Rowe, Richard Slee, Martin Smith, Emma Wolfenden. Artists should visit the gallery then send slides and CV with s.a.e. for their return.

Beaux Arts, 22 Cork Street, London W.1. Telephone 0171 (020-7 from 4/2000) 437 5799
Director: Reg Singh. Contemporary British paintings and drawings. Underground Bond Street/Green Park.

Bedford Hill Gallery, 202 Great Suffolk Street, London SE1. Telephone 0171 (020-7 from 4/2000) 403 4190.
The London Group of artists has shown here. Contemporary British painting. Undeground Borough.

Benjamin Rhodes Gallery, Mail Box 122, 37 Store Street, London WCIE 7BS. Telephone 0171 (020-7 from 4/2000) 434 1768. email: jasonrhodes @ compuserve.com
The Gillian Jason and Benjamin Rhodes partnership ended in1999. The above is a temporary contact number until the new gallery opens in Autumn 1999. The new gallery will focus on young cutting-edge British and international artists.

Ben Uri Art Gallery, 126 Albert Street, London NW1. Telephone 0171 (020-7 from 4/2000) 482 1234. Open Monday-Thursday 10-5.
Jewish art from the Society's permanent collection, as well as theme exhibitions related to Jewish artists. Underground Great Portland Street.

Berkeley Square Gallery, 23A Bruton Street, London W.1. Telephone 0171 (020-7 from 4/2000) 493 7939. Fax 493 7798.
Director: Peter Osborne. The gallery deals with original contemporary paintings, prints and sculpture, as well as Master prints. Often interesting contemporary artists on show. Underground Bond Street/Green Park.

Bernard Jacobson Gallery, 14A Clifford Street, London W.1X 1RF. Telephone 0171 (020-7 from 4/2000) 495 8575. Fax (7) 495 6210. Open Monday-Friday 10-6, Saturday 10-1.
Director: Bernard Jacobson. 20th-century British and American painting and sculpture. Artists include: Bomberg, Hitchens, King, Lanyon, Nicholson, Rauschenberg, Spencer, Stella, Sprawson, Sutherland, Tillyer, Vaux. Underground Bond Street/Green Park.

The Black Art Gallery, 225 Seven Sisters Road, Finsbury Park, London N.4. Telephone 0171 (020-7 from 4/2000) 263 1918. Open Tuesday-Thursday 11-7, Friday 11-9, Saturday 11-7, Sunday 2-7.
Director: Shakka Dedi. Work by artists from Africa, Americas, Caribbean, Britain and Europe. All media exhibited. Groups or individuals should write for application details. Underground Finsbury Park.

Blackheath Gallery, 34 Tranquil Vale, London SE3. Telephone 0181 (020-8 from 4/2000) 852 1802. Open Monday-Saturday

10-6 (closed Thursday).
Contact: JV Corless. Local gallery showing contemporary prints, paintings and sculpture. Participates in the local Lewisham Visual arts festivals.

Blains (Contemporary) Gallery, 23 Bruton Street, London W1X 7DA. Telephone 0171 (020-7 from 4/2000) 495 5050. Fax (7) 495 4050. Open Mon/Wed/Fri 10-6, Thursday 10-8, Saturday 10-5.
Director: Charlie Phillips. Young contemporary artists. Landscape, still-life, photographs, have all been shown at this gallery. Gallery artists include: Paolo Berni, Carey Burrows, Cedric Christie, Jonathan Glynn-Smith, Jonathan McCree, Jonathan Yeo. Also works in conjunction with organisations such as Ozone to promote art in venues such as restaurants. Underground Marble Arch.

Bloomsbury Galleries, University of London Institute of Education, 70 Bedford Way, London EC1. Open Monday-Friday 9.30-8, Saturday 9.30-12.
Recent work by contemporary artists. Underground Russell Square.

The Bloomsbury Workshop Ltd.,12 Galen Place, London WC1. Telephone 0171 (020-7 from 4/2000) 405 0632. Open Tuesday-Friday 9.30-5.
Bloomsbury Group and Modern British art. Paintings, drawings and prints by Vanessa Bell and Duncan Grant. Also stock of Bloomsbury Group books (first editions, secondhand and new). Underground Tottenham Court Road.

Blue Gallery, 93 Walton Street, London SW3. Telephone 01717 (020-7 from 4/2000) 589 4690.
Lively contemporary art gallery showing contemporary British art, often cutting edge. Underground Knightsbridge.

Bonhams, Auctioneers and Valuers, Montpelier Galleries, Montpelier Street, London SW7. Telephone 0171 (020-7 from 4/2000) 584 9161/4577. Open Monday-Friday 9-5.30.
Major auction house, often with paintings on show at viewings before they are sold. Underground Knightsbridge.

Bookworks, 19 Holywell Row, London EC2A 4JB. Telephone 0171 (020-7 from 4/2000) 247 2536.
Artist's book publishers mainly. They also organise contemporary artists' book exhibitions at other venues, mainly museums and galleries.

Boukamel Contemporary Art, 9 Cork Street, London W.1X 1PD. Telephone 01717 (020-7 from 4/2000) 734 6444. Fax (7) 287 1740. Open 11-6.
Director: B.Boukamel. Contemporary paintings, sculpture, prints and photography. Artists include; Ken Currie, Rainer Fetting, Luciano Castelli, Philip Braham, Joumana Mourad, Gérard Traquandi, Markus Lüpertz, Hödicke, Tatafiore, Elvira Bach. Exhibitions by all these artists are planned for 99-2001. Underground Green Park.

Boundary Gallery, 98 Boundary Road, London NW8 ORH. Telephone 0171 (020-7 from 4/2000) 624 1126. Fax 020-7 681 7663. Open Tuesday-Saturday 11-6.
Director: Agi Katz. Near the Saatchi collection in NW8. Holds lively painting exhibitions of both historical and contemporary interest. Modern British (1910-60); Jacob Epstein, Jacob Kramer, Bernard Meninsky, Sylvia Melland, Morris Kestelman. Contemporary figurative Colourists; Josef Herman, Sonia Lawson, Albert Louden, Peter Prendergast, June Redfern and Maria Pacheco. Artists can apply. Underground St Johns Wood.

Bow Arts Trust, (see The Nunnery also) 183 Bow Road, London E3 2SL. Telephone 0181 (020-8 from 4/2000) 983 9737. Fax (8) 980 7770.
A recent alternative space showing installations and events. Now called The Nunnery with a variety of curated shows.

Browse and Darby, 9 Cork Street, London W.1. Telephone 0171 (020-7 from 4/2000) 734 7984/5. Open Monday-Friday 10-5.30, Thursday 10-8, Saturday 10.30-1.
British and French drawings. Late 20th-century paintings and sculpture. Contemporary English artists include Anthony Eyton, Charlotte Verity (see interview at front of guide) and Patrick George. Underground Green Park/Bond Street.

The Bruton Street Gallery, 28 Bruton Street, London W.1. Telephone 0171 (020-7 fom 4/2000) 499 9747. Open Monday-Friday 10-6, Saturday 10-2.
Variety of exhibitions throughout the year. Contemporary art as well as 20th-century art. Underground Bond Street/Green Park.

The Building Centre Gallery, 26 Store Street, London WC1. Telephone 0171 (020-7 from 4/20000) 637 1022. Open Monday-Friday 10-5, Saturday 10-1.
Architectural and sculpture exhibitions. Underground Goodge Street.

Cable Street Gallery, 566 Cable Street, London E.1. Telephone 0171 (020-7 from mid 2000) 790 1309. Open Thursday-Sunday 12-5.

Cable street studios are based here and the gallery is in a studio setting. Cable street was once famous as the site of a battle between locals (often immigrants, including Jewish Londoners) and Mosleyite fascists in the 1930s. A nastier past than is the case at present, where artists work in peace. Underground Tower Hill.

Cadogan Contemporary Art, 108 Draycott Avenue, London SW3. Telephone 0171 (020-7 from 4/2000) 581 5451. Fax 589 3222. Open Monday-Friday 10-7, Saturday 10-5.

Director: Christopher Burness. Colourful exhibitions of work by young professional artists both British and international, usually less well-known. Underground South Kensington.

Café Gallery, 92 Webster Road, Bermondsey, London SE16. Telephone 0171 (020-7 from 4/2000) 237 2170/1230. Open Wednesday-Sunday 10-4.

Contact: Ron Henocq. Run by the Bermondsey Artists' Group, an active group of professional artists who live and work in the area. Contemporary painting and sculpture. They run an annual open exhibition for members of the group. Worth joining if you live near the area. Underground Surrey Quays.

Camden Arts Centre, Arkwright Road, London NW3. Telephone 0171 (020-7 from 4/2000) 435 2643/5224. Open Monday-Sunday 11-6, Friday 11-8, Sunday 2-6.

Director: Jenni Lomax. Contemporary art centre showing major contemporary shows of art, photography, sculpture and installations. Two large galleries. Garden space used for sculpture shows. Art classes. Underground Finchley Road.

Camerawork Gallery, 121 Roman Road, Bethnal Green, London E2 OQN. Telephone 0181 (020-8 from 4/2000) 980 6256. Open Thursday-Saturday 1-6.

Director: Philip Sanderson. Chair of Board: Joe Harper. New work considered on the first Wednesday of each month. Submit slides/cv/video. Contemporary Art and photography. Four major and eight minor photographic shows a year. Gallery artists include: Rod Dickinson, Fiona Crisp and Sarah Dobai. Underground Bethnal Green.

Catto Gallery, 100 Heath Street, London NW3. Telephone 0171 435 6660. OpenTuesday-Saturday 10-6, Sunday 2.30-6.

Director: Mrs Catto. Contemporary figurative paintings. Open to applications from figurative professional artists. Underground Hampstead.

Cecilia Colman, 67 St Johns Wood High Street, London NW8. Telephone 0171 (020-7 from 4/2000) 722 0686. Open weekdays 10-6, Saturdays 10-6.
Contemporary quality craft, jewellery, ceramics and prints. Work by top jewellery names and magnificent ceramics on display. Underground St Johns Wood.

Chalk Farm Gallery, 20 Chalk Farm Road, London NW1. Telephone 0171 (020-7 from 4/2000) 267 3300. Open Tuesday-Sunday 10-5.30.
Temporary exhibitions in the first floor gallery and large selection of limited edition prints downstairs. Framing service and art card shop also. Underground Chalk Farm/Camden Town.

Chisenhale Gallery, 64 Chisenhale Road, Bow, London E.3.5QZ. Telephone 0181 (020-8 from 4/2000) 981 4518. Fax

Kate Whiteford in her studio.

(8)980 7169. Open Wednesday-Sunday 1-6.
Director: Sue Jones. Excellent shows by avant-garde up-and-coming contemporary artists, some even Turner-Prize winners or short-listed. Consistently good exhibitions at this venue with top curators and cutting-edge work. Artists should not apply except for the annual exhibition New Work UK (applications in March). Underground Mile end/Bethnal Green.

Christies Contemporary Art, 8 Dover Street, London W.1. Telephone 0171 (020-7 from 4/2000) 499 6701. Open Monday-Friday 9.30-5.30, Saturday 10-1.
Specialises in contemporary prints. Publishes the work of some 90 artists. Branches overseas and elsewhere in Britain. The work tends to be somewhat conventional. Underground Bond Street.

The Church Gallery, Church of the Annunciation, 34 Bryanston Street, London W.1.
The gallery holds regular exhibitions of paintings, graphics by known and not so well-known artists. Framing and restoration service also available.

Commonwealth Institute, Kensington High Street, London W.8. Telephone 0171 (020-7 from 4/2000) 603 4535. Open Monday-Saturday 10-5.30, Sunday 2-5. Main galleries closed until 2002. They will then provide internet and virtual reality facilities to show what is going on in the Commonwealth today. Contact Nicola Harold for temporary exhibitions which are open in the meanwhile. The library is also still open. Restaurant and shop closed until 2002 also. Large gallery space upstairs and corridor exhibition space downstairs. Next to Holland Park. Underground High Street Kensington.

Coningsby Gallery, 30 Tottenham Street, London W.1 9PW. Telephone 0171 (020-7 from 4/2000) 636 7475. Fax (7) 580 7017. Open 10-5.30.
Director: Andrew Coningsby. Contemporary art, photography and illustration. Artists can call or send in work, but must not turn up on the gallery doorstep. Artists include; Rubin Hazelwood, Paul Slater, David Downton, Steve Geary and many others. Underground Tottenham Court Road.

Connaught Brown, 2 Albemarle Street, London W.1. Telephone 0171 (020-7 from 4/2000) 408 0362. Open Monday-Friday 10-6, Saturday 10-12.30.
Recent contemporary British art and European Post-Impressionism. Underground Green Park.

Contemporary Applied Arts, 2 Percy Street, London W.1. Telephone 0171 (020-7 from 4/2000) 436 2344.
Director: Mary La Trobe Bateman. Contemporary applied arts including the best of British glass, ceramics, silversmithing, and furniture. This organisation started 51 years ago as the Crafts Centre of Great Britain in 1948 in Mayfair. It moved to Covent Garden in the mid sixties and in the mid 90s to its current home. Underground Tottenham Court Road.

Crafts Council Gallery, 44A Pentonville Road, London N.1. Telephone 0171 (020-7 from 4/2000) 278 7700. Open Tuesday-Saturday 10-5, Sunday 2-5.
Contemporary quality British crafts and sometimes major international shows, but always lively. There are now two galleries and enlarged space within the Crafts Council, a slide library of some 20,000 slides, an Index of Selected Makers which is a register of 460 craftspeople in Britain arranged by area and kind of craft, a bookstall for magazines, postcards and craft books and a coffee bar. There is also an information centre for all craft queries about materials, courses, training, grants, galleries and assistance for conservation and commissions. Crafts Council exhibitions are toured nationally on many occasions. Underground Angel.

Crafts Council shop at the Victoria and Albert Museum, 123 Cromwell Road, London SW7. Telephone 0171 (020-7 from4/2000) 589 5070. Open Monday-Saturday 10-5.30, Sunday 2.30-5.30.
Magnificent showcase for the best of British crafts. Underground South Kensington.

Conductors Hallway, 301 Camberwell New Road, London SE5 OTF. Telephone 0171 (020-7 from 4/2000) 274 7474. Fax 274 1744.
They do invite submissions from fine artists/video/photographers. Contemporary art. 36 Bus from Victoria.

Contemporary Ceramics, Marshall Street, London W.1 Telephone 0171 (020-7 from 4/2000) 437 7605. Open Monday-Friday 10-5.30, Saturday 10.30-5.
Craftsmen and women can apply. Selection committee meets 4 times a year. UK crafts mainly. Also a craft shop for reasonably priced work. Underground Oxford Circus.

Crane Kalman Gallery, 178 Brompton Road, London SW3. Telephone 01/1 (020-7 from 4/2000) 584 7566. Open Monday-Friday 10-6, Saturday 10-4.

Andrew Kalman of Crane Kalman gallery with painting by Jenny Franklin.

Directors: Andras and Andrew Kalman. Another friendly, family-run gallery, established for many years. 20th-century established British, American and French artists. Regular colourful exhibitions. Also shows work by contemporary artists Jenny Franklin and Jonathan Huxley. Participates in the 20th century Art Fair and other British art fairs. Underground Knightsbridge.

The Crest Gallery, Dollisfield Library, Totteridge Lane, London N.20. Telephone 0181 (020-8 from 4/2000) 361 9648. Open library hours.

Contemporary art shown in a library context with the support of Bartnet Borough Arts Council. Open to local artists to apply. Underground Totteridge and Whetstone.

Curwen Gallery, 4 Windmill Street, off Charlotte Street, London W1P 1HF. Telephone 0171 (020-7 from 4/2000) 636 1459. Fax 436 3059. Open Monday-Friday 10-6, Saturday 11-5.
Directors: John and Jill Hutchings. Founded 1965. Monthly exhibitions of contemporary British art. Specialises in abstract and semi-abstract paintings, constructions and works on paper. Artists include: Paul Ryan, Thirza Kotzen, Yuji Oki, Glynn Boyd Harte, Kieron Farrow. Contemporary prints, painting,sculpture. Undergound Goodge Street.

Danielle Arnaud, 123 Kennington Rd, London SE11 6SF. Telephone/Fax 0171 (020-7 from 4/2000) 735 8292. www.daniellearnaud.com. Open Friday, Saturday, Sunday 2-6, or by appointment.
Director: Danielle Arnaud. Young international artists showing painting, drawings and photography. Artists include: Joy Anderson (perspex), Glauca Cerveira, Simon Granger, Georgie Hopton, Kirai Lau, Gerry Smith, Sarah Woodfine (drawings), David Bate, Amy Eshoo, Susan Morris, Marie-France and Patricia Martin (all photographers or video artists). The gallery is in a large Georgian house.

Davies and Tooth, (see AIR Gallery entry)
Sell contemporary art for offices, receptions and boardrooms.

David Messum, 8 Cork Street, London W1X 1PB. Telephone 0171 (020-7 from 4/2000) 437 5545. Open weekdays 10-6, Saturdays 10-4.
Contemporary and 20th century art including paintings and photoworks. Also extremely interested in Cornish paintings. Underground Bond Street/Green Park.

Delfina Gallery, 50 Bermondsey Street, London SE1. Telephone 0171 (020-7 from 4/2000) 357 6600. Open Monday-Friday 11-6, Saturday 11-3.
Delfina artists' studios are next door. The gallery shows work by contemporary artists including paitings, sculpture, prints and works on paper. A large gallery space with a café/restaurant at the entrance to the gallery. There are some interesting paintings on display in the restaurant, but the work on show in the gallery varies. It participated in the Whitechapel Open in '96. Not a central art venue but obviously popular with gallery clientele. Undeground Bermondsey (new Jubilee Line when it opens).

Diorama Gallery, 34 Osnaburgh Street, London NW1 3ND. This Regents' Park gallery is often used by various art organisations for exhibitions. Write to the gallery if interested. Underground Regents' Park.

Duncan Campbell Fine Art, 15 Thackeray Street, Kensington Square, London W8 5ET. Telephone 0171 937 8665. Open Tuesday-Friday 11-6, Saturday 10-5.
Director: Duncan Campbell. Regular shows of work by mainly figurative painters, some established, some not-so. Painting, watercolours and young and established artists. Artists include: Rowland Hilder, Eugene Palmer, Magda Kozarzewska, Ann Brunskill, Ralph Anderson, Francis Farmar, Geri Morgan, Jim Manley and others. Completely full for more than 2 years in advance. Underground High Street Kensington.

Duncan Cargill, 22 Warren Street, London W.1. Telephone 0171 (020-7 from 4/2000) 388 3603. Open Thursday-Friday 11-6, Saturday 11-3.
Director: Duncan Cargill. Contemporary art including artists such as Claude Heath and Adam Dant. Underground Warren Street.

The Eagle Gallery, EMH Arts,159 Farringdon Road, London EC1. Telephone 0171 833 2674. Open Tuesday-Friday 11-6, Saturday 11-4.
Contemporary art. Paintings and drawings, sculpture and limited edition prints. Underground Farringdon.

East West Gallery, 8 Blenheim Crescent, London W.11. Telephone 0171 229 7981.
Directors: Jill Morgan and David Solomon. Paintings, drawings and prints from Eastern Europe as well as from British artists. Friendly gallery with work on sale at accessible prices. In the heart of the Portobello Market area. Will consider looking at work, but artists must visit the gallery first and meet the directors. Most artists have at least 10 years experience as professional artists before applying. Underground Notting Hill Gate and walk down the hill/Ladbroke Grove.

The Economist Gallery, 25 St James's Street, London SW1A 1HG. Telephone 0171 839 7000. Open office hours.
Contact: Helen Mann. Applications can be made to use the spaces at the Economist, both outside and inside. Advisable to telephone first to see if your work is appropriate. Underground Green Park.

Electrum Gallery, 21 South Molton Street, London W.1. Telephone 0171 629 6325. Open Monday-Friday 10-6, Saturday 10-1.

Top British and international jewellers. Contemporary jewellery only, but some of the top British craft. Two floors. Open to jewellers to apply. Underground Bond Street.

Emily Tsingou Gallery, 10 Charles Street, London SW1. Telephone 0171 (020-7 from 4/2000)839 5320. Open Tuesday-Saturday 10-6. Director: Emily Tsingou Contemporary young artists. Underground Piccadilly.

England & Co., 216 Westbourne Grove, London W11 2RH. Telephone 0171 (020-7 from 4/2000) 221 0417. Fax (7) 221 4499. Open Tuesday-Saturday 11-6.
Director: Jane England. 20th-century Modern British paintings — 1940s, 50s and 60s. Excellent selection of works from this period with a Director who does her background research well and is well-respected. Catalogues available from past shows. Also contemporary art shows by young and established artists. Artists should phone the gallery before submitting work. Underground Notting Hill Gate.

Entwistle Gallery, 6 Cork Street, London W.1. Telephone 0171 (020-7 from 4/2000) 409 3484. Open10-6.
Holds an annual Marcel Duchamp show. Otherwise deals in contemporary artists: Siobhan Hopaska, Peter Newman, Bridget Smith, Sue Arrowsmith, Lipski, Nicky Hoberman. Open to slide applications but ring the gallery first to check the possibilities, as they are limited. Underground Green Park.

507 Gallery, 507 Kings Road, London SW10. Open Tuesday-Saturday 10-5.30. Director: Jason Brooks. Contemporary art including recent graduates and young artists, particularly painting.

Faggionato Fine Art, 49 Albemarle Street, London W.1. Telephone 0171 (020-7 from 4/2000) 409 7979. Open10-6.
A recent gallery showing paintings, drawings and sculpture by good contemporary artists. Accessible prices for first-time buyers. Underground Green Park.

Fine Art Society, 148 New Bond Street, London W.1. Telephone 0171 (020-7 from 4/2000) 629 5116. Open Monday-Friday 9.30-5.30, Saturday 10-1.
Directors: Andrew McIntosh Patrick, Peyton Skipwith. 19th and 20th-century art. Heavy emphasis on Scottish painting including the Scottish Colourists (Peploe, Cadell, Hunter JD Fergusson) Ideal gallery for private collectors or for large collections. Good selection of past catalogues on sale. Also shows contemporary artist Emma Sergeant. Underground Bond Street/Green Park.

Fine Art Trade Guild, 16 Empress Place, London SW6 1TT. Telephone 0171 (020-7 from 4/2000) 381 6616.
Publishers of Art Business Today, a trade journal. Members include galleries, publishers, framers, artists and art suppliers.

Angela Flowers Gallery at London Fields, 282 Richmond Road, London E.8. Telephone 0181 (020-8 from 4/2000) 985 3333. Open Tuesday-Sunday 10-6.
Directors: Angela Flowers, Matthew Flowers, Karen Demuth. A branch of the successful Flowers Galleries, across the road from Flowers East. Large gallery space to show more of the Flowers' artists. The Paton gallery is in the same building. Underground Bethnal Green or various buses.

Flowers East, 199-205 Richmond Road, Hackney, London E.8. Telephone 0181 (020-8 from 4/2000) 985 3333. Open Tuesday-Sunday 10-6.
Large gallery spaces for the many artists shown by Flowers East; Jack Smith, Prunella Clough, Carole Hodgson, Amanda Faulkner, Neil Jeffries, Lucy Jones, Peter Howson, Patrick Hughes, Tim Mara, Trevor Jones, John Loker, John Keane, John Gibbons, Nicola Hicks, Mikey Cuddihy, Alison Watt, Alan Gouk, Kevin Sinnott, Alan Stocker, Andrew Stahl, Henry Kondracki, John Kirby. In July every year they run an Artist of the Day show, with artists chosen by known names. There is a Graphics Gallery, a Print of the Month club and even an opportunity to become a shareholder in this growing concern. One of London's most dynamic galleries. Underground Bethnal Green.

Focus Gallery, 43 Museum Street, Bloomsbury, London WC1A1LY. Telephone 01 (020-7 from 4/2000) 242 7191. Fax (7) 242 7127. Director: Helena Kovac. A recent photography gallery near the British Museum, selling and showing contemporary, 20th century and some 19th century photography. **See interview at the front of the guide.** Shows usually by invitation but they prefer photographers to make an appointment to discuss work. Do not doorstep the gallery with your portfolio. Photographers include: Erwin Blumenfeld, Ian Berry, Dorothy Bohm, David Buckland, Bryn Campbell, Cozette de Charmoy, Franco Fontana, Joan Fontecuberta, Fay Godwin, Judy Goldhill, Sam Haskins, Marketa Luskacova, George Rodger and Magnum photographers. Underground Tottenham Court Road.

Foundry, 84-86 Great Eastern Street, London EC2. Telephone 0171 (020-7 from 4/2000) 739 6900. Open Monday-Friday 1-11, Saturday 7-11, Sunday 2-10. An alternative art venue with rising stars.

Foyles Gallery, 119 Charing Cross Road, London WC2. Telephone 0171 (020-7 from 4/2000) 437 5660. Open Monday-Saturday 10-6.
Exhibitions of craft, book illustrations and paintings in Foyles bookshop next to the art department. Underground Tottenham Court Road.

Francis Graham-Dixon Gallery, London N16 0WQ. Telephone 0181 (020-8 from 4/2000) 809 1999. By appointment only. Director: Francis Graham-Dixon. Contemporary and post-war British artists include Jennifer Durrant, Sybille Berger, Merlin James, Virginia Verran, Sheila Girling, Julia Farrer, Mali Morris and Clyde Hopkins.

Francis Kyle, 9 Maddox Street, London W.1. Telephone 0171 (020-7 from 4/2000) 499 6870/6970. Open Monday-Friday 10-6, Saturday 11-5. Director: Francis Kyle. Contemporary young British artists. Also publish lithographs by British artists. Many of the paintings and prints have a colourful, decorative quality. Underground Bond Street.

Frith Street Gallery, 60 Frith Street, Soho, London W.1. Telephone 0171 (020-7 from 4/2000) 494 1550. Open11-6.
Director: Jane Hamlyn. Set in the heart of Soho, this gallery has produced several Turner prize shortlisted artists. Works on paper, including prints, photographs and small paintings. Good innovative lively cutting-edge art. Underground Tottenham Court Road.

The Gallery at Bird and Davis Ltd., 45 Holmes Road, Kentish Town London NW5. Telephone 0171 (020-7 from 4/2000) 485 3797. Open shop hours.
A gallery in a materials-shop setting. Contemporary works on paper. Underground Kentish Town.

Gallery K, 101-103 Heath Street, Hampstead, London NW3. Telephone 0171 (020-7 from 4/2000) 794 4949. Open Tuesday-Friday 10-6, Saturday 11-6.
Variety of shows by Greek artists or artists with Greek connections. Usually paintings. Underground Hampstead.

The Gallery at John Jones, Unit 4, Finsbury Park Trading Estate, Morris Place, London N.4. Telephone 0171 (020-7 from 4/2000) 281 2380. Open Tuesday-Friday10-6, Saturday 10-2, Sunday 12-4.
This gallery space and materials store has continued to show work by unknown but promising artists, with some thought involved in the selection procedure. Underground Finsbury Park.

Galerie Vermilion, 120 Upper Tooting Road, London SW17. Telephone 0181 767 5029. Open Monday-Friday 11-6, Saturday 10-2.
Ceramics, sculpture, paintings and public art. Underground Tooting Bec.

Gasworks, 155 Vauxhall Street, The Oval, London SE11 5RH. Telephone 0171 (020-7 from 4/2000) 582 6848. Fax (7) 582 0159. Open Friday-Saturday 12-6.
Director: Peter Cross. Contemporary international art. Five exhibitions per year. Off-site projects. Proposals considered by the gallery. Ring first for details. Past exhibitions have included: David Medalla, Javier Tellez, Roberto Obregon and Audry Lisseron-Monfils. Underground Oval.

Gillian Jason, 40 Inverness Street, London NW1 7HB. Telephone 0171 (020-7 from mid 2000) 267 4835. email: gillianjason@compuserve.com
The Gillian Jason and Benjamin Rhodes partnership ended in 1999. She will continue to deal in 20th Century British and European Art and organise exhibitions for her group of contemporary artists.

Gimpel Fils, 30 Davies Street, London W.1. Telephone 0171 (020-7 from 4/2000) 493 2488. Open Monday-Friday 9.30-5.30, Saturday 10-1. Directors: Peter and René Gimpel. An established, well-respected top London gallery. The Gimpels have years of experience in art dealing. Contemporary artists including Alan Davie, Gillian Ayres, Susan Hillier, Albert Irvin and other younger lesser-known names. Underground Bond Street.

Goëthe Institut, 50 Princes Gate, London SW7. Telephone 0171 (020-7 from 4/2000) 411 3400. Contemporary German art including work by some top names such as Georg Baselitz. Underground South Kensington.

Goldsmiths College Gallery, New Cross, London SE14 6NW. Telephone 0181 (020-8 from 4/2000) 692 7171 ext 264. Open Monday-Friday 12-5.
Work by contemporary artists in an art school context. It is worth remembering that Goldsmiths' past artists are now some of London's most successful, so perhaps worth paying a visit to see what makes Goldsmiths such a special art school. Underground New Cross.

Green and Stone of Chelsea, 259 Kings Road, London SW3. Telephone 0171 (020-7 from 4/2000) 352 6521. Open shop hours.

Stockists of fine art materials, near Chelsea art school, but also holds occasional exhibitions at the back of the shop, of small works by local professional artists. Underground Sloane Square and then walk or bus.

Greengrassi, 39C Fitzroy Street, London W.1. Telephone 0171 (020-7 from 4/2000) 387 8747. Open Tuesday-Saturday 11-6. Contemporary cutting-edge art including installations, video, multi-media. Underground Warren Street.

Greenwich Printmakers Association, 7 Turpin Lane, London SE10. Telephone 0181 (020-7 from 4/2000) 858 2290. Open daily 11-5. Closed Monday and Thursday.
A group of artist-printmakers. Regular Exhibitions of professional prints.

Greenwich Theatre Gallery, Crooms Hill, London SE10. Telephone 0181 (020-8 from 4/2000) 858 4447/8. Open Monday-Saturday 10.30-10.15pm.
Professional artists can apply. Contemporary art. Contact Geoffrey Beaghen.

Grosvenor Gallery, 8 Albemarle Street, London W.1. Telephone 0171 (020-7 from 4/2000) 629 0891. Publish work by Gerald Scarfe as well as being the world representatives of Erté. Also work covering the Art Nouveau period, Mucha and 20th-century masters for sale. Underground Green Park.

Hackelbury Fine Art, 4 Launceston Place, London W8 5RL. Telephone 0171 (020-7 from 4/2000) 937 8688. Fax (7) 937 8868. Open Wednesday-Saturday 10-5.
Directors: Sascha Hackel and Marcus Bury. Contemporary photography gallery. Photographers include: Frank Horvat, Edouard Boubat, Roman Vishniac, Pascal Kern. Photographers should call first to arrange a time to drop off their portfolio. Shows for 2000 include David Michael Kennedy and Sally Mann. Underground Gloucester Road/High Street Kensington.

Hales Gallery, 70 Deptford High Street, London SE8 4RT. Telephone 0181 (020-8 from mid 2000) 694 1194. Fax (8) 692 0471. Director: Paul Hedge. Cutting edge artists; Andrew Bick, Jonathan Callan, Ian Dawson, Judith Dean, Claude Heath, David Leapman, Martin McGinn, Tomoko Takahashi, Rachel Lowe, James Hyde, Claire Carter, Richard Woods. Channel 4 showed a film in spring '99 about a year In the life of this gallery. Saatchi buys here.

Hamiltons Gallery, 13 Carlos Place, London W.1. Telephone 0171 (020-7 from mid 2000) 499 9493/4. Open Monday-Friday 10-6, Saturday 10-1.
Fashionable photography gallery. Specialists in contemporary and vintage photographs. The gallery can be hired. Underground Bond Street.

Hart Gallery, 113 Upper Street, Islington, London N1 1QN. Telephone 0171 (020-7 from mid 2000) 704 1131.
Contemporary paintings, sculpture and ceramics. Artists: Kenneth Draper, Maxwell Doig, Richard Devereux, Tom Wood, David Blackburn and others.

Hayward Gallery, South Bank, London SE1. Telephone 0171 (020-7 from 4/2000) 960 4242. Fax (7)401 2664. Open daily 10-6. Tues and Wed until 8.
Director: Susan Ferlager Brades. This is a major London art gallery, run by the South Bank Centre. It concentrates on four areas; contemporary, other cultures, single artists, historical themes and artistic movements. A variety of major exhibitions are held here, ranging from contemporary British Art to major 20th-century Masters or touring shows. Check Time Out or main newspapers for details. The small bookshop is well-stocked and also sells cards and catalogues from past exhibitions. In early 2000 there is a Lucio Fontana show. Hayward Members scheme for discounts and free entrance to shows. Underground Waterloo or Embankment and walk across the bridge.

Helly Nahmad Gallery, 2 Cork Street, London W1X 1PB. Telephone 0171 (020-7 from 4/2000) 494 3200. Fax (7) 494 3355. Open Monday-Friday 10-6, Saturday 10-1.
Director: Helly Nahmad. A magnificent gallery space on two floors, showing Impressionist paintings, 20th century and contemporary art. The Nahmads are well-known art collectors and so far major shows have complemented Picasso and Impressionist exhibitions at the Royal Academy with superb catalogues. In '99 works by Damien Hirst, Marc Quinn, Keith Coventry, Gary Hume and Angus Fairhurst were shown. Artists should not apply for exhibitions. Underground Bond Street/Green Park.

Henry Moore Gallery, Royal College of Art, Kensington Gore, London SW7. Telephone (7) 590 4444. Fax 590 4500. Open 10-6. The enormous RCA galleries holds regular exhibitions of work by established artists, sometimes connected with the college, but often not. Check the press for details of current shows. The 20th Century Art Fair and Art on Paper Fair are held here.

Underground South Kensington or High Street Kensington.

Holland Park, Orangery Gallery, London W.8. Telephone 0171 (020-7 from mid 2000) 603 1123. Opening hours vary.
Artists can apply for exhibitions in this lovely light space in Holland Park. Artists have to organise their own publicity and security. Underground Holland Park.

Honor Oak Gallery, 52 Honor Oak Park, London SE23. Telephone 0181 (8 from 4/2000) 291 6094.
Contemporary art exhibitions. Participates in local Lewisham Visual Arts Festivals.

Hales Gallery, 70 Deptford High Street, London SE8. Telephone 0181 (020-8 from 4/2000) 694 1194. Open Tuesday-Saturday 10-4.
Contact: Paul Hedge. This is a gallery within a café context but provides the area with a good series of exhibitions by professional artists. Worth visiting if in the area. Charles Saatchi has bought work from here. Sculpture, installations and cutting-edge work. A film was shown on Channel 4 about a year in the life of the gallery in '99. Underground New Cross.

Houldsworth Fine Art, 34Cork Street, London W1X1HB. Telephone 0171 (020-7 from 4/2000) 434 2333. Fax (7) 434 3636. Artists include: Richard Bray, Robin Connelly, Jonathan Delafield Cook, Richard Henman, Gavin Lockheart, Paul McPhail, Matthew Radford, Peter Randall-Page, Karl Weschke and Uwe Wittwer. Contemporary painting and sculpture. Shows at Art 2000. Underground Green/Bond Street.

Hornsey Library New Gallery, Haringey Park Road, London N.8. Telephone 0181 (020-8 from 4/2000) 348 3351. Open Monday-Friday 9.30-8, Saturday 9.30-5.
Artists can apply for exhibitions.

ICA (Institute of Contemporary Arts), The Mall, London SW1. Telephone 0171 (020-7 from 4/2000) 930 3647/0493. Recorded information (7) 930 6393. Open daily 12-9. The centre is open 12-11 every day for the theatre, cinema, bar and restaurant.
Director: Mik Flood. Membership scheme for details of events and free entry to shows. Three galleries. Not a submissions gallery but interested to see work if appropriate in form of slides/photos/documentation by professional artists. It is advisable to ring the visual arts department first. Restaurant, bookshop with good selection of art magazines and alternative reviews and catalogues. Video library. Art pass for students.

Lively arts centre in central London with international visitors as well as British visitors. Underground Charing Cross.

The Ice House, Holland Park, London W.8. Telephone 0171 (020-7 from 4/2000) 603 1123.
Artists can rent this unusual space for small exhibitions. Past exhibitors have been photographers, craftsmen and women, jewellery designers and painters. Underground Holland Park.

Indar Pasricha Fine Arts, 22 Connaught Street, London W.2. Telephone 0171 (020-7 from 4/2000) 724 9541. Open Monday-Friday 10-5, Saturday 10-1.
Director: Indar Pasricha. Islamic, Anglo-Indian and Indian art, as well as European and American art. Underground Marble Arch.

Interim Art, 21 Beck Road, London E8 4RE. Telephone 0181 (020-8 from 4/2000) 254 9607. Check for opening hours and exhibitions. Run by Maureen O. Paley. Exhibitions of work by contemporary cutting-edge artists, many who live in the East end. Exhibits at Art 2000 every January.

198 Gallery, 198 Railton Road, Herne Hill, London SE24 0LU. Telephone 0181 (020-8 from 4/2000) 978 8309. Fax (8) 652 1418. Open Tuesday-Saturday 1-6.
Chairman: Clarence Thompson. Run as a charity the gallery provides access for artists of African, Caribbean or Asian descent. Culturally diverse exhibitions. 2 gallery spaces. Print and darkroom facilities. Contact the Chairman for details about exhibiting. Underground Brixton.

Islington Central Library, 2 Fieldway Crescent, London N.5. Telephone 0181 (020-8 from 4/2000) 609 3051 ext 56. Open Monday, Tuesday, Thursday 10-7, Saturday 11-4.
Professional artists can apply. Underground Highbury and Islington.

James Colman Fine Art, at Montpelier Sandelson, 4 Montpelier Street, London SW7IEZ. Telephone 0171 (020-7 from 4/2000) 548 7488. Fax (7) 225 2280. During exhibitions open 10-6.
Director: James Colman. A new gallery space run by James Colman at Montpelier Sandelson. Contemporary artists from established to recent RCA graduates. Mainly painting but has shown other work. Denis Clarke, Caroline Kent and others. Underground Knightsbridge.

Javier Lopez Gallery, 41-42 Foley Street, London W.1. Telephone 0171 (020-7 from 4/2000) 436 9884.

James Colman at his gallery, with artist Denis Clarke.

Contemporary art gallery and has also shown installations as well as paintings. Underground Tottenham Court Road.

Jerwood Space, 171 Union Street, London SE1. Telephone 0171 (020-7 from 4/2000) 654 0171. Fax (7) 654 0172.
Director: Richard Lee. Curator: Stephen Hepworth. 25,000 square feet of magnificent gallery space near Bankside the new art area. Includes rehearsal space for several dance groups or theatre groups at a time. The gallery is at the front of the building and shows the annual Jerwood Painting Prize (winner Madeleine Strindberg in '98) and other shortlisted artists. Sculpture in the courtyard outside. There are also other Jerwood projects including the Jerwood Gallery at the Natural History Museum, at Trinity Hall Cambridge, at Witley Park, Worcester and capital grants are being awarded for arts and educational projects. There are other prizes for fashion, dance, textiles and crafts. Underground Waterloo and walk or London Bridge.

Jibby Beane Gallery, 12 Clerkenwell Road, London EC1. Telephone 0171 (020-7 from 4/2000) 689 0336.
Director: Jibby Beane Cutting-edge artists at this central space run by the dynamic, extraordinary Jibby Beane, who seems to get more coverage in the press than most dealers and artists put together! Shows at Art 2000 in January each year. Underground Old Street.

Jill George Gallery, 38 Lexington Street, London W.1. Telephone 0171 (020-7 from 4/2000) 439 7343. Open weekdays 10-6, Saturday 11-4.
Director: Jill George. The gallery deals in paintings and drawings

by established artists. Recommended by an art collector for first time and regular buyers. Underground Oxford Circus.

Jonathan Clark Gallery, 18 Park Walk, London SW10 OAQ. Telephone 0171 (020-7 from mid 2000) 351 3555.
Modern and contemporary British Art; St Ives, Camden Town Group, Euston Road School and School of London.

Julian Lax, Flat J, 37-39 Arkwright Road, London NW3. Telephone 0171 (020-7 from 4/2000) 794 9933. By appointment only.
Fine original prints; Chagall, Colquhoun, Frink, Hockney, Hodgkin, Matisse, Miró, Moore, Nicholson, Pasmore, Picasso and Piper.

Kapil Jariwala, 4 New Burlington Street, London W.1. Telephone 0171 (020-7 from 4/2000) 437 2172. Open Monday-Friday 10-6, Saturday 10-2.
Interesting variety of shows here from painting to video and photography by good contemporary artists. Underground Green Park.

Keith H. Chapman, 91 Raymouth Road, London SE16 2DA. Telephone 0171 (020-7 from mid 2000) 232 1885.
Sculptors and Abstract painters prominent during the 1950s and contemporary painting; Michael Ayrton, Rober Clatworthy, Bernard Meadows.

Kew Gardens Gallery, Royal Botanic Gardens, Kew. Telephone 0181 (020-8 from 4/2000) 332 5168.
Regular exhibitions of paintings on a botanical theme. Opening times vary, but are usually Monday-Saturday 9.30-4.45. Underground Kew.

The Kilim Warehouse, 28A Pickets Street, London SW12. Telephone 0181 (020-8 from 4/2000) 675 3122.
Old, decorative and antique kilims from Asia Minor and beyond. New kilims handwoven in the Anatolian villages using classical designs.

Kingsgate Gallery. See Artists Register.

Knapp Gallery, Regents College, Inner Circle, Regents Park, London NW1. Telephone 0171 (020-7 from 4/2000) 487 7540. Open Monday-Friday but check times.
Regular exhibitions by known and unknown artists. Often theme exhibitions or artists of one nationality. Artist can apply. Underground Baker Street.

Kufa Gallery, Westbourne Hall, 26 Westbourne Grove, London W.2. Telephone 0171 (020-7 from 4/2000) 229 1928. Open 10-6.

Middle Eastern arts; visul arts, architecture, music and literature. Changing exhibitions, sometimes traditional, sometimes contemporary art. Underground Queensway.

Lamont Gallery, 65 Roman Road, London E2 0QN. Telephone 0181 (020-8 from 4/2000) 981 6332. Open Tuesday-Saturday 11-6. Contemporary art. Paintings, prints and photographs have all been shown here. Underground Bethnal Green.

Laure Genillard Gallery, 82-84 Clerkenwell Road, London EC1M 5RF. Telephone 0171 (020-7 from 4/2000) 436 2300. Open Tuesday-Saturday11-6.
Director: Laure Genillard. Installations, conceptual and Minimal art, shown by this charming Swiss art dealer. Cutting-edge artists. Also painters. Artists include: Dan Hays, Lesley Foxcroft, Elisa Signicelli, Alice Stepanek, Steven Maslin, Lindsay Seers, Sylvie Fleury, Padraig Timoney, Dean Hughes, Douglas Allsop. Gallery policy is that they look at all work that relates to contemporary discourse, but accept very little new work. Underground Farringdon.

Laurent Delaye, 22 Barrett Street, London W.1. Telephone 0171 (020-7 from 4/2000) 629 5905. Open Tuesday-Friday 10-6, Saturday 12-6.
Director: Laurent Delaye. Good contemporary British and European artists in this established gallery. Underground Bond Street.

Lefevre Gallery, 30 Bruton Street, London W.1. Telephone 0171 (020-7 from 4/2000) 493 2107. Open Monday-Friday 10-5, Saturday 10-1.
19th and 20th-century European art and British 20th-century artists such as Edward Burra and LS Lowry. Underground Green Park.

Leighton House Museum, 12 Holland Park Road, London W14 8LZ. Telephone 0171 (020-7 from 4/2000) 602 3316.
Artists can apply for exhibitions in the temporary exhibitions space. Ideal for several artists exhibiting together. Near Holland Park. Underground High Street Kensington and walk.

Lesley Craze, 34 Clerkenwell Green, London EC1. Telephone 0171 (020-7 from 4/2000) 608 0393.
Contemporary jewellery and silverware. Wendy Ramshaw, Liz Tyler, Vicky Amber-Smith. The best of British silversmithing and design.

Liberty and Co Ltd., Regent Street, London W.1. Telephone

0171 734 1234. Open Monday-Friday 9-5.30, Thursday-7, Saturday 9.30-5.30.
Prints and paintings, also craftwork by young designers. Shows have been in the basement and on the top floor. Underground Oxford Circus.

Linda Blackstone Gallery, The Old Slaughterhouse (rear of 13 High Street), Pinner, Middlesex. Telephone 0181 (020-8 from 4/2000) 868 5765. Open Wednesday-Saturday10-6.
Director: Linda Blackstone. British contemporary representational paintings and sculpture. Artists can apply in writing with cv and illustrations and then artists will be seen by appointment only. Underground Pinner (Metropolitan line).

Lisson Gallery, 67 Lisson Street, London NW1. Telephone 0171 (020-7 from 4/2000) 724 2739. Fax 724 7124. Open Monday-Friday 10-6, Saturday 10-5.
Directors: Nicholas Logsdail, Barry Barker and Jill Silverman.
An important contemporary art gallery. Many of their artists have been shortlisted for the Turner Prize over the years, as well as winners. Conceptual, Minimal, sculpture and other recent developments in art have been shown here. Artists include: Art & Language, John Latham, Donald Judd, Sol Lewitt, Dan Graham, Robert Mangold, Grenville Davy (Turner winner), Richard Deacon (Turner winner), Shirazeh Houshiary, Anish Kapoor, Tony Cragg, Julian Opie, Richard Wentworth, Christine Borland, Jason Martin, Douglas Gordon (Turner winner), Jane and Louise Wilson, Mat Colishaw, Jonathan Monk, Simon Patterson, Pierre Bismuth, Mark Hosking, Ceal Floyer, Thomas Schütte, Jan Vercruysse, Lili Dujourie, John Murphy and others. Artists should not apply. Underground Edgware Road.

Locus Gallery, 116 Heath Street, London NW3. Telephone 0171 (020-7 from 4/2000) 435 4005. Open Monday-Friday 10.30-5.30, Saturday 11-5.
Director: Gudrun Fazzina. Professional artists can apply. Italian sculpture often on show. Two floors 5x13 metres. A small gallery situated on the main road up to Hampstead Heath. Underground Hampstead.

Loggia Gallery and Sculpture Gardens, 15 Buckingham Gate, London SW1. Telephone 0171 (020-7 from 4/2000) 828 5963. Open Monday-Friday 6-8, Saturday and Sunday 2-6.
Members of the Free Painters and Sculptors Group only. Ideal place for buyers looking for sculpture by established artists. Underground Victoria.

Logos Gallery, 20 Barter Street, London WC1A 2AH. Telephone 0171 (020-7 from 4/2000) 404 7091. Open Tuesday-Friday 11-5, Saturday 11-3.
International contemporary art; Lucien Cooper, Mitra, Ruscha, Langelaar, Alexander Putar, Helen Wilkes. The gallery also runs the Logos national art competition. Underground Holborn.

London Projects, 47 Frith Street, London W.1. Telephone 0171 (020-7 from 4/2000) 734 1723. Open Friday and Saturday 10-6. Director: Marc Jancou. This young, lively Swiss art dealer moved to London from Zurich to run his successful new gallery and participate in the boom London art scene. Contemporary art with reasonably well-known painters, such as Michelle Fierro. Underground Tottenham Court Road.

Midriver: The Bearer 94-97, Timothy Hyman.

Long & Ryle, 4 John Islip Street, London SW1. Telephone 0171 (020-7 from 4/2000) 834 1434. Fax 821 9409. Open Tuesday-Friday 10-5, Saturday 10-2.
Director: Sarah Long. Contemporary British and European artists. Colour is usually a key highlight in their exhibitions, paintings and sculpture. Artists include: Simon Casson, Matthew Rose, Sarah Stitt, Susan Light, D.Thomas, Brian Sayers, Ramiro Fernandez Saus. Artists can send slides and a copy of their cv. Underground Pimlico.

Lothbury Gallery, 41 Lothbury, London EC2P 2BP. Telephone 0171 (020-7 from 4/2000) 726 1642. Open Monday-Friday 10-4. Curator: Rosemary Harris. The Nat West Art Prize shortlisted artists are shown here every year. See details of the prize in prize section. The Nat West art collection includes work by John Bellany, Anthony Malinowski, Mary Fedden, Albert Irvin among 1500 works of art, shown in rotation in the large central gallery space. Other contemporary installations, sculpture and art exhibitions take place regularly at the National Westminster Bank headquarters in the City. Underground Bank.

Lotta Hammer, 51 Cleveland Street, London W.1. Telephone 0171 (020-7 from 4/2000) 636 2221. Fax 436 6067. Open Tuesday-Friday 11-6, Saturday 12-4.
Director: Lotta Hammer. Lively contemporary art gallery in central London space. Artists include: Tracy McKenna & Edwin

Nat West art collection, Lothbury Gallery, City of London.

Janssen, Graham Gussin, Pierre Huyghe, Liz Arnold, Jason Coburn and others. Underground Goodge Street.

Lumley Cazalet, 33 Davies Street, London W.1. Telephone 0171 (020-7 from 4/2000) 499 5058. Open Monday-Friday 10-6, Saturday by appointment.
Directors: C.Annesley, C.Cazalet, C.Hodgkinson and M. Butterwick. Prints by 20th-century Masters and also by young international artists. Young professional artists can apply to show prints by presenting their portfolios to the directors. Underground Bond Street/Green Park.

Lynne Stern Associates, 46 Bedford Row, London W.C1. Telephone 0171 (020-7 from 4/2000) 491 8905/8906. Open Monday-Friday 10-6, Saturday10-1.
Art consultancy run by Lynne Stern for companies and corporate collectors. Large selection of work on view by British contemporary artists including: Norman Adams RA, Jennifer Durrant, Jean Gibson, Adrian Heath, Howard Hodgkin, Michael Kenny ARA, William Littlejohn RSW, John Loker, Anthony Whishaw and others. Specialists in advising and assisting businesses with purchase, hire and commissioning. Underground Green Park.

Lyric Theatre, King Street, London W.6. Telephone 0171 (020-7 from 4/2000) 741 2311. Open Monday-Saturday 10-11pm, Sunday 12-11pm.
Gallery space within a theatre context. Painting, photography and print exhibitions. Professional artists can apply. Underground Hammersmith.

Malcolm Innes Gallery, 7 Bury Street, London SW1. Telephone 0171 (020-7 from 4/2000) 839 8083. 19th and 20th-century Scottish landscape. Underground Green Park.

The Mall Galleries, The Mall, London SW1. Telephone 0171 (020-7 from 4/2000) 930 6844. Open 7 days a week 10-5.
Annual exhibitions of work by members of the various art societies belonging to the Federation of British Artists (see Useful addresses — artist organisations). For hire also; 510 square metres and mailing list available. Write to 17 Carlton House Terrace, London SW1Y 5BD.

Marlene Eleini, 12/69 Westbourne Terrace, London W.2. 3UY. Telephone 0171 (020-7 from 4/2000) 706 0373. Fax 0171 (020-7 from 4/2000) 706 1241. Open by appointment only.
Marlene Eleini now deals privately showing artists such as Bob Law whose work is in the Tate gallery and the Guggenheim.

Maureen Michaelson, 27 Daleham Gardens, Hampstead, London NW3. Telephone 0171 (020-7 from 4/2000) 435 0510. Open by appointment.
Ceramics and prints by established names.

Manya Igel Fine Arts, 21-22 Peters Court, Porchester Road, London W.2. Telephone 0171 (020-7 from 4/2000) 229 1669/8429. Open Monday-Friday 10-5 by appointment only.
20th-century British paintings and watercolours. Participates in various British art fairs. Underground Queensway.

Marina Henderson Gallery, 11 Langton Street, London SW10. Telephone 0171 (020-7 from 4/2000) 352 1667. Open Tuesday -Saturday 11-6.
Theatrical and architectural designs from 1800 to today.

Mark Gallery, 9 Porchester Place, Marble Arch, London W.2. Telephone 0171 (020-7 from 4/2000) 262 4906. Open Monday-Friday 10-1, 2-6, Saturday 11-1. Director: Helen Mark. Specialises in Russian 16th century icons, but also Ecole de Paris and modern and contemporary prints. Only French artists. Underground Marble Arch.

Marlborough Fine Art, and Marlborough Graphics, 6 Albemarle Street, London W.1. Telephone 0171 (020-7 from 4/2000) 629 5161. Open Monday-Friday 10-5.30, Saturday 10-12.30.
The Graphics gallery is also based here. Directors: G.Parton, J.Erle-

The Bathers, Coney Island suite, Bill Jacklin (Marlborough Fine Art).

Drax, D.Case. 20th-century Masters, German Expressionists and contemporary artists; Auerbach, Arikha, Stephen Conroy, Davies, Enkaona, Freud Prints, Ken Kiff, Kitaj, Bill Jacklin, Christopher Le Brun, Mason, Thérèse Oulton Pasmore, Celia Paul, John Piper, Paula Rego. A major international art gallery with branches in Tokyo and Madrid. Artists should not apply but send invitations to exhibitions to the Directors. Exhibitions in late '99 include Paula Rego and Thérèse Oulton. Underground Green Park.

Matts Gallery, 44 Copperfield Road, London E3 4RR. Telephone 0181 (020-8 from 4/2000) 983 1771. Open Wednesday-Sunday 12-6. Closed Monday and Tuesday.
Robin Klassnik. 1500 square feet of space. They do not encourage unsolicited material. All exhibitions are commissioned especially for gallery spaces (all media shown). Gallery artists include: Willie Doherty, Jaroslaw Kozlowski, Kate Smith, Mike Nelson, Melanie Counsell, Juan Cruz, Lucy Gunning, John Frankland, Mel Jackson.

Mayor Gallery, 22A Cork Street, London W.1. Telephone 0171 (020-7 from 4/2000) 734 3558. Fax (7) 494 1377. Open Monday-Friday 10-5.30, Saturday 10-1 (except August when they are closed on Saturdays).
Directors: James Mayor and Andrew Murray. Please apply by sending photographs in the first instance. 20th-century Masters and contemporary British, American and European painting, and works on paper. British and European Surrealists, British and American Pop Arts, Kitchen sink painters. Usually holds some interesting exhibitions and the atmosphere is friendly. Underground Green Park/Bond Street.

McHardy Sculpture Company, Cardamon Building, Shad Thames, London SE1. Telephone 0171 (020-7 from 4/2000) 403 7555.
Run by Agi Cohen. At least 100 works of Sculpture on display. Nicola Godden, Neil Williams, Patricia Volk, Glynis Williams. Prices range from £50-£15,000.

Mercury Gallery, 26 Cork Street, London W.1. Telephone 0171 (020-7 from 4/2000) 734 7800. Open Monday-Friday 10-5.30, Saturday 10-12.30.
Director: Mrs Gillian Raffles. 20th-century Masters. Scottish artists a speciality; Elizabeth Blackadder, John Houston, David Michie and less well-known Scottish artists. Underground Bond Street/Green Park.

Merrifield Studios, 110 Heath Street, London NW3. Telephone 0171 (020-7 from 4/2000) 794 0343. Open Wednesday-Sunday 10-6.

Director: Blackie Merrifield. Paintings and prints by contemporary British artists as well as sculpture and drawings by Tom Merrifield. In Hampstead village on the way to the heath. Underground Hampstead.

Michael Goedhuis, 116 Mount Street, London W1Y 5HD. Telephone 0171 (020-7 from 4/2000) 629 2228.
The gallery specialises in contemporary Chinese art. Interesting to see the Chinese response to Western Modernism. Underground Green Park.

Michael Hue-Williams, 1st floor, 21 Cork Street, London W.1. Telephone 0171 (020-7 from 4/2000) 434 1318. Fax (7) 434 1321. Open Monday-Friday 10-5.30.
Director: Michael Hue-Williams. Contemporary sculpture, painting and photography. Artists should not apply. Past exhibitions have included Andy Goldsworthy and contemporary established sculptors and painters. Underground Bond Street/Green Park.

Mistral Galleries, 10 Dover Street, London W.1. Telephone 0171 (020-7 from 4/2000) 499 4701. Open Monday-Friday 10-6, Saturday 10-4.
The London branch of this Westerham, Kent gallery. Gallery artists include lesser-known names such as Roy Petley and Annabel Gosling. Underground Green Park.

Modern Art Inc., 73 Redchurch Street, London E.2. Telephone 0171 (020-7 from 4/2000) 739 2081. Open Thursday-Sunday 11-6. Contemporary sculpture by British artists. Underground Old Street.

Morley Gallery, 61 Westminster Bridge Road, London SE1. Telephone 0171 (020-7 from 4/2000) 928 8501 ext 30. Open 10-9 college terms, 10-6 otherwise.
All forms of art and craft are considered. 150 linear feet on one floor. Must provide own costs for publicity, private views and security. Underground Lambeth North.

Museum of Installation, 175 Deptford High Street, London SE8. Open Tuesday-Friday 12-5, Saturday 2-5.
Installation art. Underground New Cross.

National Theatre, South Bank, London SE1. Telephone 0171 (020-7 from 4/2000) 928 2033. Open Monday-Saturday 10-11pm.
Professional artists can apply for exhibitions here. Underground Waterloo.

Neffe-Degandt Fine Art, 32A St George Street, London W1R 9FA. Telephone 071 (020-7from 4/2000) 493 2630/629 9788. Fax 493 1379. Open Tuesday-Friday 10-5.30, and by appointment.
This gallery holds an annual Raoul Dufy exhibition showing some of his exqucolours and drawings. Paul Poiret dress designs 1917-19 have also been shown. Underground Oxford Circus.

New Academy Gallery, 34 Windmill Street, London W.1. Telephone 0171 (020-7 from 4/2000) 323 4700. Fax 436 3059. Open Monday-Friday 10-6, Saturday 11-5. Closed Sunday and Bank holidays.
Directors: John and Jill Hutchings. Artists include: Jane Corsellis, Donald Hamilton-Fraser, Padraig MacMiadhachain and others. Northern Graduates show annually in August. Artists should not apply. Comprehensive art service to businesses, including hire scheme and commissions. Exhibitions of work by contemporary artists. Underground Goodge Street.

New Art Centre, now **The New Art Centre Sculpture Park and Gallery at Roche Court, near Salisbury.** Telephone 01980 862244. 100 works by sculptors.

New Grafton Gallery, 49 Church Road Barnes, London SW13.8HH. Telephone 0181 (020-8 from 4/2000) 748 8850. Open Tuesday-Saturday 10-5.
Director: David Wolfers. Professional artists can apply at any time of the year by post, including slides or photographs and cv. Send sae. Modern British figurative work only, 1900-2000 Artists include: Ken Howard, Fred Cuming, John Nash, Sir Hugh Casson, Tom Coates, Todd Warmouth, Ruth Stage, Richard Pikesley, and others. One floor. Portrait painting centre. British Rail Barnes.

Northcote Gallery, 110 Northcote Road, London SW11. Telephone 0181 (020-8 from 4/2000) 748 8850. Open Tuesday-Friday 11-7, Saturday 11-6.
Contemporary paintings. British Rail Clapham Junction.

The Nunnery, See Bow Arts Trust entry.
Director: Stuart Glass. Telephone (8) 983 9737. Fax (8)980 7770. Thursday-Sunday 12-6. Unsolicited applications considered. Contemporary visual and performance art. 2000 exhibitions include Nicky Hoberman and John Frankland.

Nylon, 9 Sinclair Gardens, London W14 OAU. Telephone 0171 (020-7 from mid 2000) 601 6061. Fax (7) 602 2126.
Set up in late '98 this is a gallery in a home setting. The owner

is young and dynamic and sells work at accessible prices. Mostly young contemporary artists and has had shows in conjunction with Andrew Mummery gallery ('99).

The October Gallery, 24 Old Gloucester Street, London WC1. Telephone 0171 (020-7 from 4/2000) 242 7367. Fax (7) 405 1851. Open Tuesday-Saturday 12.30 5.30.
Director: Chili Hawes. Artistic director: Elisabeth Lalouschek. Art centre with bookshop, theatre, coffee shop, photo lab and lively gallery. Paintings, prints and sculpture. Applications are considered. Send 6 slides or photos, a c.v. and self-addressed stamped envelope. Artists from many countries shown in the gallery; El Anatsui, Ablade Glover, Emmanuel Taiwo Jegede, Elisabeth Lalouschek, Julieta Rubio, Gerald Wilde, Aubrey Williams, Xu Zhong Min. One floor of space 40x20. Variety of paintings, performance, mixed media shows. Underground Holborn.

Paton Gallery, 282 Richmond Road, London E.8. Telephone 0181 (020-8 from 4/2000) 986 3409. Fax (8) 986 0811. Open Tuesday-Saturday 11-6, Sunday 12-6.
Director: Graham Paton. This is a lively East end gallery and the director is keen to promote young, professional, exciting, new artists, but not at the expense of his established artists. Charles Saatchi buys work, corporate collections and the Met in New York, amongst others. Artists include: Rosie Snell, rising star Ellie Howitt, Alexander Guy, Julie Major, Tim Ollivier, Kate Palmer, Alex Veness. Many of Paton's artists have done well and are shown in the Metropolitan Art Museum in New York. The gallery is in a complex with Angela Flowers art gallery. British Rail London Fields or bus 38.

Peter Gwyther Gallery, 29 Bruton Street, London W1X 7DB. Telephone 01717 (020-7 from 4/2000) 495 4747. Fax 495 6232. Contyemporary art. Past shows include: Prints by Peter Blake and Andy Warhol. Underground Bond Street/Green Park.

Phillips Fine Art Auctioneers, 101 New Bond Street, London W.1. Telephone 0171 (20-7 from 4/2000) 629 6602.
Auctions and viewings held daily of paintings and prints. Also Oriental ceramics, glass, furniture, clocks, jewellery, books, miniatures, Art Nouveau, Art Deco and 20th-century art. Underground Bond Street.

Photofusion Photography Centre, 17A Electric Lane, Brixton, London SW9 8LA. Telephone 0171 (020-7 from 4/2000) 738 5774. Fax (7) 738 5509.
A wide range of contemporary and historical photography, video

and multi-media installations. The gallery is available to hire for exhibitions, book launches and events. Picture library and agency with 100,000 images and wory 100 photographers. New Media Workroom and darkroom and studio facilities. Gallery open Tues/Thurs/Friday 10-6, Wednesday 10-8, Saturday 12-4. Underground Brixton.

Photographers Gallery Ltd., 5 & 8 Great Newport Street, London WC2. Telephone 0171 (020-7 from 4/2000) 831 1772. Open Monday-Saturday 11-6.
Director: Paul Wombell. Photographers can apply at any time but decisions are made in early March and early October. Variety of work ranging from political/social documentation to historical and avant-garde contemporary. A number of spaces at both buildings. At No. 5 there is a reference library with 3000 books, slide library with 5000 slides of prints, a viewing room for buyers (Print sales are Tuesday-Saturday 12-6). The bookshop has over 1200 titles, 400 postcards, posters and the noticeboard gives details of competitions, prizes and awards available in Britain. The membership scheme is excellent value for private views and discounts. Underground Leicester Square.

Photology, 24 Litchfield Street, London W C2. Telephone 0171 (020-7 from 4/2000) 836 8600. Open Tuesday-Saturday 11-6.
Interesting photography exhibitions. Underground Covent Garden.

Piccadilly Gallery, 16 Cork Street, London W.1. Telephone 0171 (020-7 from 4/2000) 499 4632.
Director: Godfrey Pilkington. British figurative work. David Tindle, Graham Ovenden, Rosie Lee and other very British artists. Artists should make an appointment to show work, if appropriate. 500m square feet of gallery space. One of the most charming, well-mannered gallery directors in Cork Street. Underground Green Park.

Piers Feetham, 475 Fulham Road, London SW6. Telephone 0171 (020-7 from 4/2000) 381 5958. Open Tuesday-Friday 10-1 and 2-6, Saturday 10-1.
Small exhibition space, also framing. Open to applications but ring the gallery first. Underground Fulham Broadway.

Pitshanger Manor Gallery, Mattock Lane, Ealing, London W.5. Telephone 0181 (020-8 from 4/2000) 567 1227. Open Tuesday-Saturday 10-5. Closed Monday.
Subsidised by Ealing Education and Leisure Services. Applications open to West London artists. Underground Ealing Broadway.

Purdy Hicks Gallery, 65 Hopton Street, Bankside, London SE1. Telephone 0171 (020-7 from 4/000) 401 9229. Fax 401 9595. Open Tuesday, Thursday and Friday 10-5.30, Wednesday 10-8, Saturday 10-2.
Directors: Jayne Purdy and Rebecca Hicks, Nicola Shane.
Large gallery space in the newly-fashionable area that will be next to the new Tate Bankside when it opens at the millennium, also near the Globe Theatre. Artists include: Arturo di Stefano, Felim Egan, Estelle Thompson, David Hiscock, Rachel Budd, Michael Finch, Michael Porter, Andrez Jackowski, Hughie O'Donoghue, John Hubbard (Jerwood prizewinner). A dynamic gallery with refreshing shows. Underground Blackfriars (Exit Blackfriars Bridge East side).

Portal Gallery, 43 Dover Street, London W.1. Telephone 0171 (020-7 from 4/2000) 493 0706. Open Monday-Friday 10-5.45, Saturday 11-2.
Professional artists can apply at any time. Mainly 20th-century self-taught naive painters and figurative fantasy paintings. On two floors. Underground Green Park.

Portland Gallery, 9 Bury Street, St James's, London SW1. Telephone 0171 (020-7 from mid 2000) 321 0422. Open Tuesday-Friday, Saturday 9.30-5.30.
Specialises in Scottish 20th-century and also contemporary exhibitions. Underground Green Park.

Portobello Green, Portobello Road, at Westway under the bridge, London W.10.
24 small workshops run by professional craft, design and creative people. Worth a visit. Underground Westbourne Park.

Proud Galleries, 5 Buckingham Street, London WC2. Telephone 0171 (020-7 from mid 2000) 839 4942. Open Monday-Friday 10-6:15, Saturday and Sunday 11-5.
Variety of contemporary art shows including Chinese prints and British artists. Underground Charing Cross.

Pump House Gallery, Battersea Park, London SW11 4NJ. Telephone 0181 (020-8 from 4/2000) 871 7572. Fax 0171 (020-7 from 4/2000) 228 9062. Wednesday-Friday 11-3, Saturday and Sunday 11-4.
Director: Susie Gray. Gallery in Battersea park setting. Contemporary painting, Open to artists to apply in writing.

Railings Gallery, 5 New Cavendish Street, London W.1. Telephone 0171 (020-7 from 4/2000) 935 1114. Open Monday-

Saturday 9.30-6.
Director: Geihle Sander. Open to artists to apply, but ring the gallery first. Small contemporary art gallery.

Aboriginal art at Rebecca Hossack gallery in August annually.

Rebecca Hossack Gallery, 35 Windmill Street, Fitzrovia, London W1. Telephone 0171 (020-7 from 4/2000) 436 4899 Fax 323 3182. Open Monday-Saturday 10-6.
Director: Rebecca Hossack. Contemporary artists (painting, prints, photography, ceramics) but also Australian Aboriginal art every summer and non-western art occasionally. Open to artists to apply in writing with slides and photos, but ring the gallery first, to see if your work is appropriate. Artists include: Jan Williams, Sophie de Stempel, Toby Ziegler, Alasdair Wallace, Abigail McLellan. Rebecca is now the Cultural Attaché for Australia in London, so a manager runs the gallery mainly. Good place for art buyers. Underground Goodge Street.

The Redfern Gallery, 20 Cork Street, London W.1. Telephone 0171 (020-7 from 4/2000) 734 1732. Open Monday-Friday 10-5.30, Saturday 10-12.30.
Applications by professional artists should be made in the first six months of the year and an appointment should be made first. Contemporary art and established names include Patrick Procktor, Oxtoby, Preece, Kneale, Stevens and others. Underground Green Park.

Regent Street Gallery, See Concourse Gallery entry for details on applications for artists.

RIBA, 66 Portland Place, London W.1. Telephone 0171 (020-7 from mid 2000) 580 5533. Open Monday-Friday 10-6, Saturday 10-2. Exhibitions mainly of an architectural nature, but sometimes photographic. Underground Regents Park.

Richard Salmon, Studio 4, 59 South Edwardes Square, London W.8 6HW. Telephone 0171 (020-7 from mid 2000) 602 9494. International contemporary art and 20th Century Masters.

Riverside Studios Gallery, Crisp Road, Hammersmith, London W.6. Telephone 0181 (020-8 from 4/2000) 237 1000. Fax (8) 237 1001. Open 9-11. Closed Friday afternoons (seasonal), Sunday 12-10.30.
Director: William Burdett-Coutts. Administrator: Julie Beresford. Contemporary, exciting, new young British multi-media artists. Selected apllications. Please call ahead for further information. In a complex by the River Thames at Hammersmith. Underground Hammersmith.

Robert Prime, 60/61 Warren Street, London W1P 5PA. Telephone 0171 (020-7 from 4/2000) 916 636. Fax (7) 916 6369. Open Tuesday-Friday 11-6, Saturday 2-6.
Directors: Gregorio Magnani and Tommaso Corvi-Mora. Contemporary European and American artists. Artists include: Kai Althoff, Michel Auder, Angela Bulloch, Joe Cavallaro, Rachel Feinstein, Vidya Gastaldon and Jean-Michel Wicker, General Idea, Isa Genzken, Liam Gillick, Dominique Gonzalez-Foerster, Lothar Hempel, Candida Hofer, Jim Isermann, Christina Mackie, Eva Marisaldi, Philippe Parreno and Monique Prieto. Artists should not apply. Underground Warren Street.

Robert Sandelson, 5 Cork Street, London W.1. Telephone 0171 (020-7 from mid 2000) 439 1001. Fax (7) 439 2299.
Director: Robert Sandelson. In '99 Robert Sandelson opened a large new gallery at 5 Cork Street on two floors, one below the Atrium Bookshop. Previously owner of the family gallery in Knightsbridge, Robert Sandelson deals in 20th century Modern and contemporary British and International art including artists such as the international Louise Bourgeois and British artists Anne Rothenstein. On one floor contemporary international (including Russian artists) and British artists will be on show and on another 20th century Modern Art. A welcome addition to Cork street. Underground Green Park/Bond Street.

Rocket Gallery, 130 Old Burlington Street, London W.1. Telephone 0171 (020-7 from 4/2000) 434 3043. Tues, Wed, Fri, Saturday 10-6.
Innovative contemporary art. Underground Bond Street/Piccadilly.

Rona Gallery, 1/2 Weighhouse Street, London W.1. Telephone 0171 (020-7 from 4/2000) 491 3718/499 8830. Open Monday-Saturday 10.30-5.30.
Director: Stanley Harries. Naive artists including Joe Scarborough, Margaret Loxton and Dora Holzhandler.

Royal Academy, Burlington House, Piccadilly, London W.1. Telephone 0171 (020-7 from 4/2000) 300 8000. Open daily 10-6. The Royal Academy is the oldest society in Britain, founded in 1768 and devoted to the fine arts. It is famous for its annual summer exhibition of some 1000 paintings, drawings, prints and sculpture. It holds a variety of major exhibitions throughout the year and the Friends of the RA membership is very good value, to get maximum benefit from the RA. The magnificent Sackler Galleries upstairs have successfully combined modern architecture with historical. Recently shows have been far more dynamic and contemporary, as well as the major money spinning blockbusters. The main galleries hold the major international touring shows and downstairs in the basement the RA schools hold degree shows in the summer as well as displays of prizewinning work, or other similar shows. There is an excellent shop/bookshop and the restaurant in the basement is well-worth visiting. The RA magazine is not just a house magazine but covers international and national art news and reviews. Underground Piccadilly Circus/Green Park.

Royal Overseas League, Overseas House, Park Place, St James's Street, London SW1. Telephone 0171 (020-7 from 4/2000) 408 0214. As the ROSL is a club/hotel the gallery is open daily.
Contact: Roderick Lakin. The ROSL annual art exhibition is held in September in London and then tours to the ROSL in Edinburgh. Over 500 works of art are on show after a rigorous selection procedure by judges and there are many prizes from £200-£3000 and two travelling prizes. Commonwealth artists are highlighted making the exhibitions international and often unusual. There are now exhibitions all year round. If you are looking for a comfortable London hotel facing onto Green Park it is well-worth joining the ROSL. The Edinburgh ROSL is very central too in Princes Street. Underground Green Park.

Royal College of Art Gallery, Kensington Gore, London SW7. Telephone 0171 (020-7 from 4/2000) 590 4444. Fax (7) 590 4500. Open10-6.
Now known as the **Henry Moore Galleries**. Also used by other organisations such as the **20th century Art Fair** in September and the **Art on Paper Fair**. Sometimes major shows, but watch

Time Out or newspapers for details. Otherwise it is RCA graduate and postgraduate shows throughout the year. Underground High Street Kensington.

Royal Festival Hall, South Bank, London SE1. Telephone 0171 (020-7 from 4/2000) 928 3002. Open concert hall hours. There are now a variety of exhibitions at Festival Hall using the large space down from the bar and one near the café, as well as upstairs. Applications are considered and exhibitions reach a far wider public than in most galleries. Underground Waterloo.

Royal Watercolour Society, see under Bankside Gallery.

Saatchi Collection, 89A Boundary Road, London NW8. Telephone 0171 (020-7 from 4/2000) 624 8299. Open Thursday-Saturday 12-6.
A large building designed specifically for this important contemporary art collection. Charles Saatchi is one of Britain's most important contemporary art collectors. The collection is rotated and ranges from 1960s Pop Art to Damien Hirst, New Neurotic Realism and recent graduates of art school. Charles Saatchi donated 100 works by 64 artists to the Arts Council collection in 1999. These include many of the RA Sensation show artists. Charles Saatchi is one of the most important figures in the London contemporary art world. When he sells part of his collection the art world awaits with bated breath for the results. If he buys from certain galleries their future is assured for the near future.

Richard Deacon sculpture at the Saatchi gallery.

Sadie Coles HQ, 35 Heddon Street, London W1R 7LL. Telephone 0171 (020-7 from 4/2000) 434 2227. Fax 434 2222. Open Tues-Sat 10-6.

Director: Sadie Coles. Artists shown: Sarah Lucas, Elizabeth Peyton, Angus Fairhurst, Don Brown, Saul Fletcher, Nicola Tyson, Laura Owens. Sadie Coles was previously a director at Anthony d'Offay gallery and also worked in New York. She is backed by Oliver Peyton owner of the Atlantic Bar and Grill and Mash and selects art for the fashionable restaurants' walls, which encourages buyers to visit her central gallery in fashionable Heddon Street. Artists should not apply. Underground Oxford Circus/Piccadilly.

St John's Smith Square, The Footstool Restaurant Gallery, London SW1. Telephone 0171 (020-7 from 4/2000) 222 2168. Open Monday-Friday 11.30-2.45.

Busy restaurant gallery setting near the Tate Gallery and often attended by politicians from the nearby Houses of Parliament and Conservatve Central Office. Underground Westminster.

Sally Hunter, 11 Halkin Arcade, London SW1. Telephone 0171 (020-7 from 4/2000) 235 0934.

Contemporary British paintings. Open to artist applications but artists must ring the gallery first. Underground Knightsbridge.

The Showroom, 44 Bonner Road, London E2.9JS. Telephone 0181 (020-8 from mid 2000) 983 4115. Fax 981 4112. Open Wednesday-Sunday 1-6.

Director: Kirsty Ogg. A showplace for lively contemporary art, often with installations. 6/7 shows a year. Open to artist applications but artists must ring the gallery first to see if their work is appropriate. Underground Bethnal Green.

Serpentine Gallery, Kensington Gardens, London W.2. Telephone 0171 (020-7 from 4/2000) 298 1515. Fax 402 4103. Open daily10-6.

Director: Julia Peyton-Jones. The gallery has been renovated and re-opened with a far higher standing in the art community and national and international sponsorship. Now one of London's leading galleries, showing Modern and contemporary art, often cutting-edge and provocative. Past shows since it re-opened have included Mariko Mori, Cornelia Parker, Chris Ofili ('98 Turner prizewinner), Louise Bourgeois and Andreas Gursky, the '98 Citibank photography prizewinner. **Future shows include Bridget Riley, William Kentridge, the Wilsons and other contemporary leading YBAs (Young British Artists).** Well worth visiting. The bookshop specializes in art theory and philosophy. Underground Lancaster Gate or High Street Kensington and 9,10 buses.

Slaughterhouse Gallery, 63 Charterhouse Street, London EC1. Telephone 0171 (020-7 from 4/2000) 251 5888. Open Monday-Saturday 10-7.
Lively gallery showing work by young contemporary artists. Underground Barbican.

Small Mansion Arts Centre, Gunnersbury Park, Popes Lane, London W.3.
Artists can apply for exhibitions. Ideal for large group shows or local artists. Underground Acton Town.

Sotheby's, 34-35 New Bond Street, London W.1. Telephone 0171 (020-7 from 4/2000) 293 5000. Open Monday-Friday 9-4.30.
Auctions held daily of antiquities, Asian art,books,manuscripts, paintings, drawings, watercolours, prints (including contemporary art), photography, Chinese, Japanese and Islamic works of art, carpets, rugs, clocks, watches, coins, medals, arms and armour, costumes and textiles, silver, furniture and jewellery, stamps, tribal art, wine and vintage cars. Free advice and valuations given on the premises. Underground Bond Street/Green Park.

South Bank Centre, Royal Festival Hall, London SE1 8XX. See under Royal Festival Hall.

South London Art Gallery, Peckham Road, London SE5. Telephone 0171 (020-7 from 4/2000) 703 6120. Open Monday-Saturday 10-6, Sunday 3-6.
Exhibitions of contemporary art, historical and retrospectives. Permanent collection also of British painting. The gallery was shortlisted in '96 for the Prudential Awards, as it is such a well-run and dynamic gallery.

The Southwark College Gallery, Elephant and Castle Shopping Centre, London SE1. Telephone 0171 (020-7 from 4/2000) 928 9561 ext 320 or 703 2936. Open usually Monday-Friday 9.30-4.30.
Applications: The programme of exhibitions is in the process of arrangement. Used for exhibitions by staff and students. Applications from lively professional artists are welcomed. Exhibitions change monthly and the gallery is closed during the summer and Christmas periods. The gallery measures 1500 square feet but there are screens to allow variations. Two exhibitions could also be mounted at the same time. Underground Elephant and Castle.

Special Photographers Company, 21 Kensington Park Road, London W.11 2EU. Telephone 0171 (020-7 from 4/2000) 221

3489. Open Monday-Saturday 10-6.
Directors: Chris Kewbank and Catherine Turner. Stylish photography gallery near Portobello Road market, which sells photographs both to organisations and individuals, acting as agents for the photographers. Some interesting shows of fine art photography as well as commercial photography. Underground Ladbroke Grove or Notting Hill gate and walk down the hill.

The Spitz Gallery (Element 3), 109 Commercial Street, Old Spitalfields Market, London E1 6BG. Telephone 0171 (020-7 from 4/2000) 392 934. Fax 0171 (020-7 from 4/2000) 377 8915.
Director: Jane Glitre. Contemporary Art. Includes hi-tech new information shows.

Stables Gallery, Bladstone Park, Dollis Hill Lane, London NW2.6HT. Telephone 0181 (020-8 from 4/000) 452 8655. Open Thursday-Sunday 11-5. April-September 11-6.
Chairman: Peter Hammond. Gallery Manager: Chris Channing.
Open to artist applications but ring the gallery first as they are heavily-booked. Apply in spring 2000 for 2001-2002. Contemporary artists, especially recent graduates. Underground Dollis Hill.

Standpoint Gallery, 45 Coronet Street, London N.1. 6HD. Telephone 0171 (020-7 from 4/2000) 729 5272. Open Wednesday-Sunday 12-6.
Contemporary art. One of several galleries in this area. Underground Old Street.

Bartley Drey Gallery, 62 Old Church Street, London SW3. Telephone 0171 (020-7 from 4/2000) 352 8686. Open Tuesday-Saturday 11-6.30.
Directors: Stephen Bartley and Gill Drey. Small gallery off the Kings Road. Exhibitions every 2/3 weeks by a variety of artists, some fashionable and socially well-connected. Friendly gallery owners. Near the Chelsea Arts Club. Underground Sloane Square and bus.

Stephen Friedman Gallery, 25-28 Old Burlington Street, London W.1.Telephone 0171 (020-7 from 4/2000) 494 1434. Fax 0171 (020-7 from 4/2000) 494 1431. Open Tuesday-Saturday 10-6.
Director: Stephen Friedman. A cutting-edge gallery near Cork Street, with interesting shows by contemporary artists from the international mainstream of conceptual and Minimal art. Artists can apply and submit ten slides and a c.v., as well as a stamped addressed envelope. The director goes through slides 2 or 3 times a year and he never looks at an artist's work in front of him/her. Gallery artists are: Anya Gallaccio, Kerry Stewart, Peter

Fraser, Yinka Shonibare, Alexis Harding and Vong Phaophanit. Overseas artists include: Stephan Balkenhol, Jessica Stockholder, Betty Goodwin and Tom Friedman. An important contemporary gallery. Underground Bond Street/Green Park.

Stoppenbach and Delestre, 25 Cork Street, London W.1. Telephone 0171 (020-7 from 4/000) 734 3534. Fax 494 3578. Directors: Robert Stoppenbach and Francois Delestre. 19th and 20th-century French art. Corot, Courbet, Daubigny, Pissarro, Derain, Matisse, Vignon and others. No contemporary art or artists. Underground Bond Street/Green Park.

Swiss Cottage Library, 88 Avenue Road, London NW3. Telephone 0171 (020-7 from 4/2000) 278 4444 ext 2457. Open library hours.
Contemporary art by professional local artists. Artists can apply. Underground Swiss Cottage.

Tabernacle, Powis Square, London W.11. Telephone 0171 (020-7 from 4/2000) 565 7890. Open Wednesday-Saturday 12-6.
This local Notting Hill gate arts centre has been transformed with an injection of lottery money into a lively, smart venue for the arts, with café, theatre group and gallery space for local artists. The directors of "Notting Hill", the film in '99 even gave the centre money. Undergound Ladbroke Grove/Notting Hill gate and walk down the hill.

Tadema Gallery, 10 Charlton Place, Camden Passage, London N.1. Telephone 0171 (020-7 from 4/000) 359 1055. Open Tuesday, Wednesday, Friday and Saturday 10-5 or by appointment.
20th-century decorative art including Modern British and continental painting and sculpture.

Tate Gallery of British Art, Millbank, London SW1. Telephone 0171 (020-7 from 4/2000) 887 8008. Open daily 10-5.50.
The new Tate Gallery of British Art will open in summer 2001. Until this opens the current Tate gallery at Millbank will rotate parts of the Collection. There will also be access to the collection via the Internet. In early 2000 all international 20th century art moves to the Tate Gallery of Modern Art at Bankside. The Turner prize will remain at Millbank, with an exhibition annually in October/November as this comes under the British art remit. The Tate has a new Espresso Bar in the basement to cope with the growing numbers of visitors. The bookshop has an excellent selection of art books, catalogues, magazines and postcards with knowledgeable staff. Discounts at the shop for Friends of the Tate. Underground Pimlico or 88 bus from Trafalgar Square or Oxford Circus.

Tate Gallery of Modern Art, Sumner Street, Southwark, London SE1. Telephone 0171 (020-7 from 4/2000) 401 7302 (visitor centre until it opens in 2000), 887 8888 (central Tate number) Open daily 10-6.

Director: Lars Nittve. **See interview with Lars Nittve at the front of the guide.** This old Power station designed by Sir Gilbert Scott, has been transformed into a Modern Art palace, by Swiss architects Herzog and de Meuron. A magnificent new museum, the Tate Bankside becomes one of the three great modern art museums in the world in 2000. It becomes the national gallery of international modern art, continuing where the National Gallery at Trafalgar Square ends in the late19th century. As a

Sculpture by Eiji Ohubo.

landmark on riverside London at the Millennium, it will attract a large group of visitors from overseas as well as within Britain and London in particular. Although fine art is the main focus, architecture, design and film will be on display and the decorative arts. Displayed in chronological order the Tate's international modern art collection starts with artists such as Picasso (The Three Dancers), Matisse (The Snail), Salvador Dali (Metamorphosis of Narcissus), and continues through American artists such as Andy Warhol (Marilyn Diptych), Rothko and Lichtenstein to late 20th century artists such as Baselitz, Kiefer, Mimmo Paladino, Jeff Koons, Cindy Sherman and others. Some British 20th century art will move between the museums according to exhibitions and displays. The Janet Wolfson de Botton gift collection will be based here. Other facilities include an information centre, auditorium, education centre, gift shops, a café with outdoor terrace and a restaurant with views across London. A new millennium bridge is being built with sculptures by Anthony

Caro, designed by Norman Foster, to facilitate access to the Tate Bankside. A new Bankside Browser open-exhibition is open to Southwark artists, starting '99. The Tate Bankside has a strong programme involving local events at Southwark and with the Southwark community. Underground London Bridge/Blackfriars.

Thackeray Gallery, 18 Thackeray Street, London W.8.5ET. Telephone 0171 (020-7 from 4/2000) 937 5883. Fax 937 6965. Open Tuesday-Friday 10-6, Saturday 10-4. Closed Sunday and Monday.
Director: Anne Thomson. Open to applications with slides/photos and covering letter. Gallery closed January and August. Mainly British and contemporary art. Kyffin Williams, Alberto Morocco, Gordon Bryce, Emily Young, Mark Ianson, Victoria Crowe, James Morrisson, Joanna Carrington and others. Ground floor and basement. Underground High Street Kensington.

Todd Gallery, 1-5 Needham Road, London W.11. Telephone 0171 (020-7 from 4/2000) 792 1404. Open Tuesday-Friday 11-6, Saturday 11-5.
Director: Jenny Todd. Consistently good cutting-edge exhibitions by lesser known contemporary artists, as well as established names. Exhibits at international art fairs. Underground Notting Hill Gate/Queensway.

Tom Allen Arts Centre, Grove Crescent Road, Stratford, London E15. Telephone 0181 (020-8 from 4/2000) 519 6818. Open Monday-Friday 12-7, Saturday 12-5.
Contemporary, young and often struggling artists.

Tom Blau Gallery, 21 Queen Elizabeth Street, London SE1 2PD. Telephone 0171 (020-7 from 4/2000) 378 1300.
Photography exhibitions mainly from Camera Press photographers and Focal Point.

The Taylor Gallery, 1 Bolney Gate, London SW7. Telephone 0171 (020-7 from 4/2000) 581 0253. Open Monday-Friday 10-5. Annual exhibition of Irish art, which is usually worth visiting. Also deals in contemporary paintings. Underground South Kensington.

The Gallery, 28 Cork Street, London W1X 1HB.
This gallery can be hired for exhibitions. Underground Green Park.

The Old School, 17 Hoxton Square, London N.1. Telephone 0171 (020-7 from 4/2000) 483 4461. Open Wednesday-Sunday 12-6. Has shown work by photographers and filmmakers in this

Hoxton venue. Hoxton has become a very lively area with bars, restaurants and gallery spaces. Underground Old Street.

Timothy Taylor Gallery, Bruton Place, London W.1. Telephone 0171 (020-7 from 4/2000) 409 3344. Open Monday-Friday 10-6, Saturday 11-2.
Directors: Timothy Taylor and Helen Windsor. Contemporary painting with established artists such as Sean Scully and lesser known British artists. Underground Bond Street.

Tricycle Theatre Gallery, Tricycle Theatre, 269 Kilburn High Road, London NW6.7JR. Telephone 0171 (020-7 from 4/2000) 372 6611. Fax 328 0795. Open theatre hours,11-11.
Exhibitions by young, unknown local contemporary artists. Good selling outlet. Artists must be studying at or recently graduated from a recognised art school and that this will be their first exhibition, or, that the artist is resident in the London Borough of Brent. Also shows disabled artists, artists from ethnic minorities within the local community (Asian/Irish/Afro-Caribbean), work from local schools and occasional exhibitions by artists of national or international stature.

Tryon and Swann, 23 Cork Street, London W.1. Telephone 0171 (020-7 from 4/2000) 734 6961. Open Monday-Friday 9.30-6.
Contact: A.D.Tryon. Applications considered at any time. Exhibitions: All artists paint sporting and natural history subjects and include David Shepherd, Susan Crawford, Roger McPhail. Space: One floor. Underground Green Park/Bond Street.

Unicorn at Space 8, 8 Hollywood Rd, London SW10 9HY. Telephone 0171 (020-7 from 4/2000) 376 3195. Open Tuesday-Saturday 11-8, Sundays 12-5.
Consultants to Corporate and Parliamentary contemporary art collections. The gallery shows work by award-winning artists in the contemporary art field. Underground Fulham Broadway/Earls Court and bus.

30 Underwood Street, 30-34 Underwood Street, London N1 7JX. Telephone 0171 (020-7 from mid 2000) 336 0884. email: sidust@aol.com
An avant-garde cutting-edge gallery showing contemporary art including audio, video and film. The live launch of "cd one" was held here in '99.

Victoria Miro Gallery, 21 Cork Street, London W.1. Telephone 0171 (020-7 from 4/2000) 734 5082. Fax 494 1787. Open

Monday-Saturday 9.30-6, Sunday 1-6.
Director: Victoria Miro. Painting, sculpture and conceptual art by top British and European artists. Artists include: Marina Abramovic, Peter Doig, Ian Hamilton Finlay, Andreas Gursky, Abigail Lane, Chris Ofili and Stephen Willats among others. Well worth a visit as the shows are more dynamic than many other Cork Street exhibitions. Underground Bond Street/Green Park.

Waddington Galleries Ltd., 11 Cork Street, London W1X1PD. Telephone 0171 439 6262/437 8611. Fax 734 4146. Open Monday-Friday 10-5.30, Saturday 10-1. Thursday open until 7. Directors: Leslie Waddington, A.Bernstein, Sir Thomas Lighton, Lord McAlpine, Hester van Royen, S.Saunders. The galleries have consolidated to concentrate on contemporary artists and dealing in 20th-century Masters such as Picasso and Matisse. This is one of London's most important galleries, run by Leslie Waddington and associates. Many of the owners of smaller contemporary art galleries centrally, have spent some time working at Waddington's in the past, so he deserves some credit for the expansion of contemporary art in London. Regular shows introduce less well-established and recently established names such as Zebedee Jones, Ian Davenport, Fiona Rae (wonderful, colourful abstract paintings). Other artists include: Josef Albers, Peter Blake, Michael Craig-Martin, Patrick Caulfield, Ivon Hitchens, Mimmo Paladino, Lisa Milroy and William Turnbull. It is essential to visit these galleries and Anthony d'Offay galleries on Dering Street (off Oxford Street), to gain some perspective on important contemporary and late 20th-century artists. Underground Bond Street/Green Park.

Watermans Arts Centre, 40 High Street, Brentford, Middlesex, TW8 ODS. Telephone 0181 (020-8 from 4/2000) 847 5651. Open Monday-Friday 12.30-8.30, Saturday and Sunday 11-9.
Contact: Visual arts officer. Applications in the form of slides and c.v. are considered quarterly from artists and photographers working in any medium. The gallery space is 250 linear feet/1000 square feet. The centre also has a theatre, cinema, foyer areas, restaurant and bar. Underground Gunnersbury Park/South Ealing.

White Cube Gallery, 44 Duke Street, St James's London SW1Y 6DD. Telephone 0171 (020-7 from 4/2000) 930 5373. Fax (7) 930 9973. Open gallery hours11-6.
Directors: Jay Jopling and Julia Royse. A phenomenally successful gallery dealing in cutting-edge art. The White Cube is one of the smallest exhibition spaces in Europe, on the first floor of London's very traditional Old Masters art dealing street. The

White Cube was designed by minimalist architect Claudio Silvestrin. The space provides an intimate setting for the gallery artists to show their ideas. Jay Jopling introduced the legendary Damien Hirst, once "enfant terrible" in the contemporary art world, to a wider international public. He deals in other cutting-edge artists, although Damien is his star artist. Many of the artists shown in the RA "Sensation" show can be seen here. Artists include: Darren Almond, Ashley Bickerton, Sophie Calle, Tracey Emin, Brian Eno, Antony Gormley, Marcus Harvey, Mona Hatoum, Gary Hill, Damien Hirst, Gary Hume, Sarah Lucas, Sarah Morris, Richard Prince, Marc Quinn, Jessica Stockholder, Hiroshi Sugimoto, Marcus Taylor, Sam Taylor-Wood, Cerith Wyn Evans, Gavin Turk, Jeff Wall and others. Underground Green Park.

Whitechapel Art Gallery, 80-82 Whitechapel High Street, London E.1. Telephone 0171 (020-7 from 4/2000) 522 7888. Fax 377 1685. Open Tuesday-Sunday 11-5 Wednesday 11-8. Closed Monday.
Director: Catherine Lampert. Application forms are available from the gallery. The Whitechapel Open happens every 2 years (last one '98) and is a major event all over the East end of London. The gallery shows major exhibitions of 20th-century and contemporary art. Two floors of gallery space with educational facilities. Artists should not apply except for the Whitechapel Open. Underground Aldgate East.

Wigmore Fine Art, 104 Wigmore Street, London W.1. Telephone 0171 (020-7 from 4/2000) 224 1962. Open Tuesday-Friday 10-6, Saturday 11-5.
Director: Mary Los. This magnificent two floor space is near Selfridges, tucked away behind Oxford Street. Shows predominantly contemporary Greek-related artists such as Nayia Frangouli and John Stathatos, but recently other British and European artists. Underground Bond Street.

Wilson Stephens Fine Art, 11 Cavendish Road, London NW6 7XT. Telephone 0181 (020-8 from mid 2000) 459 0760.
Modern British and contemporary art; Richard Winkworth, Ben McLaughlin, Deborah Tarr, Emma McClure, Andrew Johnstone, Sabrina Skinner.

Wiseman Originals, 34 West Square, Lambeth, London SE11.4SP. Telephone 0171 (020-7 from 4/2000) 587 0747. Open by appointment.
Directors: Caroline and Garth Wiseman. The directors open their Georgian house as a gallery. The Modern Art Collectors Club enables visitors to browse through original prints and works on

ákea: atonements,1995, John Stathatos (Wigmore Fine Art).

paper by international Masters such as Miró, Picasso, Matisse. They also sell British Master prints and works by younger artists such as Eileen Cooper and Peter Howson. Underground Lambeth North.

Wolseley Fine Arts, 12 Needham Rd, London W.11 2RP. Telephone 0171 (020-7 from 4/2000) 792 2788. Fax 792 2988. Drawings and prints specialist in 20th century art. Exhibits at the Art on Paper Fair in February. Underground Notting Hill Gate and walk/bus.

Zelda Cheatle Gallery, 99 Mount Street, London W1. Telephone 0171 (020-7 from 4/2000) 408 4448. Open daily except Sunday 11-6.
Zelda Cheatle runs this friendly photography gallery in a larger

space in Mount Street, after moving from Cecil Court. Zelda has a wealth of experience behind her and holds regular exhibitions of work by top names and recent contemporary photographers. Prints are reasonably priced and her knowledge and expertise are invaluable. Also sells photography catalogues and books. Underground Bond Street.

Zella 9, 2 Park Walk, London SW10. Telephone 0171 (020-7 from 4/2000) 351 0588. Open Monday-Saturday 9.30-6, Sunday 11.30-5.30.
Director: Mozzella Gore. Prints of all kinds and sizes by British and European printmakers. Excellent place to sell prints and to buy them at reasonable prices. Professional printmakers can submit work for sale. Contact gallery for details. Underground South Kensington/Fulham Broadway.

National
Centres&Institutes

This section has been included so that overseas visitors can see that there are various centres throughout London that specialise in art from one particular country. Many are still affiliated to Embassies, with government support, but others are quite separate.

In many cases artists from the appropriate country or with work associated with that country, may be considered for exhibitions. Contact the gallery director first to find out.

Africa Centre, 38 King Street, London WC2. Telephone 0171 (0207 from 4/2000) 836 1973. Open Monday-Friday and weekends, ring gallery for times.
An educational charity that runs a very lively arts centre in Covent Garden. Classes in dance, literature, movement and evening meetings. The gallery upstairs shows a variety of shows covering painting, sculpture, weaving, masks and craft. Africa Centrepoint, a monthly newsletter gives updated information about the centre. Variety of prices for membership. The Calabash restaurant is well-worth a visit. Underground Covent Garden.

Canada House, Trafalgar Square, London SW1. Telephone 0171 (0207 from 4/2000) 629 9492. Contact Michael Reagan 258 6537 about visual arts information and exhibitions. Telephone 0171 (0207 from 4/2000) 258 6366. Artsnews magazine edited by Gillian Licari. Cultural Attaché Diana Jervis-Read. Canada House Cultural Centre re-opened in 1998 with magnificent restoration work on the building designed by Sir Robert Smirke in 1824. The visual arts programme will mean about 4 major exhibitions a year and links to Canadian music and film events in London. Artnews magazine covers all details of Canadian events in London. Underground Bond Street.

Canning House Centre, 2 Belgrave Square, London SW1X 8PJ. Telephone 0171 (0207 from 4/2000) 235 2303. Closed at weekends.
The centre holds a number of exhibitions throughout the year to promote the arts and culture of Latin America, Spain and Portugal. Artists and organisations can apply to the Culture and Education Department. £150 booking fee payable. Ideal for painting, photography, textiles and craft.

Monsieur de Norvins, Ingres (National Gallery).

The Czech Centre, 95 Great Portland Street, London W.1. Telephone 0171 (020-7 from 4/2000) 291 9920. Open Monday-Friday 10-6.
A variety of events and exhibitions with a Czech connection. Underground Great Portland Street.

Commonwealth Institute, High Street Kensington, London W.8. Telephone 0171 (0207 from 4/2000) 603 4535. Recorded information 602 3257. Open Monday-Saturday 10-4.30, Sundays 2-5.
The Commonwealth Institute galleries are closed until 2002 but temporary exhibitions are still being held. Contact Nicola Harold for details. The institute was set up to record the development and history of the British Commonwealth and also has a shop, restaurant (both closed until 2002) and gallery space for exhibitions by Commonwealth artists (Canadian, Australian, New

Zealand, African and Indian mainly). Underground High Street Kensington.

Daiwa Anglo-Japanese Foundation, 13-14 Cornwall Terrace, London NW1 4QP. Telephone 0171 (020-7from 4/2000) 486 4348. Open Monday-Friday 9-5.
A variety of exhibitions have been held here recently including work by British artists connected with Japan and Japanese artists visiting Britain. Underground Baker Street.

French Institute, Cultural Centre, 17 Queensberry Place, London SW7. Telephone 0171 (0207 from 4/2000) 838 2144. Open10-9.30, Saturday 12-9.30 (hours vary for the cinema, library and other facilities). Closed Sunday and Monday. Language Centre for French classes 0171 (0207 from 4/2000) 581 2701.
A cinema, library, theatre, concerts, lectures, and now a café with newspapers to read while you wait for friends. Ciné Lumière has a regular programme of French films and also talks by authors and film-makers. Underground South Kensington.

Goethe Institut, 50 Princes Gate, Exhibition Road, London SW7. Telephone 0171 (0207 from4/2000) 581 3344/7. Open Monday-Friday12-8, Saturday 10-1.
The gallery has exhibitions by top German artists such as Kiefer, Baselitz and artists known to the art world. The newsletter gives details of other German films, books and events. Underground South Kensington.

Foundation for Hellenic Culture, 60 Brook Street, London W.1. Telephone 0171 (0207 from 4/2000) 499 9826.
This centre has some excellent exhibitions of Greek art, both historical and contemporary. Also a centre for Greek contacts and language classes. Underground Bond Street.

New Zealand House, Haymarket, London SW1. Telephone 0171 (0207 from 4/2000) 930 8422. Open Monday-Friday 9-5.
New Zealand High Commission has a large area for concerts, theatre productions, recitals and a gallery on the mezzanine floor. New Zealand professional artists can apply to the Cultural Affairs Department all year round. Underground Charing Cross/Piccadilly.

Polish Institute, 34 Portland Place, London W.1. Telephone 0171 (0207 from 4/2000) 636 6033/4. Open Monday-Friday 10-6.
The gallery shows work by Polish artists ranging from painting to posters. Underground Oxford Circus.

Photography Galleries

Henri Cartier-Bresson; photographs from the Americas and Asia, Canon Photography Gallery, V&A Museum.

Photography has mushroomed in London in recent years and the V&A's photography collection, The **Canon Photography Gallery**, gives the public a chance to see many of the photographs from the Henry Cole Wing, that had never been on display, through lack of space. Commercial photography galleries show a complete range of photographs now from reportage, social documentation to fine art, advertising and even collage. **See Collecting Photographs**, at the front of the guide, as well as the **interview with Focus Gallery** (Helena Kovac), to see the range of photographs for sale. **The Special Photographers Company**, off Portobello Road is well-worth a visit, **Zelda Cheatle Gallery** and of course the **Photographers Gallery**, is a must with its excellent bookshop, galleries and print advice and viewing room.

Association Gallery, 9-10 Domingo Street, London EC1. Telephone 0171 (0207 from 4/2000) 608 1441.
Variety of shows, mainly by members. Underground Old Street.

Barbican Centre Art Gallery, Silk Street, London EC2. Telephone 0171 (0207 from 4/2000) 638 4141 ext 306. Open Tuesday-Saturday 11-7, Sunday 12-6.
Curator: John Hoole. Major gallery on two floors. Ansel Adams, French photography ,Eve Arnold, Blumenfeld, Picasso's

Photography, and other photography shows have been seen here. See Galleries section for full details about the centre. Underground Barbican/Moorgate/Bank.

Wall Street, New York 1915, Paul Strand (Photographers Gallery).

Camden Arts Centre, Arkwright Road, London NW3. Telephone 0171 (0207 from 4/2000) 435 2643/5224. Open Monday-Saturday 11-6, Friday 11-8, Sunday 2-6.
Director: Jenni Lomax. Arts centre with occasional photo shows. Underground Finchley Road.

The Camera Club, 16 Bourden Street, London SE11. Telephone 0171 (0207 from 4/2000) 587 1809. Open Monday-Saturday 11-11.
Facilities for photographers to take classes and access to other useful information.

Camerawork Gallery, 121 Roman Road, Bethnal Green, London E.2. Telephone 0181 (0208 from 4/2000) 980 6256. Open Tuesday 1-6, Wednesday-Saturday 11-6.
Workshop facilities and classes. Keen to encourage young photographers concerned with social documentation. Also run Camerawork magazine. New work considered on the first Wednesday of each month. Phone for an appointment first. Four major and eight minor shows each year and 48 touring shows for hire. Write for details. Underground Bethnal Green.

Focus Gallery, 43 Museum Street, London WC1. Telephone 0171

(0207 from 4/2000) 242 7191. Open 11-6 Tuesday-Saturday.
Directors: Helena Kovac and Dorothy Bohm. A welcome addition to the photography scene, established photography dealer Helena Kovac shows contemporary and 20th century photography with regular shows. **See interview at front of guide.** Underground Tottenham Court Road.

Hackelbury Fine Art, 4 Launceston Place, London W.8. Telephone 0171 (0207 from 4/2000) 937 8686. Open Wednesday-Friday 10-5.
Another new gallery that has shown Roman Vishniac photographs in 1998, as well as more contemporary work. Underground Gloucester Road.

Hamiltons Gallery, 13 Carlos Place, Grosvenor Square, London W.1. Telephone 0171 (0207 from 4/2000) 499 9493. Run by Tim Jefferies. Represents top commercial photographers and the gallery is often attended by celebrities. Underground Bond Street.

Hulton Getty, 3 Jubilee Place, London SW3. Telephone 0171 (020-7 from 4/2000) 376 4525.
A chance to see photographs from this famous collection. Underground Sloane Square.

Imperial War Museum, Lambeth Road, London SE1. Telephone 0181 (0208 from 4/2000) 735 8922.
Photography exhibitions in relation to war. Underground Lambeth North.

Institute of Contemporary Arts, The Mall, London SW1. Telephone 0171 (0207 from 4/2000) 930 0493. Open 12-late. Closed Mondays. The ICA is supposed to be moving to Bankside in the early 21st century.
Interested to see work in the form of slides/photos/documentation by professional artists and photographers. Photography exhibitions regularly in the corridor near the restaurant and upstairs. Very good central venue visited by international and national public. Video library, cinema, theatre as well as a restaurant and bar. Good bookshop. Underground Charing Cross.

Marlborough Fine Art, 6 Albemarle Street, London W.1. Telephone 0171 (0207 from 4/2000) 629 5161.
Primarily a top fine art dealer, but has shown photographs, sometimes connected with book launches. Underground Green Park.

Michael Hoppen Photography, 3 Jubilee Place, London SW3. Telephone 0171 (020-7 from mid 2000) 352 3649. Open 11-6.

157

Director: Michael Hoppen. The gallery opened in 1994 and shows 19th and 20th century photography. Excellent shows, such as the Lartigue one in '99. Underground Sloane Square and walk.

National Portrait Gallery, Trafalgar Square, London WC2. Telephone 0171 (0207 from 4/2000) 930 1522. Open Monday-Friday 10-5, Saturday 10-6 and Sunday 2-6.
Quite a number of photography exhibitions recently and holds the exhibitions for the Kobal and ICI photography awards. Underground Charing Cross.

National Theatre, South Bank, London SE1.
Photography shows in a busy theatre complex, reaching a wide public. Underground Waterloo.

The Photographers Gallery, 5 & 8 Great Newport Street, London WC2. Telephone 0171 (0207 from 4/2000) 831 1772. Open Tuesday-Saturday 11-7. Closed Mondays.
Director: Paul Wombell. Photographers can apply at any time, but decisions are made twice a year in March and October. Exhibitions cover the complete spectrum of photography from commercial to social documentation, fine art, reportage. At No. 8 there is an excellent bookshop and gallery space and at No. 5 there is a gallery downstairs with a café and upstairs a slide library with 5000+ slides, a reference library with 3000+ books and a viewing room for buyers, where advice can be given about particular photographs. The staff are well-informed and helpful. Membership scheme. Underground Covent Garden/Leicester Square.

Photology, 24 Litchfield Street, London WC2. Telephone 0171 (020-7 from 4/2000) 836 8600. Open Tuesday-Saturday 11-6.
Variety of photography shows here. Underground Covent Garden.

Serpentine Gallery, Kensington Gardens, London W.2.3XA. Telephone 0171 (0207 from 4/2000) 402 6075 / 298 1515 (recorded information). Open daily 10-6.
After a massive £4million renovation programme the gallery is now very much ready for the millennium. Julia Peyton-Jones, the dynamic director has worked hard to make this a key London contemporary art venue. The lawn holds site-specific works. Photography and video shown in a contemporary art situation. The bookshop now specialises in art criticism and theory and holds evening lectures and events. Underground Lancaster Gate or South Kensington.

Special Photographers Company, 21 Kensington Park Road, London W.11. Telephone 0171 (0207 from 4/2000) 221 3489.
Run by Catherine Turner and Chris Kewbank. The gallery acts as

Bibi, Hendaye, Jacques-Henri Lartigue (Michael Hoppen Photography).

an agency for photographers and as a gallery. Commercial and fine-art photography. Underground Notting Hill Gate or Ladbroke Grove. See Portobello Arts Map.

Stock Exchange Visitors' Gallery, Threadneedle Street, London EC2.
Occasional photography shows here, mostly of a financial nature and by financial photojournalists. Underground Bank.

Victoria and Albert Museum (Canon Photography Gallery), South Kensington, London SW7. Telephone 0171 589 6371. Open Monday-Saturday 10-5.50, Sunday 2.30-5.50.
The Canon Photography Gallery opened with a historical show and contemporary photography. Gradually we have been shown parts of the collection in small interesting exhibitions. Visual display units allow visitors to look at works not on display to see the extent of the V&A's collection. Underground South Kensington.

Untitled, 1990, Melanie Manchot (Zelda Cheatle Gallery).

Zelda Cheatle Gallery, 99 Mount Street, London W1. Telephone 0171 (0207 from 4/2000) 408 4448. Open 11-6. Director: Zelda Cheatle. Friendly photography gallery, now in a new setting in the heart of Mayfair. Zelda shows contemporary unknowns and top world names. Exhibitions by invitation only. Underground Leicester Square.

Organisations such as Art for Offices (See Galleries section), will look at photographers work for selling to business clients. Contact them first to make an appointment.

160

Alternative Art Spaces

In the last three years there has been a rapid growth in alternative art spaces all over London as conceptual and Minimal work, installations and site-specific work became fashionable and popular. Many are possibly temporary so check before visiting, as by the very nature of being alternative they are not run along conventional lines and are often in spaces that are temporarily vacant. **Artangel** is a well-known organisation that arranges unusual events and exhibitions in public spaces all over London, often by well-known British or international artists.

Annexed, 1 Hoxton Street, London N.1. Telephone 0171 (0207 from 4/2000) 256 1566. Mainly installations.

Artangel, 36 St John's Lane, London EC1M 4BJ. Telephone 0171 (0207 from 4/2000) 336 6801. Run by James Lingwood. A high profile organisation that arranges innovatiove events and exhibitions in public spaces. Well-funded.

Bishop's Wharf, 49 Parkgate Road, London SW11. Telephone 0171 (0207 from 4/2000) 978 7878. Open Monday-Friday 10-5. British Rail Battersea Park.

Bow Arts, 181-183 Bow Road, London E.3. Telephone 0181 (0208 from 4/2000) 981 0744. Open Thursday-Sunday 1-6. Gallery known as The Nunnery.

The Conductors Hallway, 301 Camberwell New Road, London SE5. Telephone 0171 (0207 from 4/2000) 703 8385. Open Thursday-Sunday 11-5.
Installations, video and sound shows.

Curtain Road Arts, 96A Curtain Road, London EC2. Telephone 0171 (0207 from 4/2000) 613 5303. Open Thursday-Sunday 12-6. Installations and other exhibitions. Underground Old Street.

Gasworks, 155 Vauxhall Street, London SE11. Telephone 0171 (0207 from 4/2000) 735 3445. Open Friday-Sunday 12-6. Exhibitions of paintings in a studio context.

Many of the above also operate as venues for Performance/Live Art. Instead of listing a separate section for Live Art the following may be useful:

BAC
Camden Arts Centre
Chisenhale
ICA
London Musicians Collective
Oval House
Riverside Studios
Serpentine Gallery
Tate Gallery (Millbank and Bankside)
Whitechapel Gallery

Addresses of the above are in the "Galleries" section.

The Arts Council of England, considers applications from artists for Live Art or shows in alternative spaces. ACE,14 Gt Peter Street, London SW1. Telephone 0171 (0207 from 4/2000) 333 0100.

Studios

SPACE Studios, (Head Office), 8 Hoxton Street, London N.1. Telephone 0171 (0207 from 4/2000) 613 1925. Fax 613 1996. See useful addresses (artist' organisations) for details. Studio space for artists, but not living accommodation.

SPACE Studio sites:
16 Belsham Street, London E.9.
Britannia Works, 80 Dace Road, Old Ford London E.3.
15 Milborne Street, London E.8.
199 Richmond Road, London E.8.
49 Columbia Road, London E.2.
282A Richmond Rd, London E.8.
10 Martello Street, London E.8.
7 Winkley Street, London E.2.
142 Vauxhall Street, London SE11.
142D Leabridge Road, London E.5.
Eastway Studios, 80 Eastway, London E.9.
Deborah House, Retreat Place, London EC1.
Sara Lane Studios, 60 Starway Street London N.1.

All phone numbers of the above studios are in the phone book under SPACE Studios.

ACME Housing Association, (main office), 44 Copperfield Road, London E.3. Telephone 0181 (0208 from 4/2000) 981 6811. Fax 0181 (0208 from 4/2000) 983 0567.
Some 250 houses for artists, five studio blocks.

ACME Studios, also at Brixton, Camden, North Shoreditch and Stratford East. Childers Road.
Old Church Hall Studios, Redhill Street, London NW1.
105 Carpenters Rd, London E.15. Telephone 0181 (0208 from 4/2000) 519 5240/5808.
2 & 3 Jubilee Terrace, London E.1.
Bonner Rd Studios, 44 Bonner Road London E.2. Telephone 0181 (0208 from 4/2000) 980 0189.
Larnaca Works, Grange Walk, London SE1. Telephone 0171 (0207 from 4/2000) 252 2027.
11-31 Orsman Road, London N1 5RA. Telephone 0171 (0207 from 4/2000) 739 5976.
Ring the main office for details of the latest studio space and to be put on the waiting list after an interview.

Independent Studio Blocks

Barbican Arts Group, 12/14 Hertford Road, London N.1. Telephone 0171 (0207 from 4/2000) 241 0651. 25 studio spaces.

Kingsgate Workshops, 110-116 Kingsgate Road, London NW6. See Artists Register Galleries section for details. 35 studios and a waiting list.

Pixley Street Studios, 14 Pixley Street, London E.14.

Park Studios, 34 Scarborough Road, Finsbury Park, London N.4. 4LT.

A2 Arts, 143A Greenwich South Street, London SE10. Also 101 Blackheath Road, SE10.

Arbutus Studios, 1A Arbutus Street, London E.8.4DT.

Arch 339 Studio, 337 Medlar Street, London SE5.

ASC Studios, 6-8 Rosebery Avenue, London EC1R 4TD.

Baches Street Studios, 10 12 Baches Street, London N.1. 6D.

Bow Arts Trust, 181-183 Bow Road, London E.3 2SJ.

Cable Street Studios, Thames House, 566 Cable Street, London E1 9HB.

Lance Smith, artist.

Chisenhale Studios, 64-84 Chisenhale Rd, London E.3. 5QZ.

City Studios, 40 Underwood Street, London N1 7QJ.

Colosseum, 1A Beechwood Road, London E.8.

Cubitt Studios, 2-4 Caledonia Street, London N1 9DZ.

Fashion Street Studios, 11 Fashion Street, London E.1.

Hanbury Street Studios, Top Floor, 49 Hanbury Street, London E.1 5JP.

Hartley House Studios, Hartley House, Green Walk, London SE1.

Hertford Road Studios, 12-14 Hertford Rd, London N1 5SH.

Left Bank, 84-86 Great Eastern Street, London EC2.

Lewisham Art House,140 Lewisham Way, London SE14 6PD.

Limehouse Arts Foundation, Towcester Rd, London E3 3ND.

Maryland Studios, 22 Grove Crescent Road, London E15.

Not Cut, Not Cut House, 36 Southwark Bridge Rd, London SE1.

Southgate Studios, 2-4 Southgate Road, London N1 3JJ.

Tram Depot Studios, 38/40 Upper Clapton Rd, London E.5.

Globe Studios, 62A Southwark Bridge Road, London SE1. Telephone 0171 (0207 from 4/2000) 261 9066.

Delfina Studios, Maryland Works, 22 Grove Crescent Road, London E.15. Telephone 0181 (0208 from 4/2000) 519 8814. Run by the same organisation that owns the Delfina Gallery in Bermondsey.

Artsplace Trust, Chisenhale Works, Chisenhale Road, Bow, London E.3. Telephone 0181 (0208 from 4/2000) 981 4518. 38 studios.

Greenwich Murals Workshop, MacBean Centre, MacBean Street, London SE18. Telephone 0181 (0208 from 4/2000) 854 9266. Contact: Steve Lobb. Publish a useful murals handbook.

Hetley Road, London W.12. Telephone 0181 (0208 from 4/2000) 743 1843. Studios and a gallery.

Fremantle, Kenneth Lauder (studio 01568 615818).

Faroe Road, London W.12. Waiting list.

Clapham Studios, 590 Wandsworth Road, London SW8. Telephone 0181 (0208 from 4/2000) 720 7817.

Fulham Studios, 101 Farm Lane, London SW6. Telephone 0171 (0207 from 4/2000) 381 4000.
For hire commercially for photography or exhibitions.

Print Publishers

The list following covers print publishers that publish limited editions of etchings, silkscreens, lithographs, photo-silkscreens and occasionally woodcuts. Many of them are also listed under the contemporary galleries section. Flowers gallery runs a print-of-the-month club to encourage print buyers. Some also publish artist' books.

Advanced Graphics, Faircharm C103 8-12 Creekside, London SE8 3DX. Telephone 0181 (0208 from 4/2000) 691 1330. Print artists' books as well as prints.

Alan Cristea, 31 Cork Street, London W.1. Telephone 0171 (0207 from 4/2000) 439 1866. Fax 0171 (0207 from 4/2000) 734 1549. Open Monday-Friday 10-5.30, Saturday 10-1 (except August). Alan Cristea took over Waddington Graphics and publishes European and American prints by most of the top names: Hockney, Lichtenstein, Jasper Johns, Mimmo Paladino, Stella, Warhol, Tapies, Dine, Picasso, Matisse, Leger, Braque, Nicholson. The gallery holds some excellent shows.

Anderson O'Day Graphics, 5 St Quintin Avenue, London W.10. Telephone 0171 (0207 from 4/2000) 969 8085. Open by appointment. Norman Ackroyd, Mandy Bonnell, Michael Carlo, Yvonne Cole, JD Winter, Delia Delderfield, Brendan Neiland, Alison Neville, Carl Rowe, Donald Wilkinson.

Bernard Jacobson, 14A Clifford Street, London W.1. Telephone 0171 (0207 from 4/2000) 495 8575. Two branches in New York and Los Angeles. Ivor Abrahams, Maggi Hambling, Denny, Auerbach, Heindorff, Smith, Tucker and others.

Christies Contemporary Art, 8 Dover Street, London W.1. Telephone 0171 (0207 from 4/2000) 499 6701. Open Monday-Friday 9.30-5.30, Saturday 10-1. Probably one of the largest European print publishers of contemporary lithographs, etchings and screenprints and certainly one of the most promotion-conscious publishers. Also in New York. Colour catalogue sent with details of the artists, on request. Branches in Farnham and Oxford.

Marlborough Graphics, 6 Albemarle Street, London W.1. Telephone 0171 (0207 from 4/2000) 629 5161. See Marlborough Fine Art (Galleries section) for details. A top, major international art gallery with overseas branches.

New Academy Gallery, 34 Windmill Street, London W.1. Telephone 0171 (0207 from 4/2000) 323 4700. Prints by a variety of established contemporary artists.

Studio Prints, 159 Queens Crescent, London NW5. Telephone 0171 (0207 from 4/2000) 485 4527. Ayrton, Trevelyan, Wilkinson, Wight, Greaves and Chris Penny among others.

Print Studios

Some of these studios have either a membership scheme or access for professional printmakers.

London Contemporary Art, 132 Lots Road, London SW10ORJ. Telephone 0171 (0207 from 4/2000) 351 7696.
300 new editions a year.

Half Moon Printmakers, 10 Beckwith Road, London SE24. Telephone 0171 (0207 from 4/2000) 733 9166.

South Hill Park Arts Centre, Bracknell, Berkshire. Telephone 01344 27272.

Prue O'Day with sculpture by Mario Rossi.

Printers Ink and Associates, 27 Clerkenwell Close, Unit 355, London EC1. 0171 (0207 from 4/2000) 251 1923.
Etching workshops and Printmakers Association.

Studio Prints, 159 Queens Crescent, London NW5. Telephone 0171 (0207 from 4/2000) 485 4527.
Studio facilities for etching editions.

Workshops/
Film Workshops

London Filmakers' Co-op, 42 Gloucester Avenue, London NW1. Telephone 0171 (0207 from 4/2000) 586 8516.
Film and video production, distribution and exhibition. Offers all these facilities to others. Accent on experimental and art-based films.

Useful Addresses

Artisits' Organisations

Alternative Arts, 202 B Brushfield Road, Spitalfields, London E.1. Telephone 0171 (0207 from 4/2000) 375 0441. This organisation is truly amazing, having started in West Soho, where it set up exhibitions in shops and alternative West end outlets. Now it operates from Spitalfields and continues to set up alternative temporary venues all over London.

SHAPE, 356 Hollywood Road, London N.7. Telephone 0181
Shape introduces professional visual artists, musicians, actors and dancers, also puppeteers to hospitals, prisons, youth centres, day centres and to elderly, mentally and physically-handicapped people and to homeless, disturbed adolescents and offenders.

ACME Housing Association, 44 Copperfield Road, Bow, London E.3. Telephone 0181 (0208 from 4/2000) 981 6811. Fax 0181 (0208 from 4/2000) 983 0567.

Lovers in a little café, Brassai (Photographers Gallery).

Directors: Jonathan Harvey and David Panton. A non-profitmaking charity that houses artists, mainly in the East end of London. Currently has some 250 houses and two studio blocks. Waiting list after the artist has been interviewed and if accepted. See Studios section for details.

AN Information, PO Box 23, Sunderland SR4 6DG. Telephone 0191 567 3589.
Caroline Lambert is in charge of Artists' Newsletter visual arts information service. They sell lists of contact addresses, recommend publications and offer resource packs — not free of course. Phone 10-12 or 2-4 Tuesday-Friday. Send an sae if writing.

SPACE Studios, 8 Hoxton Street, London N.1. Telephone 0171 (0207 from 4/2000) 613 1925.
Space Studios was set up in 1968 to help artists find cheap studio space. See studios section for details. Waiting list and interview for studios first.

National Artists Association, 21 Steward Street, Spitalfields, London E1 6AJ. Telephone 0171 (0207 from 4/2000) 426 0911. Membership organisation with an access point for practising artists. Handbook and Code of Practice for Artists available.

Artists' Agency, 18 Norfolk Street, Sunderland, SR1 1EA. Telephone 0191 510 9318.
Offers advice to artists about setting up residencies and placements.

Axis, Leeds University, Calverley Street, Leeds LS1 3HE. Telephone 01132 833125. Also based in London at The Building Centre, 26 Store Street London WC1. Telephone 0171 (0207 from 4/2000) 637 1022.
Multimedia text and image database holding the work of visual artists, craftspeople and photographers in England, Scotland and Wales. 3 images per artist.

INIVA (Institute of New International Visual Arts), 12-14 Whitfield Street, London W1P 5RD. Telephone 0171 (0207 from 4/2000) 636 1930.
Development project with the Arts Council working towards a major Visual Arts organisation to promote contemporary artists worldwide.

African and Asian Visual Artists Archive, University of East London, Greengate Street, London E13 OBJ. Telephone 0181 (0208 from 4/2000) 548 9146.
Information on contemporary artists of African and Asian origin living and working in Britain.

The Association of Black Photographers, Zetland House, 5/25 Scrutton Street, London EC2A 4LP. Telephone 0171 (0207 from 4/2000) 739 1777.

Federation of British Artists, 17 Carlton House Terrace, London SW1. Telephone 0171 (0207 from 4/2000) 930 6844. A Federation of British Art Societies, including many Royal Art Societies. Leases the Mall Galleries where members have the opportunity to submit work for exhibitions. Membership by subscription.

National Society of Painters, Sculptors and Printmakers, 17 Carlton House Terrace, London SW1.

Industrial Painters Group, (as above) also the following:
Royal Institute of Oil Painters
Royal Institute of Painters in Watercolour
Royal Society of British Artist
Royal Society of Marine Artists
Royal Society of Miniature Artists
Royal Society of Portrait Painters
Senefelf Group of Artist Lithographers
Society of Mural Painters
Society of Women Artists
United Society of Artists
Society of Architect Artists

The Florence Trust, St Saviours Church, Aberdeen Park, London N.5. Telephone 0171 (20207 from 4/2000) 354 4771. A trust that provides artists' studios and sells work at auction occasionally, to help keep them going.

New English Art Club, 17 Carlton House Terrace, London SW1.

Women Artists Slide Library, Fulham Palace, Bishops Avenue, London SW6. Telephone 0171 (0207 from 4/2000) 731 7618.
Register of slides of work by British women artists, in all media. They also have a library of catalogues and books by women artists and about them. Their magazine is well-edited and in full colour.

Organisation for Black Arts Advancement and Leisure Activities (OBAALA), 225 Seven Sisters Road, London N.4. Telephone 0181 (0208 from 4/2000) 263 1918.
A non-profit organisation to promote Black African art and artists. Membership.

Landscape and Art Network, c/o Treasurer Frank Hodgson, 21 Gloucester Road, Kew, Richmond, Surrey TW9 3BS.

Concerned with the quality of the urban and natural environment. Quarterly newsletter and reduced prices for books, events and site visits.

Free Painters and Sculptors, 15 Buckingham Gate, London SW1.

Royal Society of British Sculptors, 108 Old Brompton Road, London SW7.
230 sculptors are members.

The Sculpture Company, also at this address.
It advises on corporate and private commissions.

Society of Industrial Artists and Designers, 12 Carlton House Terrace, London SW1.

Society of Designers and Craftsmen, 6 Queen Square, London WC1.

Royal Society of Painters in Watercolours, Royal Society of Painters, Etchers and Engravers, c/o Bankside Gallery, 48 Hopton Street, Blackfriars, London SE1. Telephone 0171 (0207 ftom 4/2000) 928 7521.

Royal Academy of Arts, Burlington House, Piccadilly, London W.1. Telephone 0171 (0207 from 4/2000) 300 8000.
RA membership is by election only. Membership scheme for Friends of the Royal Academy for discounts on private views, materials, magazines.

Greenwich Printmakers Association, 7 Turpin Lane, Greenwich, London SE10. Telephone 0181 (0208 from 4/2000) 858 2290.

Printmakers Council, 31 Clerkenwell Close, London EC1. Telephone 0171 (0207 from /2000) 250 1927.
Regular bulletin and promotion of printmakers' interests. Professional membership. Publishes the Handbook of Printmaking Supplies, a must for printmakers.

The London Group, Box 447, London SE22.
An exhibition association of artists. Exhibitions annually in London with occasional cash prizes. The shows are usually at the Barbican Concourse Gallery.

Artists General Benevolent Institution, Burlington House, Piccadilly, London W.1. Telephone 0171 (0207 from 4/2000) 744 1194.

Artist-run to provide financial assistance to professional artists in old age or in times of misfortune. Also Artists' Orphan Fund.

Artists' League of Great Britain, c/o Bankside Gallery, Hopton Street, London SE1. Telephone 0171 (0207 from 4/2000) 928 7521.

VARS, Visual Artists Rights Society, 108 Old Brompton Road, London SW7. Telephone 0171 (0207 from 4/2000) 373 3581.

The Corporate Arts, 6 Peto Place, Dionis Road, London SW6. Telephone 0171 (0207 from 4/2000) 384 2727.
Helps artists exhibit work in offices. Non-profit. Director: Sarah Hodson. Advises corporations about office exhibitions.

Audio Arts, 6 Briarwood Road, London SW4. Telephone 0181 (0208 from 4/2000) 720 9129.
Bill Furlong has been documenting contemporary art since 1973. Beuys, Duchamp, Richter and Long and sound art works.

Design and Artists' Copyright Society (DACS), 2 Whitechurch Lane, London E1 7QR. Telephone 0171 (0207 from 4/2000) 247 1650.

Art for Offices, 15 Dock Street, London E.1. Telephone 0171 (0207 from 4/2000) 481 1337.
Run by Andrew Hutchinson and Peter Harris. Deals with multi-national corporations and city offices providing paintings, drawings, prints, photographs to brighten the workplace. Artists can submit work but ring for advice first.

Art Agencies

Public Art Development Trust, 12-14 Whitfield Street, London W.1. Telephone 0171 (0207 from 4/2000) 580 9977 / 580 8540. Non-profit organisation. Encourages and organises commissions for works of art in public places. Also runs art in hospitals scheme for London.

Common Ground, The London Ecology Centre, 45 Shelton Street, London WC2H 9HJ. Telephone 0171 (0207 from 4/2000) 379 3109.
A charity to encourage works of art in public places.

Other Useful Art Addresses

Arts Council of England, 14 Great Peter Street, London SW1. Telephone 0171 (0207 from 4/2000) 333 0100. For awards ring 0171 (0207 from 4/2000) 921 0600.
Helps promote cultural activities in England. Professional artists can apply for grants and awards. Addresses of Regional Arts Associations can be obtained from the Arts Council. See Awards and grants section for details.

The Art Loss Register, 13 Grosvenor Place, London SW1. Telephone 0171 (0207 from 4/2000) 235 3393. If you have had art stolen then they will help trace whatever is missing and give advice.

British Council, 11 Spring Gardens, London SW1. Telephone 0171 (0207 from 4/2000) 930 8466

Fine Art Department, 11 Portland Place, London W.1. Telephone 0171 (0207 from 4/2000) 389 3043.
Organises British exhibitions overseas. Awards several scholarships and publishes a booklet on scholarships — available from Spring Gardens address above for approximately £4.

Visting Arts Unit, 11 Portland Place, London W.1. Telephone 0171 (0207 from 4/2000) 636 6888.
Funded by the Foreign office, Calouste Gulbenkian Foundation and the British Council.

Central Bureau for Educational Visits and Exchanges, Seymour House, Seymour Mews, London W.1H 9PE. Telephone 0171 (0207 from 4/2000) 486 5101.
Assists educational exchanges overseas. Art teachers should enquire about art teaching exchanges in Europe.

Association of Business Sponsorship for the Arts, Nutmeg House, Gainsford Street, London SE1. Telephone 0171 (0207 from 4/2000) 378 8143.
They have a list of companies that sponsor the arts. Congratulates large companies for sponsoring the arts with awards.

London Arts Board, Elme House, 133 Long Acre, London WC2E 9AF. Telephone 0171 (0207 from 4/2000) 240 1313.
Artists can apply for grants. The information girl is very overworked so don't rely on quick return of information!

Scottish Arts Council, 12 Manor Place, Edinburgh EH3 7DO. Telephone 0131 226 6051.

Sorting work at an art competition.

Welsh Arts Council, Holst House, Museum Place, Cardiff. Telephone 012222 394711.

The Arts Council of Northern Ireland, 181A Stranmillis Place, Belfast. Telephone 01232 663591.

Arts Council in Eire, 70 Merrion Square, Dublin 2. Telephone Dublin 764695.

British American Arts Association, 116 Commercial Street, London E.1 6NF. Telephone 0171 (0207 from 4/2000) 247 5385. Director: Jennifer Williams. Useful organisation for artists travelling to the USA and needing information prior to departure on scholarships, art schools etc.

British Chinese Artists Association, Dalby Street, London NW5. Telephone 0171 (0207 from 4/2000) 267 6133.

Insight Arts Trust, 9 Islington Green, London N.1. 2XH. Telephone 0171 (0207 from 4/2000) 359 0772.
An arts organisation for ex-offenders and people on probation. Contact: Bernardine Evaristo.

Gulbenkian Foundation, 98 Portland Place, London W1N 4ET. Telephone 0171 (0207 from 4/2000) 636 5313.

British Film Institute, 21 Stephen Street, London W1P 1PL. Telephone 0171 (0207 from 4/2000) 255 1444.

176

Chelsea Arts Club, 143 Old Church Street, London SW3. Telephone 0171 (0207 from 4/2000) 376 3311. Secretary Dudley Winterbottom. Private club open to arts world people to apply for membership. Many famous artists are members here, but you will also see the BBC and Channel 4 arts-mafia. Lovely garden in summertime. The yearbook shows work by Arts Club artists.

The Arts Club, 40 Dover Street, London W.1. Telephone 0171 (0207 from 4/2000) 499 8581.
Established private arts club. Open to arts world people for membership. Gracious dining and drawing room and garden at the back. They run regular exhibitions.

International Association of Art Critics, c/o Membership secretary Miriam Kramer, 54 the Vineyard, Richmond TW10 6AN. Membership open to art critics in the UK. Meets regularly and discusses problems relating to art criticism. The Bernard Denvir Prize is awarded to a critic, every 3/4 years. The international AICA Congress will be held in London in 2000 in September. Membership provides a press card for use internationally at museums and galleries for free entry. £30 annual fee. There are annual congresses held every year in a different country.

Contemporary Art Society, 20 John Islip Street, London SW1. Telephone 0171 (0207 from 4/2000) 821 5323.
Acquires works by living artists so that they can lend them to public galleries. They run an annual Art Market, usually at the Royal Festival Hall in November. Membership £30 per annum.

Council for National Academic Awards, 344-354 Grays Inn Road, London WC1. Telephone 0171 (0207 from 4/2000) 278 4411. Lists courses currently being offered by colleges and polytechnics throughout the UK.

Crafts Council, 44 A Pentonville Road, London N.1. Telephone 0171 (0207 from 4/2000) 278 7700.
Advises craftsmen and women and gives awards annually. Holds a register of craftsmen and women. Gallery next to the offices. Useful information service.

Museums Association, 34 Bloomsbury Way, London WC1. Telephone 0171 (0207 from 4/2000) 404 4767.

National Art Collections Fund, 7 Cromwell Place, London SW7. Telephone 0171 (0207 from 4/2000) 225 4800.
Helps galleries and museums acquire works of art of historical interest. Membership scheme.

National Association of Decorative and Fine Arts Societies, c/o Secretary 8A Lower Grosvenor Place, London SW1. Telephone 0171 (0207 from 4/2000) 233 5433.

National Society for Art Education, Champness Hall, Drake Street, Rochdale, Lancashire.
Represents the interests of teachers of art and design.

Royal Society of Arts, 6-8 John Adam Street, London WC2. Telephone 0171 (0207 from 4/2000) 839 2361.
Holds occasional art exhibitions, but acts as a link between the practical arts and the sciences.

The Society of London Art Dealers, c/o Secretary OT Galloway, 41 Norfolk Avenue, Sanderstead, South Croydon.
Founded to uphold the good name of the art trade.

Sotheby's, Fine Art Courses, 34-35 New Bond Street, London W.1. Telephone 0171 (0207 from 4/2000) 408 1100.
Variety of specialised courses open to students.

The City University, Centre for Arts and Related Studies, St John Street, London EC1. Telephone 0171 (0207 from 4/2000) 253 4399.
Arts administration courses. Applicants should be 21 or over and hold a degree or equivalent.

Association of Art Historians, c/o Peter Fitzgerald, Dept. of Art History, University of Reading, London Road, Berkshire.
Annual subscription which includes 4 issues of Art History magazine.

Art Fairs

Art 2000, Business Design Centre, 52 Upper Street, Islington London N.1. 0QH. Telephone 01717 (020-7 from 4/2000) 359 3535. The largest contemporary art fair in the UK which takes place in January every year. Over 100 leading galleries and a variety of special exhibitions featuring topical artists.

20th Century British Art Fair, Telephone 0181 (020-8 from 4/2000) 742 1611. Takes place every September at the Royal College of Art at Kensington Gore and is the only fair covering British Art from 1900 to today. About 60 leading dealers take part and contemporary and Modern British art are both on view. Also the **Art on Paper Fair**.

Art Teaching Courses

Goldsmiths College, Lewisham Way, London SE14. Telephone 0181 (0208 from 4/2000) 692 0211.
Secondary education.

Middlesex, Trent Park, Cockfosters, Herts.
Secondary and Higher education.

University of London, 1 Malet Street, London WC1.

Garnett College, Roehampton Lane, London SW15.
Higher and further education.

Artists' Materials

Painting Materials

Brodie and Middleton, 68 Drury Lane, London WC2. Telephone 0171 (0207 from 4/2000) 836 3289.

London Graphics, 16-18 Shelton Street, London WC2. Telephone 0171 (0207 from 4/2000) 240 0095.
Variety of art materials.

A.S.Handover Ltd, 37 Mildmay Grove, London N.1. Telephone 0171 (0207 from 4./2000) 359 4696.
Brushmakers.

Cornelissen & Son Ltd., 105 Great Russell Street, London WC1. Telephone 0171 (0207 from 4/2000) 636 1045. Fax 636 3655. Materials for painters, printmakers, gilders, also pastel tints. Direct mail orders also. Ring for details.

Daler-Rowney, 12 Percy Street, London W.1. Telephone 0171 (0207 from 4/2000) 836 8241.
Most art materials.

Winsor and Newton, 51 Rathbone Place, London W.1. Telephone 0171 (0207 from 4/2000) 636 4231. Head office 0181 (0208 from 4/2000) 427 4343.
Most art materials.

Print production at a factory, Winsor and Newton.

Reeves, 178 Kensington High Street, London W.8. Telephone 0171 (0207 from 4/2000) 937 5370.
Most art materials.

Bird and Davis, 45 Holmes Road, London NW5. Telephone 0171 (0207 from 4/2000) 485 3797.
Stretchers, machinist-joiners. Stretchers have to be ordered.

Russell and Chapple Ltd., 23 Monmouth Street, London WC2. Telephone 0171 (0207 from 4/2000) 836 7521.
Canvas suppliers.

Ploton Supplies, 273 Archway Road, London N.6. Telephone 0181 (0208 from 4/2000) 348 0315.

Lawrence, 117-119 Clerkenwell Road, London EC1. Telephone 0171 (0207 from 4/2000) 242 3534.
Acrylic, oils, canvas, brushes, paper.

Tiranti, 27 Warren Street, London W.1. Telephone 0171 (0207 from 4/2000) 636 8565.
Sculpture materials specialist.

Rohm and Haas (UK) Ltd., Lenning House, 2 Masons Avenue, Croydon, Surrey. Telephone 0181 (0208 from 4/2000) 686 8844.

180

Acrylic mediums (large quantities).

Binney and Smith (Europe) Ltd., Ampthill Road, Bedford.
UK wholesalers for liquitex.

C.Roberson and Co. Ltd., 1A Hercules Street, London N.7.
Telephone 0171 (0207 from 4/2000) 272 0567.
Recommended by a reader as the "best art supply shop in London." Stretchers, paint, paper etc.

Green and Stone, 259 Kings Road, London SW3. Telephone 0171 (0207 from 4/2000) 352 0837.
All materials.

General Section

Atlantis, 146 Brick Lane, London E.1. Telephone 0171 (0207 from 4/2000) 377 8855.
All art materials. Along the road from the Whitechapel Gallery.

Yates, 146 Kensington Church Street, London W.8. Telephone 0171 (0207 from 4/2000) 229 4276.
Woodyard-hardboard etc.

Ryman, 96 and 227 Kensington High Street, London W.8.
Telephone 0171 (0207 from 4/2000) 937 1107.
Branches throughout London. Stationers, office equipment and general office supplies.

Morse, 264 Lee High Road, London SE13. Telephone 0181 (0208 from 4/2000) 852 4183.
Artists' materials and framing.

Winton, 36 Earls Court Road, London W.8. Telephone 0171 (0207 from 4/2000) 937 2024.
Hardboard, picture glass etc.

Cowling and Wilcox, 26-28 Broadwick Street, London W.1.
Telephone 0171 (0207 from 4/2000) 734 9558.
Graphics specialists.

Rank Xerox, 20 Edgware Road, London W.2. Telephone 0171 (0207 from 4/2000) 402 7647.
HQ Rank Xerox can do colour xerox printing and also at certain branches.

Rymans, 66 Tottenham Court Road, London W.1. Telephone 0171 (0207 from 4/2000) 636 7306.

Neal Street East, 5 Neal Street, London WC2. Telephone 0171 (0207 from 4/2000) 340 0135.
Calligraphic materials — brushes, paper, ink. An eastern paradise.

Green and Stone, 259 Kings Road, London SW3. Telephone 0171 (0207 from 4/2000) 352 0837.
All art materials and friendly staff.

Art Transport

Rees Martin Art Services, Unit 4, 129-131 Coldharbour Lane, London SE5 9NY. Telephone 0171 (0207 from 4/2000) 274 5555.
Storage, transport and packing.

Art Move, Unit 3, Grant Road, London SW11 2NU. Telephone 0171 (0207 from 4/2000) 585 1801.
Transport, hanging and shipping.

Transnic, 434 Gordon Grove, London SE5 9DU. Telephone 0171 (0207 from 4/2000) 738 755.
Transport, picture hanging and storage.

Insurance

Crowley Colosso, Ibex House, Minories, London EC3. Telephone 0171 (0207 from 4/2000) 782 9782 .
Art world specialists.

Windsor Insurance Brokers, 160-166 Borough High Street, London SE1 1JR. Telephone 0171 (0207 from 4/2000) 407 7144.
Art specialists.

Framing

Abbey Frames, 26-28 Abbey Business Centre, Ingate Place (off Queenstown Road), London SW8 3NS. Telephone 0171 (0207 from 4/2000) 622 4815.
Established trade framers specialising in decorative mounts.

Green and Stone of Chelsea, 259 Kings Road, London SW3. Telephone 0171 (0207 from 4/2000) 352 6521.
Specialist picture framers, carvers, gilders and artists' colourmen.

Sebastian d'Orsai, 39 Theobalds Road, WC1. Telephone 0171 (0207 from 4/2000) 405 6663. Also 8 Kensington Mall, London W.8. Telephone 0171 (0207 from 4/2000) 229 3888.

Frame, Set and Match, 113 Notting Hill Gate, London W.11.

Telephone 0171 (0207 from 4/2000) 229 7444. Open Monday-Saturday 9.30-6, Thursday-7. Good local framers.

John Jones Frames Ltd., 4 Morris Place (off Stroud Green Road), Finsbury Park, London N.4.3JG. Telephone 0171 (0207 from 4/2000) 281 5439. Fax 0171 (0207 from 4/2000) 281 5956. The UK's most comprehensive framing service. Mouldings, manufactured and hand-finished to order. Gilding, studio, art photographic service. In-house conservator, collection and delivery. Parking facilities. Also Fine art photographic service. They also hold exhibitions regularly.

Frame Store, 33 Great Pulteney Street, London W.1. Telephone 0171 (0207 from 4/2000) 439 1267.

Frame Factory, 132 Talbot Road, London W.11. Telephone 0171 (0207 from 4/2000) 229 8263. Branches elsewhere also.

Many galleries also do framing if you buy work from them.

Shipping

Momart, 199 Richmond Road, London E.8. Telephone 0171 (0207 from 4/2000) 985 4509/533 0121.
Art specialists.

Ol Fine Art Services, 282 Richmond Road, London E.8. Telephone 0171 (0207 from 4/2000) 533 6124.

Featherston Shipping, 24 Hampton House, 15-17 Ingate Place, London SW8. Telephone 0171 (0207 from 4/2000) 720 0422. Arts specialists.

Printers

Ranelagh, Park End, South Hill Park, London NW3. Telephone 0171 (0207 from 4/2000) 435 4400.
Invitations, publicity cards, catalogues, posters and limited edition prints.

Z Cards, 1-2 Great Chapel Street, London W.1. Telephone 0171 (0207 from 4/2000) 437 1533/1544.
Fine art print and design company. Invitations, postcards, brochures, catalogues, posters.

Abacus, Lowick House, Lowick, Near Ulverston, Cumbria. Telephone 01229 885361.
Good printers, but note that they are out of London.

Paper

Paperchase, 213 Tottenham Court Road, London W.1. Telephone 0171 (0207 from 4/2000) 580 8496.
Excellent variety of cards, paper etc.

Atlantis, 146 Brick Lane, London E.1. 6RU. Telephone 0171 (0207 from 4/2000) 377 8855. Fax 0171 (0207 from 4/2000) 377 8850.
All art materials, including paints and paper.

Falkiner Fine Papers, 76 Southampton Row, London WC1B 4AR. Telephone 0171 (0207 from 4/2000) 831 1151.
Good variety of handmade papers. Also sell art books and magazines.

RK Burt, 57 Union Street, London SE1. Telephone 0171 (0207 from 4/2000) 407 6474.
Large quantities of handmade paper.

GF Smith, 2 Leathermarket, Weston Street, London SE1. Telephone 0171 (0207 from 4/2000) 407 6174.

Barcham Green and Co. Ltd., Hayle Mill, Maidstone Kent.

Photography and Film

Check the Photographers Gallery noticeboard for useful addresses, also photographic magazines.

Process Supplies, 13-21 Mount Pleasant, London WC1. Telephone 0171 (0207 from 4/2000) 837 2179.
General photo supplies. Excellent for darkroom equipment.

Vic Oddens, 5 London Bridge Walk, London SE1. Telephone 0171 (0207 from 4/2000) 407 6833.
Cameras, film, enlargers. Good secondhand selection (speaking from experience).

Brunnings, 133 High Holborn, London WC1. Telephone 0171 (0207 from 4/2000) 831 2846.
Secondhand equipment. Photo dealers.

Keith Johnson & Pelling, 175 Wardour Street, London W.1 Telephone 0171 (0207 from 4/2000) 380 1144.
Excellent stock of professional film.

Frida Kahlo, Imogen Cunningham (Photographers Gallery).

Leeds Camera Centre, 20-26 Brunswick Centre, Bernard Street, London WC1. Telephone 0171 (0207 from 4/2000) 833 1661.

Fox Talbot Cameras, 154 Tottenham Court Road, London W.1. Telephone 0171 (0207 from 4/2000) 387 7001. Also at 443 Strand WC2. Telephone 0171 (0207 from 4/2000) 379 6522. Main Nikon retailers. Good range of quality used equipment.

ETA Labs, 216 Kensington Park Road, London W.11. Telephone 0171 (0207 from 4/2000) 727 2570.
Colour and b/w processors. Reliable and good.

Sky Photographic Services, 2 Ramillies Street, London W.1. Telephone 0171 (0207 from 4/2000) 434 2266. Also branches elsewhere in London.
B/w and colour processors. They do extra-large contact sheets.

Mounting, framing and display services. Used by top professional and commercial photographers.

Dark Side, 4-8 Helmet Row, London EC1. Telephone 0171 (0207 from 4/2000) 250 1200.
B/w and colour processing.

City Camera Exchange, 43 Strutton Ground, London SW1. Telephone 0171 (0207 from 4/2000) 222 0521. Excellent secondhand camera shop.

Jessop, 67-69 New Oxford Street, London WC1. Telephone 0171 (0207 from 4/2000) 240 6077. Helpful advice for buyers of cameras and film supplies.

Sendean, 105-109 Oxford Street, London W.1. Telephone 0171 (0207 from 4/2000) 439 8419.
Excellent repair service at reasonable rates. Friendly and helpful advice too.

Quicksilver, 8 Flitcroft Street, London WC2. Telephone 0171 (0207 from 4/2000) 836 7420.
Good cibachrome processing.

Superchrome, 154 Drummond Street, London NW1. Telephone 0171 (0207 from 4/2000) 388 6303/7779.
Cibachrome prints.

Flash Photographic, 6-8 Colville Mews, London W.11 2DA. Telephone 0171 (0207 from 4/2000)727 9881.
All photo services.

West End Cameras, 168 Tottenham Court Road, London W.1. Telephone 0171 (0207 from 4/2000) 387 0787. Small photo shop with second hand and new cameras and batteries for old cameras.

Printmaking

Printmakers would be well-advised to buy the Handbook to Printmaking Supplies published by the Printmakers Council, Clerkenwell Close (if it's not out of print). See Useful addresses for details.

General

Atlantis, 146 Brick Lane, London E.1 6RU. Telephone 0171 (0207 from 4/2000) 377 8050.

Wimbledon School of Art print workshop.

Handmade paper for printmakers.

L.Cornelissen, 105 Great Russell Street, London WC1. Telephone 0171 (0207 from 4/2000) 636 1045.
Printmaking and fine art supplies. Beautiful shop. Near the British Museum.

T.N.Lawrence and Son, 119 Clerkenwell Road, London EC1. Telephone 0171 (0207 from 4/2000) 242 3534.

C.Roberson and Co Ltd., 1A Hercules Street, London N.7. Telephone 0171 (0207 from 4/2000) 272 0567.
Plates cut to order on the premises. Charbonnel distributor.

Intaglio (Printmakers), 62 Southwark Bridge Road, London SE1. Telephone 0171 (0207 from 4/2000) 928 2633/2711.

Sculpture Materials

Metals
Lazdan, 218 Bow Common Lane, London E.3. Telephone 0181 (0208 from 4/2000) 981 4632.

Steel
Strand Glass and Co Ltd, 524 High Road, Ilford, Essex.

Fibreglass Resins
McKechnie Metal Powders, PO Box 4, Widnes, Cheshire WA8 OPG.

Hecht, Heyworth and Alcan Ltd., 70 Clifton Street, London EC2. Telephone 0171 (020-7 from 4/2000) 377 8773. Resins and rubbers.

Tools
Parry and Son (Tools) Ltd., 329 Old Street, London EC1. Telephone 0171 (020-7 from 4/2000) 739 8301.

Charles Cooper, 23 Hatton Wall, London EC1. Telephone 0171 (020-7 from /2000) 405 5928.

Stone
Stone Firms, 10 Pascal Road, London SW8.

Plaster Merchants
Bellman Ivy & Carter, 358-374 Grand Drive, Raynes Park, London SW20. Telephone 0181 (020-8 from 4/2000) 540 1372. Plasters, latex and wax.

John Myland Ltd., 80 Norwood High Street, London SE27. Telephone 0181 (020-8 from 4/2000) 670 9161. Also at 128 Stockwell Road, London SW9. Telephone 0181 (0208 from 4/2000) 274 2468.

EF Burke and Sons, Unit 12, Newlands End, London north Industrial area, Basildon. Telephone 0126841 5071. Plaster of Paris.

General
Alec Tiranti, 27 Warren Street, London W.1. Telephone 0171 (020-7 from 4/2000) 636 8565. Tools, waxes, plasters, Gelflex, flexible mouldmaking materials.

Sculpture waxes
Poth Hille and Co. Ltd., 37 High Street, London E.15. Telephone 0181 (020-8 from 4/2000) 534 7091. Waxes.

Plasterers Merchants
A. Randall, Supremacy House, Hurstwood Road, Golders Green, London NW11. Scrim, brushes, mixing bowls.

Timber
Moss, 104 King Street, London W.6. Telephone 0181 (020-8 from 4/2000) 748 8251. Hardwoods.

CF Anderson and Son Ltd., Harris Wharf, 36 Graham Street, London N.1. Telephone 0171 (020-7 from 4/2000) 226 1212. General

Buck and Ryan Ltd., 101 Tottenham Court Road, London W.1. Telephone 0171 (020-7 from 4/2000) 636 7475. Machine tools.

Video and Film

Film Makers Co-op, 42 Gloucester Avenue, London NW1. Telephone 0171 (020-7 from 4/2000) 734 7410. Advice for film makers on reduced prices for 16mm film. Membership scheme. See Film Workshop section.

Art Magazines

The main international art magazines include Artnews USA, Flash Art International and Artforum among others. In Britain the following are useful. There are also many small art magazines that come and go, so check the gallery bookshops in London.

Apollo, 1-2 Castle Lane, London SW1E 6DR. Telephone 0171 (020-7 from 4/2000) 233 8906. Glossy monthly art and antiques publication for collectors.

Arts Research Digest, Research Services Unit, University of Newcastle, 1 Park Terrace, NE1 7RU. Telephone 0191 222 5220. Published three times a year. Information on the arts.

The Artists and Illustrators Magazine, 6 Blundell Street, London N.7. Telephone 0171 (020-7 from 4/2000) 609 2222. Buyer's guide, artsnews and practical projects. For amateurs and professionals. They run an Art Materials Fair in July annually.

Artists Newsletter, PO Box 23, Sunderland SR4 6DG. Telephone 0191 567 3589. Published by Artic Producers and grant-aided by many Regional Arts Associations. Useful magazine for artists listing suppliers, news on awards, competitions, art events, book reviews and an art information service. They also publish a very useful series of artists' books.

Art Monthly, Suite 17, 26 Charing Cross Road, London WC2. Telephone 0171 (020-7 from 4/2000) 240 0389.
10 issues per annum. Art news magazine with news, reviews, interviews, criticism, artlaw and correspondence from the art world.

The Art Newspaper, 22-29 Vauxhall Grove, London SW8. Telephone 0171 (020-7 from 4/2000) 735 3331.
Part of the Umberto Allemandi publishing business in Italy. 10 issues per annum covering art news internationally, features, reviews in newspaper format, also auction news.

The Artist, 102 High Street, Tenterden, Kent. Telephone 015806 3673.
Art magazine mainly for amateur artists, but could be useful also for professionals. Technical art articles and reviews.

Art Review, 23-24 Smithfield St, London EC1A 9LB. Telephone 0171 (020-7 from 4/2000) 236 4880. Fax 236 4881.
Editor David Lee. Art reviews in Britain and an Art under £1000 section. They also publish an Art Buyer's Guide booklet annually, Print supplement and an Art Directory.

Arts and The Islamic World, 144-146 Kings Cross Road, London WC1X 9DH. Telephone 0171 (020-7 from 4/2000) 833 8275.
Editor Jalal Ahmed. Extensive coverage of the arts in the Islamic world with colour photographs.

Audio Arts, 6 Briarwood Road, London SW4. Telephone 0181 (0208 from 4/2000) 720 9129.
Bill Furlong has been documenting contemporary art since 1973. Audio cassettes available on subscription.

The British Journal of Aesthetics/Oxford Art Journal, Oxford University Press, Walton Street, Oxford OX2 6DP. Telephone 01865 26795.

The Black Art Magazine, 225 Seven Sisters Road, Finsbury Park, London N.4. Telephone 0171 (020-7 from 4/2000) 263 8016. Art news, reviews, exhibitions, interviews and interaction. Published quarterly by OBAALA, an organisation for Black Arts Advancement and leisure activities.

Block, Art History Department, Cat Hill, Cockfosters, East Barnet, Herts. Telephone 0181 (020-8 from 4/2000) 440 7431 ext 224. Articles on art historical research, live art and exhibitions.

British Journal of Photography, 58 Fleet Street, London EC4.

Telephone 0171 (020-7 from 4/2000) 583 0175.
Established weekly photographic magazine with listings of photographic exhibitions every fortnight and reviews, technical news and features.

Burlington Magazine, 6 Bloomsbury Square, London WC1 2BR. Telephone 0171 (020-7 from 4/2000) 430 0481.
Monthly art journal for art historians and students. Academic.

Camera, Bretton Court, Peterborough. Telephone 01733 264666. Editor Richard Hopkins. Articles on equipment and portfolios in black and white of work by British photographers. Practical Photography, also at this address.

Contemporary Visual Arts, Suite K101, Tower Bridge Business Complex, Clements Road London SE16 4DG. Telephone 0171 (020-7 from 4/2000) 740 1704. Editor Keith Patrick. An excellent readable contemporary art magazine. Reviews, previews, book reviews and feature articles.

Crafts, 44A Pentonville Road, London N.1. Telephone 0171 (020-7 from 4/2000) 278 7700.
Published every two months with reviews and book news. Annual subscription UK and overseas.

Flash Art, UK contact Telephone 0171 (020-7 from 4/2000) 351 5981.
Available at newsagents and art bookshops. Published in Italy by Giancarlo Politi and covers international art reviews, news and up-to-the-minute features on the latest art trends.

frieze, 21 Denmark Street, London WC2H 8NA. Subs Telephone 0171 (020-7 from 4/2000) 379 1533. A contemporary culture and art magazine.

Galleries, 54 Uxbridge Road, London W.12. Telephone 0181 (020-8 from 4/2000) 740 7020.
Monthly guide to London and British exhibitions. Free at galleries. Art features and reviews at the front, otherwise a listings magazine.

Impress, 31 Clerkenwell Close, London EC1. Telephone 0171 (020-7 from 4/2000) 250 1927.
Printmakers Council publishes this magazine at their Clerkenwell workshop.

Modern Painters, Central Books, 14 Leather Market, London SE1 3ER. Telephone 0171 (020-7 from 4/2000) 407 5447.

Editorial address: 10 Barley Mow Passage, London W.4 4PH. Editor: Karen Wright. A glossy quarterly set up by the late Peter Fuller. Features, reviews, interviews, often by people outside the art world with views on art. The board includes writer William Boyd, who now writes about art as well as fiction and film scripts.

Printmaking Today, Farrand Press, 50 Ferry Street, Isle of Dogs, London E14 3DT. Telephone 0171 (00-7 from 4/2000) 515 7322.
Quarterly magazine for the printmaking world.

Public Art Journal, Manchester M4 9BY. Telephone 01237 470 440. A twice-yearly new art journal, in March and October, with features/reviews for professionals with an interest in art and the public domain. Writers include Sacha Craddock, Jonathan Darke, Brian Catling and Paul Bonaventura. Subs £7.90

RA Magazine, Burlington House, Piccadilly, London W.1. Telephone 0171 (020-7 from 4/2000) 300 8000.
Editor: Nick Tite. Art magazine for Friends of the Royal Academy. One of the largest circulation UK art magazines. Interesting art features, reviews and news.

Transcript, School of Fine Art, Duncan of Jordanstone College, Perth Road, Dundee, DD1 4HT. Telephone 01382 223261.
An art magazine in catalogue format with interviews and features on contemporary art.

Undercut, c/o London Film Makers Co-operative, 42 Gloucester Avenue, London NW1. Telephone 0171 (020-7 from 4/2000) 586 4806.
Magazine for film makers.

Untitled, 29 Poets Road, London N.5. 2SL. Telephone 0171 (020-7 from 4/2000) 359 6523.
Editor John Stathatos. Excellent reviews and unpretentious art features.

Women's Art, Women's Art Library, Fulham Palace Road, Bishops Avenue, London SW6 6EA. Telephone 0171 (020-7 from 4/2000) 731 7618.
Features on women's art, reviews and interviews in full colour magazine.

Press Contacts

Daily Express, Ludgate House, Blackfriars Road, London SE1 9UX. Telephone 0171 (020-7 from 4/2000) 928 8000.
Features editor.

Daily Mail, Northcliffe House, 2 Derry Street, London W.8. Telephone 0171 (020-7 from 4/2000) 938 6000.

The Daily Telegraph, South Quay Plaza, 181 Marsh Wall, Isle of Dogs, London E.14 9SR. Telephone 0171 (020-7 from 4/2000) 538 5000
Art critic: Richard Dorment

The Sunday Telegraph, address as above.
Art critic: John McEwan.

The Financial Times, Number One, Southwark Bridge, London SE1. Telephone 0171 (020-7 from 4/2000) 407 5700.
Art critic: Bill Packer.

The Guardian, 119 Farringdon Road, London EC1. Telephone 0171 (020-7 from 4/2000) 278 2832.
Art critic: Adrian Searle.

The Observer, Chelsea Bridge House, Queenstown Road, London SW8 4NN. Telephone 0171 (020-7 from 4/2000) 278 2332.
Art critic: Laura Cumming

The Times, 1 Virginia Street, London E.1. Telephone 0171 (020-7 from 4/2000) 782 5000.
Art critics: Richard Cork, John Russell-Taylor, Rachel Campbell-Johnston. Arts correspondent: Dalya Alberge.

The Sunday Times, address as above.
Art critic: Waldemar Januszczak.

The Independent, 1 Canada Square, Canary Wharf, London E14 5DL. Telephone 0171 (0207 from 4/2000) 345 2000.
Art critic: Tom Lubbock. Art news: Charlotte Mullins.

The Independent on Sunday, address as above.
Art critic: Charlotte Mullins.

The friendliest news vendor in London, outside Selfridges, Oxford Street.

The Evening Standard, 2 Derry Street, London W.8. Telephone 0171 (020-7 from 4/2000) 938 6000.
Art critic: Brian Sewell.

The Friday ES magazine, (Hot Tickets) is also useful for listings, but check the front of it as the listings are done elsewhere i.e. don't send them to the ES office!

Time Out magazine, 251 Tottenham Court Road, London WC1. Telephone 0171 (020-7 from 4/2000) 813 3000.

Art critic: Sarah Kent. Other regular reviewers include Martin Coomer, Sue Hubbard and Mark Currah.

Apart from the **art side** there may well be a possible **news angle**, in which case you must work out whether you have a feature or news story to sell and contact the appropriate editor. Newspapers are frenetically busy, so be prepared to talk at high speed if you ring them direct. It is also best to send a press release and possibly a b/w photo to the arts editor as well as the critic. The **Arts editor** runs all the arts pages, whereas the art critic is often freelance and works from home. If you have a photo that could be useful for the **picture editor**, contact him/ her separately.

Television and radio

BBC radio, Portland Place, London WIA 1AA. Telephone 0171 (020-7 from 4/2000) 580 4468.
Future events unit send 12 copies of a press release well in advance. Today and Woman's Hour, are at this address.

BBC World Service, Bush House, The Strand, London WC2. Telephone 0171 (020-7 from 4/2000) 240 3460. Any story with international appeal, especially third world, could be of interest.

BBC TV, TV Centre, Wood Lane, London W.12 7RJ. Telephone 0171 (020-7 from 4/2000) 743 8000
Rosie Millard and Nick Higham cover arts news and features on the main news. Any other arts programmes are also at this address.

Channel 4, 124 Horseferry Road, London SW1. Telephone 0171 (020-7 from 4/2000) 396 4444.
Nicholas Glass covers the arts on the main Channel 4 news at 7 each evening.

London Weekend Television, Kent House, Upper ground, London SE1. Telephone 0171 (020-7 from 4/2000) 261 3434.
South Bank show: Melvyn Bragg.

Carlton Television, 101 St Martin's Lane, London WC2N 4AZ. Telephone 0171 (020-7 from 4/2000) 240 4000.
Arts and entertainment editor: Ken Andrew.
Women's magazines are also useful, and men's (GQ, Arena etc) but many need press releases and photos (colour transparencies without glass) at least 4 months in advance, if not 6 months in advance. The Features editor or the Editor should be contacted and they will pass details on to the appropriate critic or editor.

Public Relations

In London there are three companies that deal with most of the major museums, galleries and art competitions.

Bolton and Quinn, 8 Pottery Lane, London W.11 4JZ. Telephone 0171 (020-7 from 4/2000) 221 5000. Erica Bolton and Jane Quinn run a very professional PR agency. They have promoted exhibitions organised by Artangel, Whitechapel Open, the Serpentine, Scottish Art Galleries and many more.

Parker Harris, 15 Church Street, Esher, KT10 8QS (for competitions). Telephone 01372 462190.
Emma Parker and Penny Harris do the PR for the Jerwood Prize, Singer Friedlander competition and Hunting Group Prizes. They also deal with all the entries and applications for the above. PR also for galleries, museums and arts events.

Sue Bond, Boxted Hall, Boxted, Suffolk. Telephone 01787 282 288. Sue Bond's company works with the Estorick Collection, Cork Street open weekend in November, overseas art fairs and major touring exhibitions such as the Annie Leibowitz international exhibition or the Chinese Art month.

Claire Sawford PR, Studio 6E, The Courtyard, 44 Gloucester Avenue, London NW1 8JD. Telephone 0171 (020-7 from 4/2000) 722 4114. Fax 483 3838. Claire has worked for various arts publishing companies and does art books PR for the V&A Museum and various London arts book publishers. Very efficient and enthusiastic. She also develops merchandising potential for museums and galleries.

Art Bookshops

Atrium Bookshop, 5 Cork Street, London W.1. Telephone 0171 (020-7 from 4/2000) 495 0073.
Excellent Cork Street arts bookshop. Well-stocked, informative staff. Book launches often held here.

Dillons Arts bookshop, 8 Long Acre, London WC2. Telephone 0171 (020-7 from 4/2000) 836 1359. Open Monday-Saturday 10-7.45.
Good selection of art books, magazines, photography books, literature, poetry, art postcards and posters. The staff are very friendly and helpful and well-informed about the arts in London.

ICA Bookshop, Institute of Contemporary Arts, The Mall, London SW1. Telephone 0171 (020-7 from 4/2000) 930 0493. Open 12 onwards.
Selection of books, catalogues, arts magazines, books covering video, dance, film and installations. Also general fiction and cards.

Hayward Gallery Bookshop, Hayward Gallery, South Bank, London SE1. Telephone 0171 (020-7 from 4/2000) 928 3144.
Arts bookshop at the front of the gallery, stocking catalogues, books and cards. Helpful staff.

Marcus Campbell Art Books, 43 Holland Street, London SE1 9JR. Telephone 0171 (020-7 from 4/2000) 261 0111. Fax 261 0129.
The friendly Marcus Campbell has opened a new art bookshop next to the Tate Bankside. Well worth a visit if in the area.

W & G Foyle Ltd., Art department (2nd floor), 119 Charing Cross Road, London WC2. Telephone 0171 (020-7 from 4/2000) 437 5660.
Large selection of art books in this enormous bookstore. Foyles usually has a copy of nearly every book on the market.

Shipley (Books) Ltd., 70 Charing Cross Road, London WC2. Telephone 0171 (020-7 from 4/2000) 836 4872.
Specialist art booksellers. Most art history and art criticism books.

Neal Street East, 5 Neal Street, London WC2. Telephone 0171 (020-7 from 4/2000) 240 0135.
3000 books about the Orient. Art, design, craft, textiles, theatre, costume, architecture and landscape. Enjoyable art and craft emporium.

Tate Gallery bookshop, Tate Gallery, Millbank, London SW1. Telephone 0171 (020-7 from 4/2000) 887 8000. Large bookshop stocking a vast collection of art postcards, posters, books, slides, calendars. Reduction if you are a Friend of the Tate, on books. Well-run and helpful staff.

Royal Academy bookshop, Royal Academy, Burlington House, London W.1. Telephone 0171 (020-7 from 4/2000) 300 8000.
Art shop selling not only art books and magazines but cards and craft, jewellery and goods associated with specific exhibitions. Friendly and helpful.

Zwemmers, 24 Litchfield Street, London WC2. Telephone 0171 (020-7 from 4/2000) 379 7886.
Art bookshop with a large collection of arts books. Also Zwemmers at the Barbicon and Estorick collection now.

Zwemmers at the Whitechapel, Whitechapel Art Gallery, Whitechapel High Street, London E.1. Telephone 0171 (020-7 from 4/2000) 247 6924.

Photographers Gallery, 8 Great Newport Street, London WC2. Telephone 0171 (020-7 from 4/2000) 831 1772.
Large photography specialist bookshop, also selling cards and photographic magazines.

Dillons, branches at: Malet Street, WC1, Oxford Street, Barbican centre, Trafalgar Square, Piccadilly, Kings Road, Finchley, and many others.
Good art departments in all these branches.

Waterstones, Art Department (1st floor), 193 Kensington High Street, London W.8. Telephone 0171 (020-7 from 4/2000) 937 8432.
One of London's best art departments, with sections on art, architecture, design, photography, art criticism, theatre, film. Other branches in Hampstead, Old Brompton Road, Earls Court, Covent Garden, Harrods,Camden, Charing Cross Road, Wimbledon and Richmond.

Peter Stockham, 16 Cecil Court, London WC2. Telephone 0171 (020-7 from 4/2000) 836 8661.
Secondhand art books in this street of secondhand bookshops.

St Georges Gallery, 8 Duke Street, St James's, London SW1. Telephone 0171 (020-7 from 4/2000) 930 0935.
Rare and contemporary art books.

Serpentine Gallery bookshop, Telephone 0171 (020-7 from 4/2000) 402 6075.
Since the completion of renovations, the Serpentine bookshop has become a specialist art criticism, philosophy and aesthetic theory centre, but also sells catalogues for their exhibitions.

Crafts Council, 44 A Pentonville Road, London N.1. Telephone 0171 (020-7 from 4/2000) 278 7700.
Specialist Crafts bookshop with magazines and some general arts books.

Bookshops, Royal Opera Arcade, near Haymarket SW1.

Falkiner Fine Papers, 76 Southampton Row, London WC1.
Telephone 0171 (020-7 from 4/2000) 831 1151.
Downstairs in this art materials shop, there are art books for sale.
Near the Central St Martins art school building.

Art Publishers

All the publishers listed below will send catalogues on request to potential buyers. Most of the books that they publish are on sale at Dillons, Waterstones and museum and gallery bookshops, as well as bookshops throughout the country. **Catalogues** are usually published twice a year to promote autumn and spring books.

A&C Black, 35 Bedford Row, London WC1R 4JH. Telephone 0171 (020-7 from 4/2000) 242 0946.
Writers and Artists Yearbook, practical amateur art books. Also guides, music and reference books including Who's Who. Artists' Materials reference book. Also distributes the V&A Museum books.

Arts Council of England, 14 Great Peter Street, London W.1. Telephone 0171 (020-7 from 4/2000) 333 0100.
Catalogues mainly and reports.

Artic Producers, PO Box 23, Sunderland, SR4 6DG. Telephone 0191 567 3589.
Artists' Newsletter magazine and many artists' books to offer practical advice to artists.

British Museum Publications, British Museum, London WC1. Catalogues and books.

Constable, 3 The Lanchesters, 162 Fulham Palace Road, London W6 9ER. Telephone 0181 (020-8 from 4/2000) 741 3663. Art history, practical books, biographies and fiction.

Estamp, 204 St Albans Avenue, London W.4 5JU. Telephone 0181 (020-8 from 4/2000) 994 2379.
Publisher of books on printmaking, papermaking and bookbinding.

Ink Sculptors, 34 Waldemar Avenue, London SW6 5NA. Telephone 0171 (020-7 from 4/2000) 736 6753.
Publishes artists' books. Contact Patricia Scanlan.

Dorling Kindersley, 9 Henrietta Street, London WC 2E 8PS. Telephone 0171 (020-7 from 4/2000) 240 5151.

Richard Drew, 6 Clairmont Gardens, Glasgow G3 7LW. Telephone 0141 333 9341.
Charles Rennie Mackintosh books and guides.

Ebury Press, Random Century House, 20 Vauxhall Bridge Road, London SW1. Telephone 0171 (020-7 from 4/2000) 840 8763. Practical art books.

Faber and Faber, 3 Queen Square, London WC1 N3AU. Telephone 0171 (020-7 from 4/2000) 465 0045. Art criticism, reviews, biographies, poetry. Old established publisher.

John Murray, 50 Albemarle Street, London W.1. Telephone 0171 (020-7 from 4/2000) 493 4361. Art history, general art as well as travel and fiction. Established publisher.

Lawrence King, 71 Great Russell Street, London WC1. Telephone 0171 (020-7 from 4/2000) 831 6351. Art, design and craft books. Interesting titles.

Lund Humphries, Park House, 1 Russell Gardens, London NW11 9NN. Telephone 0181 (0208 from 4/2000) 458 6314. Art history and contemporary art books.

Phaidon, 18 Regents Wharf, All Saints Road, London N1 9PA. Telephone 0171 (0207 from 4/2000) 843 1000. General art, art history. Major list.

Reaktion Books, 11 Rathbone Place, London W1P 1DE. Books on art criticism and essays on art and culture.

Ridinghouse Editions, 63 Riding House Street, London W.1. Telephone 0171 (020-7 from 4/2000) 255 1160. Artists' books. Multiples and genral publications.

Sotheby's Publications, Russell Chambers, London WC2. Art sales, art history, auction catalogues.

Tate Gallery Publications, Millbank, London SW1. Telephone 0171 (020-7 from 4/2000) 887 8870. Art catalogues and books usually related to exhibitions.

Thames and Hudson, 181A High Holborn, London WC1 V7QX. Telephone 0171 (020-7 from 4/2000) 845 5000. General art books, art history, contemporary. Major art publisher.

Victoria and Albert Museum Publications, South Kensington, London SW7. Catalogues mainly.

Yale University Press, 23 Pond Street, London NW3. Telephone 0171 (020-7 from 4/2000) 431 4422. Major art history book publisher. Also distributes the National Gallery publications.

Art Schools

The **Art and Design Directory** covering details of all art school courses in Britain is available from Avec Designs Ltd., PO Box 1384, Long Ashton, Bristol BS18 9DF. Telephone 01275 394639. £19.

Art schools in the London area offer a variety of BA (Hons), Postgraduate, foundation and other courses in painting, sculpture, printmaking, photography, video, film, design, fashion design, ceramics, jewellery, textiles and television.

The London Institute, 65 Davies Street, London W.1Y2DA. Telephone 0171 (020-7 from 4/2000) 514 6000. Fax 514 6131. Rector: John McKenzie. Camberwell, Central St Martins, Chelsea, London College of Fashion, London College of Printing and the College for Distributive Trades are now amalgamated as one body, but still at separate addresses.

Camberwell College of Arts, Peckham Road, London SE5 8UF. Telephone 0181 (020-8 from 4/2000) 514 6300. Fax 514 6310. BA (Hons) courses in most departments and postgraduate courses.

Chelsea College of Art and Design, Manresa Road, London SW3 6LS. Telephone 0171 (020-7 from 4/2000) 514 7400. Fax 514 7484.
BA (Hons) courses in painting, sculpture, printmaking. Postgraduate courses in all of these and postgraduate art history course. Good art library. Visiting lecturers. BTec and HND also.

Central St Martins College of Art and Design, Southampton Row, London WC1B 4AP. Telephone 0171 (020-7 from 4/2000) 514 7000. Fax 514 7006.
BA (Hons) courses in most departments. Also postgraduate courses.

Sir John Cass School of Art, Central House, Whitechapel High Street, London E.1. Telephone 0171 (0207 from 4/2000) 283 1030.

Cordwainers Technical College, Mare Street, Hackney, London E.8. Telephone 0171 (020-7 from 4/2000) 985 0273/4. 2/3 year courses in footwear design to SIAD. Leathergoods design. No Fine Art courses.

Film students.

Byam Shaw School of Fine Art, 2 Elthorne Road, London N.19 4AG. Telephone 0181 (020-8 from 4/2000) 281 4111. Fine art courses in painting, sculpture, printmaking and 3D design. Postgraduate courses. Visiting lecturers. 30,000 square feet of studio space.

London College of Fashion, 20 John Princes Street, London W.1. Telephone 0171 (020-7 from 4/2000) 629 9401.

London College of Printing and Distributive Trades, Elephant and Castle, London SE1 6SB. Telephone 0171 (020-7 from 4/2000) 514 6500. Fax 514 6535.

London International Film School, 24 Shelton Street, London WC2H 9HP. Telephone 0171 (020-7 from 4/2000) 836 9642. 2-year film-making diploma.

Middlesex (Hornsey), Fine Art department, 114 Chase Side, London N.14. Telephone 0181 (020-8 from 4/2000) 886 6599.

Royal College of Art, Kensington Gore, London SW7. Telephone 0171 (020-7 from 4/2000) 584 5020.
Post graduate courses in painting, sculpture, graphics, ceramics and glass, environmental design, furniture design, industrial design, silversmithing and jewellery, fashion design, film, photography, video and television. All 2/3 year courses. Master of Arts (RCA), Master of Design (RCA), PHd (RCA) and Dr (RCA).

Saint Martins School of Art (now Central Saint Martins),107 Charing Cross Road, London WC2. Also Long Acre WC2. Telephone 0171 (020-7 from 4/2000) 753 9090.
BA (Hons) courses and postgraduate courses in Fine Art.

Royal Academy Schools, Burlington House, London W.1. Telephone 0171 (020-7 from 4/2000) 300 8000.
Postgraduate Fine Art courses only. Annual summer show of work in the lower galleries at the RA.

University of London, Goldsmiths College, School of Art and Design, New Cross, London SE14. Telephone 0181 (020-8 from 4/2000) 692 7171.
BA (Hons) Fine Art courses and postgraduate courses.

Slade School of Art, University College, Gower Street, London WC1. Telephone 0171 (020-7 from 4/2000) 387 7050.
Postgraduate and undergraduate courses in Fine Art, also stage design, film, video, photography.

Wimbledon School of Art, Merton Hall Road, London SW19. Telephone 0181 (020-8 from 4/2000) 540 0231.
BA (Hons) Fine Art courses, also theatre design.

Kingston, Art and Design department, Knights Park, Kingston on Thames, Surrey. Telephone 0181 (020-8 from 4/2000) 549 6151. BA (Hons) courses in Fine Art, 3D design, graphic design, fashion design.

Hounslow Borough College, Art department, London Road, Isleworth, Middlesex. Telephone 0181 (020-8 from 4/2000) 568 0244. Foundation Fine Art course, also other combined courses in design.

Day and Evening Classes

Information about all classes within the London area can be found in Floodlight magazine, obtainable at most newsagents or at a public library.

John Cass Art School, Central House, Whitechapel High Street, London E.1. Telephone 0171 (020-7 from 4/2000) 283 1030. Printmaking classes for overseas artists and art students, as well as many other classes.

Hampstead School of Art, King's College Campus, 19-21 Kidderpore Avenue, London NW3 7ST. Telephone 0171 (027 from 4/2000) 431 1292. Fax 794 1439.

Photofusion Photography Centre, 17a Electric Lane, Brixton, London SW9 8LA. Telephone 01717 (020-7 from 4/2000) 738 5774. £85 (£55 concessions). Beginners class on black and white printing.

The London Glassblowing Workshop, 7 Leather Market, Weston Street, London SE1. Telephone 01717 (020-7 from 4/2000) 403 2800. Monday nights, £75, includes tuition, materials and tools.

Morley College, 61 Westminster Bridge Road, London SE1. Telephone 0181 (020-8 from 4/2000) 938 6863. Good printmaking courses, also other Fine Art classes. There is a gallery on the premises.

Camden Arts Centre, Arkwright Road, London NW3. Telephone 0171 (020-7 from 4/2000) 435 2643. Art classes at various levels.

The City Lit Institute, Stukeley Street, London WC2. Variety of classes.

Several art schools run evening classes, also adult education centres throughout London.

Further Education Colleges

Brixton, (South London), 56 Brixton Hill, London SW2. Telephone 0181 (020-8 from 4/2000) 737 1166.

Kingsway Princeton College, (Central London), Sidmouth Street, London WC1. Telephone 0171 (020-7 from 4/2000) 837 8185.

North London, Camden Road, London N.7. Telephone 0181 (020-8 from 4/2000) 609 0041.

South West London, Tooting Broadway, London SW17. Telephone 0181 (020-8 from 4/2000) 672 2441.

Woolwich (South London), Villas Road, London SE18. Telephone 0181 (020-8 from 4/2000) 855 3933.

Higher Education Colleges

Also includes art schools (see ART SCHOOLS).

London College of Furniture, 41 Commercial Road, London E.1. Telephone 0171 (020-7 from 4/2000) 247 1953.

London College of Fashion and Clothing Technology, 20 John Princes Street, London W.1. Telephone 0171 (020-7 from 4/2000) 493 8341.

London College of Printing, Elephant and Castle, London SE1. Telephone 0171 (020-7 from 4/2000) 735 8484.

South London College, Knights Hill, London SE27. Telephone 0181 (020-8 from 4/2000) 670 4488.

Paddington College, Paddington Green, London W.2. Telephone 0171 (020-7 from 4/2000) 402 6221.

Hackney College, Hackney, London E.1.

College of the Distributive Trades, 107 Charing Cross Road. London WC2.

South East London College, Lewisham Way, London SE4.

South West London College, Tooting Broadway, London SW17.

School of Building and Vauxhall College of FE, Belmore

Street, London SW8.

City and East London College, Pitfield Street, London N.1.

Wandsworth College, London SW12.

Hammersmith and West London College, Airlie Gardens, London W.8. Telephone 0171 (020-7 from 4/2000) 727 4550.

Westminster College, Battersea Park Road, London SW11.

Southwark College, 209 Blackfriars Road, London SE1. Telephone 0171 (020-7 from 4/2000) 928 9441.

Royal College of Music, Prince Consort Road, London SW7. Telephone 0171 (020-7 from 4/2000) 589 3643.

Central School of Speech and Drama, 64 Eton Avenue, London NW3. Telephone 0171 (020-7 from 4/2000)722 8183.

Membership Schemes

Most galleries have a private view (and sometimes also a press view) for gallery contacts, members and friends of the artists. This is a good way to meet other artists and to make valuable contacts for the future. Sometimes it is quite a social event, as at the Royal Academy, and at The Tate Gallery, but at smaller galleries it is possible to meet other artists and find out about other art events. For art buyers it is a chance to meet a different work world and meet the artists. Some galleries that have membership schemes are listed below. Check for up-to-date prices first before sending a cheque!

The ICA, Nash House, The Mall, London SW1. Telephone 0171 (020-7 from 4/2000) 930 0493.
Full membership is £30 per annum. Full membership includes invitations to private views, advance mailing about exhibitions, cinema, theatre and other events. Art pass for students also. There are plans for the ICA to move to Bankside in 2001.

Friends of the Tate, The Tate Gallery, Millbank, London SW1. Telephone 0171 887 8752.
Member. New system for basic membership or extras. Young friend (under 26). Includes invitations to private views, advance mailing of Tate Gallery events, lectures, overseas visits, and a copy of Tate magazine. Young Friends also organise visits to the theatre, cinema and other events. Reductions on catalogues and calendars, also books at the Tate shop.

Friends of the Royal Academy, Royal Academy of Arts, Burlington House, Piccadilly, London W.1. Telephone 0171 (020-7 from 4/2000) 494 5668 / 300 8000.
Friends £40. Museum staff £35/teachers. £35 for young friends and for pensioners. Friends receive free admission to all exhibitions, plus a guest and up to 4 children, catalogues at a reduced price and other benefits. Discount also on RA summer show submissions, discounts at other shops.

Photographers Gallery, 5 & 8 Great Newport Street, London WC 2. Telephone 0171 (020-7 from 4/2000) 831 1772.
Member £25. Supporter £900, Associate £75, collector £200, Patron £675, Benefactor £375. Wine for members at openings. Details of lectures/workshops/photo sales/competitions/ discounts.

Friends of the Victoria and Albert Museum, Victoria and Albert Museum, London SW7. Telephone 0171 (020-7 from 4/2000) 589 4040.
Member £30. Educational/museum staff £30. Corporate membership and family membership also. Late night views at the V&A have become very popular. Invitations to openings and details of gallery events and lectures.

Friends of the Courtauld Institute, Somerset House, Strand, London WC2. Telephone 0171 (020-7 from 4/2000) 873 2243. £20 or students (under 26) £10. Life members £300.

Friends of the Hayward Gallery, Telephone 0171 (020-7 from 4/2000) 450 2009. Free unlimited entry to the Hayward Gallery exhibitions, private views, talks and lectures. Discount at the shop and at Aroma cafés throughout London.

The British Museum Society, The British Museum, London WC1. Telephone 0171 (020-7 from 4/2000) 637 9983.
Member £30. Family £40. Invitations to openings, details of gallery and museum events and lectures. Also reduction on catalogues. Visits abroad and within Britain.

Contemporary Art Society, 20 John Islip Street, London SW1. Telephone 0171 (020-7 from 4/2000) 821 5323.
Member £30. Joint family membership £50.

Friends of the Café Gallery, By the pool, Southwark Park, Bermondsey, London SE16. Telephone 0171 (020-7 from 4/2000) 232 2170.
Invitations to private views, discount on submissions to open exhibitions and gallery events. Also Bermondsey Artists Group (BAG), if you are an artist living in that area. Opportunities to exhibit in the group shows, private views at the gallery and possible exchanges overseas.

Friends of the Federation of British Artists, 17 Carlton House Terrace, London SW1. Telephone 0171 (020-7 from 4/2000) 930 6844.
£24 or life membership £240. Benefits include private views, free catalogues and admission, free newsletter, reduced rates for room hire and prizes of works of art.

Friends of the Iveagh Bequest, Kenwood House, Hampstead Lane, London NW3. Telephone 0181 (020-8 from 4/2000) 348 1286.
Member £10. Private views, lectures and visits to country houses. Newsletter.

National Art Collections Fund, Millais House, 7 Cromwell Place, London SW7 2JN. Telephone 0171 (020-7 from 4/2000) 225 4800.
Member £25, joint £30. Reductions for OAPs and under 25s £15 or £20 joint.

Information about other Friends' organisations in Britain can be obtained at:

The British Association of Friends of Museums, 66 The Downs, Altrincham, Cheshire. Telephone 0161 928 4340.

Degree shows at art schools in London take place in June and July. The Royal College of Art's show is the most outstanding for its variety of work. You can buy items of interest, knowing that they will give lasting pleasure and that they have been made by the country's top, talented designers. Work at most other colleges covers ceramics, sculpture, fashion design, jewellery, painting, printmaking, photography, film, video and furniture. See **ART SCHOOLS** section for addressses and phone numbers. Works of art can be bought at most shows. By doing this you can help an artist at the beginning of his/her career and in return own an original one-off work of art. Time Out lists the dates and times of the degree shows in the summer months.

Scholarships, Grants, Awards, Prizes

London

Arts Council of England, 14 Great Peter Street, London SW1.
Telephone 0171 (020-7 from 4/2000) 333 0100.
For up-to-date details contact the appropriate officer. Dates for
deadlines may change.

Visual Arts. Development grants for visual arts touring exhibitions and events. Deadline April1st. Contact 0171 (020-7 from 4/2000) 973 6566.

Exhibitions and events. Deadline December 4th. Contact 0171 (020-7 from 4/2000) 973 6566.

Touring exhibitions and events travel grants. Deadline April1st. Contact 0171 (020-7 from 4/2000) 973 6566.

Visual Arts (photography and new media) publishing grants.
Deadline March. Contact 0171 (020-7 from 4/2000) 333 0100 ext 425.
First-time publications. Deadline October 9th. Contact 0171 (020-7 from 4/2000) 333 0100 ext425.

Symposia grants. Deadline December 4th. Contact 0171 (020-7 from 4/2000) 333 0100 ext 425.

Photography publishing grants. Deadline March18th. Contact 0171 (020-7 from 4/2000) 973 6474.

Live-Art commission fund. Contact 0171 (020-7 from 4/2000) 973 6512.

Live-Art travel and research fund. Contact 0171 (020-7 from 4/2000) 973 6512.

Live-Art in Higher education. Contact 0171 (020-7 from 4/2000) 973 6512.

There are also film, video, broadcast, drama, music and literature awards. Telephone 0171 (020-7 from 4/2000) 333 0100.

The Lottery

The arts receive revenues generated by the National Lottery for capital projects such as construction of a new building, refurbishment of an existing building or buying equipment. Telephone 0171 (020-7 from 4/2000) 312 0123 for details.

Crafts Council, Awards Officer, 44 A Pentonville Road, London N.1. Telephone 0171 (020-7 from 4/2000) 278 7700.
Similar awards scheme to the Arts Council of England relating to equipment for craftwork and training, maintenance. Open to craftsmen and women throughout England.

London Arts Board, Elme House, 133 Long Acre, London WC2E 9AF. Telephone 0171 (020-7 from 4/2000) 240 1313.
Awards to individuals (painting, sculpture, photography, live-art, video, installations). Deadline currently 29th November. Ring to check though. Awards for these categories up to £2000. Send an sae to the Visual Arts Unit.

London exhibitions and events fund, Open to organisations and individuals.
There are no residency schemes at present.

Competitions

Check with the main newspapers, as they often run art or photography competitions. **The Independent (photography), The Sunday Times (Singer Friedlander watercolours), The Observer (painting), The Guardian (exhibitions and prizes) and The Spectator** have all run competitions in the past.

The Times/Artangel Open Commissions, Artangel, PO Box 18103, London EC1M 4JQ. Telephone 0171 (020-7 from 4/2000) 490 0226. Open to practising artists, living and working in the UK, to propose ambitious ideas or projects in any form or medium. Outline your project on no more than 3 sheets of A4 paper and supplement with 35mm slides (maximum 24). Projects will be completed in 1999 and 2000. Proposals should be sent with an sae.

The Jerwood Painting Prize, 15 Church Street, Esher, KT10 8QS. Telephone 01372 462190. Annual deadline June. Started in 1994. One artist receives £30,000 after judges select a shortlist of 7 artists. The 7 artists show work in a final exhibition at the new Jerwood Space, where the winner is announced in September each year. Entry fee £15 per artist. Send an sae for details. Organised by Parker Harris PR company.

Lucie Cookson, artist, at her first exhibition in London.

The Singer Friedlander Sunday Times Painting Competition, PO Box 1390, London SW8 1QZ. Telephone 01372 462190. Send an sae for details.
£25,000 worth of prizes, awarded at an annual exhibition of shortlisted paintings, usually at the Mall Galleries, where the paintings are then on sale to the public.

The Hunting Art Prizes, 15 Church St, Esher, KT10 8QS. Telephone 01372 462191. Send an sae for details. Prizes totalling £20,500 with a first prize of £10,000. Also a travel award. Handing in points at Belfast, Bristol, Cardiff, Cornwall,

Edinburgh, Manchester, Yorkshire and London. Final exhibition at the Royal College of Art in February.

Turner Prize, Tate Gallery, Millbank, London SW1.
£20,000 prize and a major help to your career. Past winners have included Richard Deacon, Damien Hirst, Rachel Whiteread. Sponsored by Channel 4. Artists are nominated by people in the art world and chosen by a panel of international judges. The artist must be under 50. Not open to artists to apply.

John Moores, Exhibition Secretary, Walker Art Gallery, Liverpool. Three major prizes and 10 smaller ones. This is a prestigious prize and a great help to the artist's career.

Royal Overseas League, Overseas House, Park Place, St James's, London SW1. Telephone 0171 (020-7 from 4/2000) 408 0214 ext 219.
Ist prize £3000 and many other prizes including a travel award. Exhibition in September at the ROSL London and then Edinburgh ROSL, where all works are for sale. Open to professional artists under 35, who are citizens of the UK, the Commonwealth or former Commonwealth countries. Deadline for entry forms July.

South Bank Photo Show, Royal Festival Hall, London SE1.
Contact: Susan Toft. Send an sae for an application form. Deadline early April. Exhibition of entrants work. £6000 in prizes.

Logos National Art Competition, Logos Art Gallery, 20 Barter Street, London WC1A 2AH. Telephone 0171 (020-7 from 4/2000) 404 7091.
Aims to promote contemporary artists working in the UK. Finalists' summer show and one-person exhibition awarded.

Citibank Photography Prize, at The Photographers' Gallery, 5 Great Newport Street, London WC2H 7HY.
Awards of £10,000 annually and an exhibition for winners at the Photographers' Gallery. Past winners include Andras Gursky and Richard Billingham. Send an sae for details. A prestigious prize.

Photographers Gallery Transition Optical Annual Exhibition, 5 Great Newport Street, London WC2H 7HY. Telephone 0171 (020-7 from 4/2000) 831 1772.
Fee £15 per print. Free to Photographers' Gallery members. 1st prize £2000, 2nd prize £750, 3rd prize £100. Deadline late August. Send an sae for details.

Fitzrovia Open, 26 Hanson Street, Fitzrovia, London W.1P

7DD. Telephone 0171 (020-7 from 4/2000) 323 3596. Deadline June, exhibition in July. Send an sae for details if you live in Fitzrovia.

ICI Photography Awards, National Museum of Film and Photography, Bradford. Telephone 01274 307611.
Total prize money of £35,000 for the best of British photography, called the Fox Talbot prize. Entry by nomination only and the International photography prize nominated worldwide. Exhibition of work by entrants at the National Portrait Gallery in London.

Printmakers Miniature Print Exhibition, Printmakers Council, Clerkenwell Close, London EC1. Telephone 0171 (020-7 from 4/2000) 250 1927.
Prizes and exhibition. Printmakers should send an sae for details.

Cleveland Drawing Biennale, Cleveland Art Gallery, Victoria Road, Middlesbrough, Cleveland TS1 3QS. Telephone 01642 225408.
Total of £15,000 in prizes. Works for sale. Send an sae for details.

International Print Biennale, Cartwright Hall, Bradford. Entry Fee. Send an sae for details. Closing date 30th September. Sending in day 31st December.

Royal Academy Summer Show, Burlington House, Piccadilly, London W.1. Telephone 0171 (020-7 from 4/2000) 300 8000.
Send an sae for details. Annual summer exhibition with total of £50,000+ of prizes. Work is also for sale — about 1000+ works! Mixture of work by amateur and professional artists, including RA elected members.

BP Portrait Awards, National Portrait Gallery, London WC2. Send an sae for details. £8 entrance fee. Winner receives £10,000 in cash and a commission of £3000 to paint a well-known sitter. The painting then becomes part of the NPG contemporary, 20th century collection. Second prize £5000, 3rd £3000 and another 5 awards of £1000 each. Also the BP travel award. The exhibition usually receives good publicity in the media.

National Westminster Prize for Art competition, Nat West Bank, 41 Lothbury, London EC2P 2BP. Telephone 0800 (080 from 4/2000) 200 400/734 4455.
Artists must be between 18 and 35. 1st prize £26,000 and 10 prizes of £10,000. An exhibition of work by the ten finalists is held at the gallery.

Artifact, 163 Citadel Road, The Hoe, Plymouth, Devon PL1 2HU. Telephone 01752 228727.

Philip Saunders. For a subscription per annum Artifact will send you details about some 140 open art competitions, prizes and shows both in the UK and internationally. A form is completed about your work and then page sheets of information are sent to give all the necessary details in a simple format.

Benson and Hedges-Illustrators Gold Competition, Association of Illustrators, 1 Colville Place, London W1P 1HN. Money prizes. Send an sae for details.

Oppenheim-John Downes Memorial Awards, 36 Whitefriars Street, London EC4 Y 8 BH.
Awards to deserving painters, sculptors, writers, craftsmen and women, dancers and musicians unable to pursue their vocation due to poverty. Must be over 30 and a British subject. By 31st October for December annually.

John Kobal Photographic Portrait Award, National Portrait Gallery, London WC2.
Send an sae for details. Sponsored by the Independent on Sunday. £5500 in awards. Deadline June. Can also write to John Kobal Award, PO Box 3838, London NW1 3JF. Telephone 0171 (020-7 from 4/2000) 383 2979. Exhibition of finalists at the NPG. A prestigious and well-respected prize and exhibition. The exhibition tours to the Royal Photographic Society in Bath and the Midlands Arts Centre in Birmingham.

John Laing Painting competition, Page Street, Mill Hill, London NW7 2ER.
£15,000 prize total. Send an sae for details.

Villiers David Prize, Parker Harris Partnership for details. 01372 462190.
A travelling prize with an exhibition at the Hart Gallery in Islington. Won by Maxwell Doig in1997.

Artist in Residence Schemes

London Arts Board, Elme House, 133 Long Acre, London WC2E 9AF. Telephone 0171 (020-7 from 4/2000) 240 1313.
At present they do not run any residency schemes.

Crafts Council, 44A Pentonville Road, London N.1. Telephone 0171 (020-7 from 4/2000)278 7700.
Assists residencies through the Regional Arts Associations. Special projects category also.

Gulbenkian Foundation, 11 Portland Place, London W.1. Telephone 0171 (020-7 from 4/2000) 636 5313. Video fellowships attached to art schools and universities.

Arts Council of England, 14 Great Peter Street, London SW1. Telephone 0171 (020-7 from 4/2000) 333 0100. Ring for details or advice about residencies.

Henry Moore Fellowship in Sculpture, Henry Moore Institute, 74 The Headrow, Leeds LS1 3AA. Centre for the Study of Sculpture, 0113 246 9469. Henry Moore Sculpture Trust, 0113 246 7467. Send an sae for details or telephone first.

Lowick House Print Workshop, Lowick Green, near Ulverston, Cumbria. Telephone 01229 85898. 2 short-term residencies.

Durham Cathedral Artists' Residency, County Hall, Durham DH1 5UF. Telephone 0191 386 4411.

European Pepinières Awards, Judith Staines, 9-11 rue Paul Leplat, 71860 Marly-le-roi, France. 3-9 month residencies in 31 cities of Europe. 2800 appointments in 17 cities last year. Worth applying if you are interested in Europe.

Brasenose College, Oxford, Director, Museum of Modern Art, 30 Pembroke Street, Oxford. Artists over 35.

Digswell Arts Trust, Digswell House, Monks Rise, Welwyn Garden City, Herts. Telephone Welwyn 21506. Studio space and workshops.

Grizedale Forest, Northern Arts, 10 Osborne Terrace, Jesmond, Newcastle on Tyne. Telephone 0191 281 6334. Artist receives £3500 for 3-6 months.

Kielder Forest Photography Residency, Northern Arts, 10 Osborne Terrace, Newcastle on Tyne.

Manchester Polytechnic, Art Dept., Manchester Polytechnic, Manchester. Textiles fellowship.

Norwich College of Art, John Brinkley Fellowship. Printmaking/painting/mixed media.

Exeter College of Art, Exeter.
Part-time teaching rates paid.

Kettles Yard, Dr Bullock, Kings College, Cambridge.
£5000 visiting fellowship.

Artists Agency, 18 Norfolk Street, Sunderland SR1 1EAs.
Telephone 0191 510 9318.
Channels awards to artists, photographers and sculptors.
Provides placements and commissions. Supported by Northern
Arts, The Arts Council and Sunderland Borough Council.

Art and Work Awards, Wapping Arts Trust, 15 Dock Street,
London E.1. 8JL. Telephone 0171 481 1337.
Falls into three categories; an art collection sponsored by a company for a corporate building, a work of art commissioned for a
specific site and the most outstanding contribution to art in the
working environment.

Gulbenkian Award, Calouste Gulbenkian Foundation, 98
Portland Place, London W1N4ET. Telephone 0171 635 5315.
Forms available from the Assistant Director. £15,000 available
for ten awards, for initial research for artists to develop large-
scale works for specific sites. Subsequently three further awards
totalling £45,000 towards final production costs.

Public Art Development Trust, 14 Whitfield Street, London
W.1. Telephone 0171 (020-7 from 4/2000) 580 9977.
Encourages works of art in public places, which is a growth area
in recent years. If your work is appropriate then ask their advice.

National Gallery, Trafalgar Square, London WC2.
Artist-in-residence. £4000 for 6 months. Now called Associate
Artist. Past ones have been Paula Rego, Peter Blake, Jock
McFadyen.

Open-exhibitions

Bankside Browser, Telephone 0171 (020-7from 4/2000) 401
7275 (Tate Bankside visitor centre, Sumner St SE1). Artists have
to live in Southwark and work can be in any medium but should
fit into an archive box 15 x 5 x 10. Exhibition April-May in SE1.

Whitechapel Open, Telephone 0171 (020-7 from 4/2000) 522
7888. Fax (7) 377 1685. Held every two years (2000/2002 etc).
Open to artists who live in the East end of London.

Overseas

The British Council, publishes **Scholarships Abroad,** a booklet giving details of awards in some 33 countries. Check for latest price of the booklet from 10 Spring Gardens London SW1. Telephone 0171 930 8466. Send an sae for details.

Useful addresses for information on Overseas Scholarships:

British Council, Fine Art Department, 65 Davies Street, London W.1.
For scholarships Abroad write to 10 Spring Gardens, London SW1., enclosing an sae.

British American Arts Association, 116 Commercial Street, London E.1 6NF. Telephone 0171 (020-7 from 4/2000) 247 5385. Director: Jennifer Williams. Directories available for reference, listing awards, scholarships in the USA, art schools, art organisations etc. Phone first 0171 (020-7 from 4/2000) 247 5385 for an appointment.

Central Bureau for Educational Visits and Exchanges, Seymour House, Seymour Mews, London W.1. Telephone 0171 (020-7 from 4/2000) 486 5107.
Art teaching bursaries for Europe and elsewhere. Educational exchanges mainly.

Association of Commonwealth Universities, 36 Gordon Square, London WC1.
Details of Commonwealth scholarships.

French Embassy, Cultural Attaché, 27 Wilton Crescent, London SW1.
Scholarships to postgraduate students in Fine Art.

Italian Institute, 39 Belgrave Square, London SW1.
Send an sae for details of scholarships open to art students and artists.

Japan Information Centre, 9 Grosvenor Square, London W.1.
Scholarships to Japan. Many well-known artists have been on them.

Royal Netherlands Embassy, 38 Hyde Park Gate, London SW7.
Scholarships to Holland. The Stedelijk Museum offers artists studio space each year in Amsterdam.

German Academic Exchange Service (DAAD), 1-15 Arlington Street, London SW1. Telephone 0171 (020-7 from

Greek priests at Pitsidia, Crete.

4/2000) 493 0614.
15 scholarships to UK Artists to study at art academies and other German art institutions. Up to 32 years old. Closing date March.

The Greek Embassy, 1A Holland Park, London W.11.
Scholarships to Greece open to art students and artists.

British Council, 10 Spring Gardens, London SW1.
Apply for details about Hungarian summer schools in art. Send an sae.

Elizabeth Greenshields Foundation, 1814 Sherbrooke Street West, Montreal, Québec, Canada.
1 year scholarship to an artist from any country. 30 awards.

Harkness Fellowships, Harkness House, 38 Upper Brook Street, London W.1.
20 offered annually for advance study and travel in the USA. Art is one of the subjects. 2 academic years and three months travel. Age 21-30. Closing date October 20th. Enclose a 9x7 envelope and sae with £1 postage and covering letter asking for details.

English Speaking Union of the Commonwealth, 37 Charles Street, London W.1. Telephone 0171 (020-7 from 4/2000) 629 0104.
Scholarships for Commonwealth countries.

Winston Churchill Memorial Trust, 15 Queens Gate, London SW7. Telephone 0171 (020-7 from 4/2000) 584 9315.
100 fellowships for travel and work abroad. Various categories which change each year. Send an sae for details.

USA/UK Educational Commission, 6 Porter Street, London W.1. Telephone 0171 (020-7 from 4/2000) 486 7697.
Runs the Fulbright Hays Awards, as well as others.

Abbey Major and Minor Awards, 1 Lowther Gardens, Exhibition Road, London SW7.

David Murray Scholarships, Royal Academy Schools, Burlington House, London W.1.
For travel, landscape painting and drawing.

Boise Scholarship, Slade School of Art, University College, Gower Street, London WC1.

The Leverhulme Trust, The Secretary, Research Awards Advisory Committee, 15-19 New Fetter Lane, London EC4. Telephone 0171 822 6952.

Up to 6 studentships overseas (not UK, Europe or USA). Closing date January 15th. Under the age of 30.

Yale University School of Art, 180 York Street, New Haven, Connecticut 06520, USA.
Advanced scholarship in British Art. 3 months and upwards. November annually.

Fulbright Awards, UK/USA Educational Commission, 6 Porter Street, London W.1. Telephone 0171 (020-7 from 4/2000) 486 7697. 1 year and travel. Maintenance. Exchange visitor visa. Closing date November 23rd. Interviews February. Several scholarships.

Institute of International Education, 809 United Nations Plaza, New York, NY 10017, USA.
For further details of USA awards.

British Film Institute, 21 Stephen Street, London W.1.
Grants £15,000. Film grants.

Kodak Ltd., PO Box 66, Kodak House, Station Road, Hemel Hempstead, Herts.
Awards of £2500 and 2 of £3500. Open to UK photographers.

Courtauld Institute, Somerset House, Strand, London WC2.
12 scholarships annually. Open to students of art history and architecture.

Canada Council, Cultural Exchange Section, PO Box 1047, Ottawa, Ontario.
Various grants.

Pratt Graphics Center, 831 Broadway, New York, NY 10003, USA.
Open to USA and foreign nationals.Opportunity to study there.

Arts Council of New Zealand, PO Box 6032, Te Aro, Wellington, New Zealand.
Write for details of awards to study in New Zealand.

Grants Register, St James's Press, 3 Percy Street, London W.1. Available for reference at most libraries. If you are looking for scholarships, fellowships, etc. Artists Newsletter see Art magazines, is very useful. Art fellowships are often advertised in the main newspapers.

ACME Housing Association, helps artists find studio space and housing and **SPACE Studios** only studio space. See **STUDIOS** section.

Riverside London

In the last decade the riverside East end of London has changed dramatically, with many new wharfside developments around **Docklands** and the **Isle of Dogs** and downriver towards Greenwich. Old warehouses, once storage for spices or clothes, have been converted in **Wapping** and **Limehouse** into luxurious, spacious loft apartments. Designer studios and architects' homes and offices predominate, in what were once in the 70s and 80s artists' studios. Professional warehouse dwellers are living side by side with poorer council house tenants and the areas are gradually changing. Docklands is now an area with city offices at **Canary Wharf**, surrounded by wine bars and fashionable restaurants and nearby small town houses for young families.

Some of London's oldest and most quaint pubs are situated next to the River Thames and in summertime visitors flock to them to cool off and taste ale that the Pilgrim Fathers might have quaffed, prior to embarkation for America. The **Mayflower pub** in **Rotherhithe** was named after the pilgrims' ship and many of the crew came from the area. Outside the pub, next to the tidal Thames, you can sit and watch barges or pleasure boats passing by. Nearby visit St Mary's Rotherhithe, which was built in 1715. At that time the area was a shipbuilding village and the church has examples of work by skilled shipwrights.

Across from Rotherhithe is **Wapping**, once an artists' area with warehouses chock-a-block with artists, designers and creative people, trying to make a living and often paying exorbitant rents. Some studios looked out onto the Thames and had superb views, but now these are mostly only owned by successful designers and photographers,or celebrities.

On leaving the studios on Wapping High Street, wander down to the **Prospect of Whitby**, which dates back to Henry VIII. Smugglers, thieves and the infamous hanging Judge Jeffries drank here, at one time or another. Judge Jeffries used to execute criminals by tying them to stakes in the river, where the rising tide slowly drowned them. Upstairs today in the pub, taste the pancakes or scampi provençale and you might even meet a famous face or two. Cher has stayed nearby when in London and David Owen the politician lives along the road.

Further down Wapping High Street, visit the **Town of Ramsgate** pub, a 17th century tavern with a riverside garden. Nearby on Wapping Old Stairs Captain Blood was caught running away with the Crown jewels. This area is often used by British and American film crews for Dickensian London settings.

Back over on the south side at **Bermondsey**, the 16th century **Angel** pub also has a few tales to relate. Samuel Pepys is reputed to have drunk here, as did Captain Cook. Bermondsey is still very much an area where 'real' Londoners live, though at times it is hard to know who real Londoners are these days. Cockneys seem to have moved to outer London suburbs and immigrants and refugees replace previous immigrants in the east end of London. The east end has always been a fascinating mix of ethnic minorities, dating from London's early days as a port. Immigrants have often lived here in appalling conditions until they find work: wandering along Brick Lane today, it would appear that times have not really changed.

St Katherine's Dock.

Heading back towards London, **St Katherine's Dock**, across the river, has become a fashionable city dockside, with cafés and restaurants near the Tower Hotel. New yachts nestle close to old sailing ships with rigging and make an attractive sight for city workers on their lunch break.

By the riverside in the city, employees can escape to pubs such as the **Bouncing Banker**, while upriver the scenery begins to change from industrial warehouses to leafy, attractive whitewashed houses at **Hammersmith, Putney, Richmond** and **Twickenham**. A boat trip upriver from **Westminster** to **Kew Gardens** or **Hampton Court** is as worthwhile as one downriver to **Greenwich** to visit the **Cutty Sark**.

At Hammersmith, walk along the Mall to the **Old Ship, the Dove, the Rutland** and **the Blue Anchor**. There are several rowing clubs here and hearty, strapping crews often stop here for a drink, before skimming down river. On the way to **Chiswick**, where **Hogarth's House** can be seen, pass by scented jasmine, lilac, wisteria and crisp pink and white magnolia trees, next to 17th and 18th century houses. **Kelmscott House** in Chiswick Mall, built in 1790, was once the home of William Morris, the great textile designer. Kelmscott Press produced many very fine mediaeval-inspired designs with birds, flowers and trees.

Queen Elizabeth I visited the Keeper of the Great Seal at Kew in1594. Queen Anne gave money for building a church at **Strand on the Green** and George III's sons were tutored here in Kew. The painters Zoffany and Gainsborough lived at Strand on the Green, which was once a fishing village and is now luckily a conservation area. **The City Barge** pub was built in 1497 in Henry VII's reign and the **Bull's Head** is reputed to be the scene of a council meeting, held by the Roundhead leader Oliver Cromwell, during the Civil War. There are cricket matches on the green in summer nowadays.

Both in London and outside there are many attractive pubs and restaurants. At Twickenham visit the **White Swan**, at Isleworth the **Londoner's Apprentice**, at Teddington **The Angler**. Outside London visit **Windsor, Egham, Marlow** and **Henley on Thames**, where the annual July regatta takes place.

St Pauls from Bankside.

The Hidden Backstreets of
Village London

One of the charms of living in London is gradually getting to know the city, area by area. In my student years, when I was at art school in London in the late 70s and short of money, I used to work for a market research company interviewing in Chelsea, Brondesbury, north London, Kensington and even on Victoria to Dover boat train services. It was certainly a way to discover inner and outer areas and get to know a variety of Londoners. Other areas of village London, such as Kentish Town, Wimbledon, Chelsea, Holland Park, Portobello, Hampstead and Richmond became familiar through visiting friends. Taking a walk to a park with a toddler or finding an obscure pub with friends would divulge attractive cul de sacs, or courtyards with balconies clad in wrought ironwork and often be a haven of peace from nearby noisy traffic.

Campden Hill, off Holland Park Avenue, is my local village. It is typical of village London that such a quiet, historical quarter could be hidden behind a main traffic artery to central London. If you wander up Aubrey Road, you will pass quaint cottages that

Aubrey Road, Campden Hill.

were once near the Notting Hill toll gate, on the grounds of the Aubrey House estate, but are now inhabited by the wealthy. **Aubrey House** is still there at the top of the hill and its grounds border Holland Park, allowing squirrels to leap across and play in local chestnut trees. The cottages on Aubrey Road have interesting wrought-iron balconies, some original, some as in Van Morrison, the rock singer's old cottage, now under different ownership, mock Charles Rennie Mackintosh. Further up at the top of the hill look back across to local church spires on Ladbroke Grove. To your left you will find **Campden Hill Square**, one of London's most famous squares. The reason for its celebrity is due to its longstanding inhabitants, including Lady Antonia Fraser the historian and novelist and her husband Harold Pinter, the internationally-renowned playwright, among other Labour supporters dubbed "champagne socialists" by the press after their June 20th meetings with literary friends in the 1980s. On Christmas Eve the square dwellers all light candles in their windows in memory of a 1930s event, when Mosleyite mobs hurled bricks at a Jewish hospital celebrating the Festival of Light. In 1975 an IRA bomb intended for Antonia Fraser's husband, an MP, sadly killed cancer specialist Professor Hamilton Fairley by mistake, so the area has had an unfortunate violent past. In1999 a Kurdish siege took place at the nearby Greek Embassy, with a15-year-old girl setting herself alight. Luckily the siege ended safely, but for a time it felt as though the whole area was in danger, as the world's press waited with bated breath to see what would happen.

At the top of Campden Hill, Aubrey House, which I have already referred to, was once the home of the two attractive Alexander sisters, who were painted when young by Whistler. After being owned for over 200 years by the Alexander family, the house was sold in 1997 to the Rausing family, millionaire entrepreneurs from Sweden, but does not appear to be occupied very often. After the bend, along towards Campden Hill tennis club, you will find more attractive houses, including what was once Patrick Lichfield's studio; nearby ivy-clad walls and balconies nestle close to the local church. Aubrey Walk was an artists' colony in Edwardian days. Queen Anne's household and Swift the famous writer lived in the area and Turner painted the sunset from the top of the hill.

The house I live in was built in 1829, during the Georgian era, and was owned by the Earl of Gainsborough. He divided the house in the 1970s, giving each member of his family a flat. Now the inhabitants are of humbler origin, but when I first moved in in 1986, there were hundreds of letters to all sorts of members of the aristocracy: this caused some amusement, until the house's past history was slowly unravelled. I think that the postman thought that the house was a refuge for newly-poor lords and ladies!

Also in Kensington, but near High Street Kensington, is **Kensington Church Walk**, which is another tranquil backwater for busy high street shoppers. Many visitors would hardly know that it existed, unless they ventured off a small side street, next to an Arab bank. The shops have changed and many of the more creative ones have moved, Manguette the jeweller to just round the corner, but others have moved in.

Kensington Church Walk.

Near the V&A Museum wander along towards Brompton Oratory, the main Catholic church in the area, turn off at Village Walk and wander past Holy Trinity Brompton until you come to Ennismore Gardens Mews. This mews is typical of many in London, where once horses were kept in stables, but now are attractive homes with colourful facades and beautifully designed balconies and doors.

Another quiet area that I have already referred to is Little Venice in Maida Vale. Warwick Avenue is the nearest tube station and then follow signs to Warwick Place, which houses the old Warwick Castle pub and some quaint shops. When I was an art student we had to paint landscapes based around the canal and the pub was our lunchtime meeting place. I've been back many times since with friends from Australia and Europe, before taking a barge from Blomfield Road. The houses in the area were once brothels, run by the Church Commissioners, a marvellous piece of Victorian hypocrisy! The houses by the canal are now elegant white-stuccoed Victoriana. Many celebrities live in the area and have included John Mortimer, Barry Humphries (alias Dame Edna Everage) and more recently rock group managers and rock stars.

Ennismore Gardens Mews, SW7.

Covent Garden is a well-trodden tourist path, but how many visitors venture up the winding side streets, near the **Lamb and Flag** pub on Rose Street? This pub has a fascinating clientele, giving plenty of food for gossip, although in recent years it has changed. **Goodwin's Court** now houses offices, but is a quaint row with bulging windows straight out of a period piece drama. You almost expect Nell Gwynne or Eliza Doolittle to pop out selling flowers with a Cockney charm and comment. Nearer the market **St Paul's Church**, the actors' church, is a surprise after the busy market. Designed by Inigo Jones the back of the church looks onto the Piazza, but it is the garden which is used by locals for a peaceful break or chance to talk, away from the hordes of tourists visiting the market stalls.These two areas in Covent Garden offer another side to the area and its now fashionable shops in Neal Street, Long Acre and Floral Street where Paul Smith's clothes shops are very popular. Agnès B and

Armani are also now in the area. The Royal Opera House refurbishment will add more glamour in the early next century.

Hampstead's High Street is the busy centre for the village near the famous heath. Wander up towards the heath, but turn off sharp left up stairs by village cottages towards Golden Yard and Fenton House, which is a late seventeenth century elegant house overlooking the heath. It is well-worth visiting to see paintings, musical instruments and has spectacular views across London.

On the other side of Heath Street turn up New End towards Christchurch Hill and back to **Flask Walk**. Many artists and writers lived in Hampstead such as DH Lawrence, the artist Mark Gertler and today Emma Thompson the actress, various playwrights and authors and Boy George, the rock musician in a Gothic house by the heath. The village atmosphere still exists, despite changes in the shops and restaurants. Hampstead has varying memories for me, ranging from being a blushing bridesmaid in a peach, Laura Ashley dress in the early 80s at Hampstead Parish Church, where Constable the artist is buried, to walks on the heath with my diabetic Australian-artist boyfriend who had a bad coma on the heath and was luckily found by a doctor who saved his life; visits to the fairground in May and August, swimming in the mixed pool after cycling energetically from Notting Hill Gate and endless discussions on the heath about life and future plans.

Golden Yard, off Heath Street, Hampstead.

Pied Bull's Yard in Bloomsbury, off Bloomsbury Square, is virtually opposite the British Museum and yet you would hardly be aware of this attractive courtyard unless you were visiting one of the shops or restaurants. I first visited it at a friend's birthday party and then Austin Desmond Gallery moved in. Bloomsbury has other secrets to offer with its Georgian houses and squares. In the mid 80s the publishing companies based aound here organised an annual Bookrest walk, for publishing employees to help earn charity money for indigent, retired book trade employees. We used to wear fancy dress and walk around some 20 publishing companies in London, mainly in this area, singing through backstreets, serenading astonished passers-by and quaffing wine and sangría at each stop. The bow window shops in **Woburn Walk**, designed by Cubitt and the **Lamb pub** are all landmarks in this literary area. Surprisingly the Italian community has also been in this area since the 17th century, adding a colourful flavour to the neighbourhood shops. There are also processions and celebrations in the summer by Italian Londoners. (See the Guide to Ethnic London by Ian MacAuley).

In the city of London at the weekends there are many areas to visit that busy city workers would hardly know existed, as they rush back to their suburban homes. In the early 80s I used to meet a friend who worked in the city for lunch occasionally. We would explore backstreets looking for unusual architecture. **Bunhill Fields**, near Wesley's House, which has been out of use since 1852, is one such surprise. John Bunyan is buried here, Daniel Defoe, William Blake, the artist and John Wesley, the founder of Methodism's mother. Milton wrote "Paradise Regained" in Bunhill Row. I hope that it gave him more joy than "Paradise Lost" gave me at school! What a contrast this historical backwater makes with the Lloyds of London landmark, designed by Richard Rogers, a more dynamic late 20th century building.

London has many arcades including the **Burlington Arcade** off Piccadilly, which houses many jewellery shops; expensive cashmere sweaters obviously find a market here but Georgina von Etsdorf has exquisite materials and Russian Palekh boxes are on display as is antique jewellery. The **Royal Opera Arcade** stretches from Pall Mall to Charles II Street near the Haymarket. Bookshops and gift shops flourish here and the New Zealand community magazine. Somehow however, the arcades in London seem very refined and correct compared to the wonderful Parisian "passages", where you can walk for several miles following them across several districts. They also contain rambling bookshops, shops with bizarre masks and other paraphernalia and photo galleries, cards, clothes. The London arcades are not full of antique shops, rather of correct country clothes, guns, swords and to attract a smart clientele looking for tablecloths Victorian style. Maybe foreigners find them charming!

London will always have its secret addresses, known to residents and adventuruous visitors, but discovering them for the first time is always a pleasure.

Little Venice to Camden Lock

Little Venice is a quiet Backwater haven on hot days in London. Take the tube to Warwick Avenue and follow signs to Warwick Place. **The Warwick Castle pub**, next to a restaurant and shops in a peaceful lane, is an ideal place for a glass of cider or beer, before catching the barge along the canal. Smell the scent of the roses and other flowers in the gardens of the large houses looking onto the canal, and take in the fact that this area is so peaceful for central London.

The houses on the canal at Little Venice were once brothels, run by the Church Commissioners; a marvellous piece of hypocrisy in Victorian England! Now these houses are elegant, well-maintained and mostly owned by successful London actors, actresses, rock world impresarios and writers. Lulu the singer, Tom Watkins the manager of the Pet Shop Boys, East 17 and Bros are both in this category and John Mortimer the writer and Barry Humphries the comedian have also lived in this area. Richard Branson, the owner of Virgin, once lived on a barge for nine years on the canal. He moved to Millionaire's Row in Holland Park after the barge sank and he lost cherished family photos and other belongings. Living on barges in London can be a cheap way to cope with city expenses.

Catching a barge along the peaceful canal from Little Venice requires a choice of barge company. I prefer **Jason's** on Blomfield Road, around the corner from the Warwick Castle pub, but there is also the **Zoo Waterbus** next to a barge café, nearby. Jason's barge, painted red and green, starts from Blomfield Road and you can order lunch or drinks while you admire the leafy green waterway. Children love the trip as there is so much to see.

The Regent's Canal was opened in 1820; a waterway joining the Grand Union Canal to the River Thames at Limehouse.At that time horses pulled the colourful barges, while men pushed the heavily-laden boats through the tunnels. The Grand Union Canal has been well-cared-for on the route that the boat takes and you start with gardens lush with flowers trailing down to the

Little Venice canal scene.

water. Passing through Maida Hill tunnel under Edgware Road, the mosque next to Regent's park soon comes into view; a magnificent golden-domed building facing Mecca. Blow-up bridge comes next, where a barge blew up years ago and soon the Aviary designed by Lord Snowdon (Princess Margaret's ex-husband) appears at the Zoo. Zoo animals are clearly seen as you pass by. Some boats stop at the zoo, but Jason's barge travels on past the floating Chinese restaurant, quite a unique sight in London, towards Camden Lock. The Pirates Castle is a wonderful fantasy playground for local children, who can play in canoes and boats, with a mock castle on the canal. They can pretend that passing boats are their future victims. Finally Camden Lock comes in to sight and travellers can get off the boat here and either return later, or stay and explore Camden Market and area.

The barge trip can of course be taken the other way round from Camden Lock, by taking the bus to Chalk Farm or Camden Town tube stations. Camden Lock itself has small shops and restaurants by the canal. Avanti Italian restaurant is ideal for taking children to, as the waiters love children. During the week the small square is peaceful, but at weekends it is buzzing with grunge and hip people. Hordes of people, especially students, come to buy cheap Doc Martens, 1970 clothes, retro fashion, handmade jewellery, records, books, craftwork, pottery and candles. This area has a real buzz about it and a slightly retro hippy feel, like Amsterdam.

Belgo Noord restaurant has good moules frites and Belgian beers, Marine Ices have the best ice-cream in London, Dôme usual bistro food and atmosphere and L'Ecluse terrific crêpes. The shops on the main road sell specialist shoes, pottery, Catalan gifts, Latin American crafts, pine shops, furniture, lighting, records and clothes. You won't have a chance to be bored here and all ages will find something to look at.

Little Venice

Jason's Trip
60 Blomfield Road
London W.9.
0171 (020-7 from 4/2000) 286 3428

Zoo Waterbus
Camden Lock Place
London NW1.
0171 (020-7 from 4/2000) 482 2550

General Information

There are numerous guides to help tourists and visitors to London. Perhaps the best of these are the **Time Out** guides and the **Evening Standard** guides. Time out is published weekly and covers virtually everything you could think of needing to know about, with features appropriate to that particular week. The Evening Standard paper is a daily and has restaurant and pub reviews weekly, as well as art, theatre, music and dance reviews and a Hot Tickets listings magazine on Thursdays.

Please note telephone changes in mid 2000. Noted as (020-7 from 4/2000) or (020-8 from 4/2000) ie from April (4th month) 2000! 0345 also becomes 084. See telephone directory for other changes.

Specialist Guides

Stanfords Bookshop, Long Acre, Covent Garden, has an excellent selection of maps and guides to London and world-wide, also the **Britain Visitor Centre**, 1 Regent Street, London SW1Y 4NX has a useful bookshop and information centre. Piccadilly Circus tube station.

Time Out
London Guide
Restaurant Guide
Shopping Guide
London Walks
Time Out also publishes excellent guides to Berlin, Amsterdam, Paris, New York, Barcelona and other cities.

Evening Standard
The Best of London Guide
Childrens London (with discount vouchers)
Restaurant Guide by Fay Maschler
Pub Guide by Andrew Jefford

Guide to Ethnic London by Ian MacAuley. Immel Publishers. This guide covers the following communities: Italian, Irish, Greek and Turkish, Black, Asian, Chinese and Jewish. Recommended.

London's Good Coffee Shops £2.99. Available from Hot Spot publications 0171 221 4669. A rather pleasant little guide if you are a coffee addict and need to know where to find a cappuccino or caffe latte.

Information about London

London Tourist Board, National Tourist Information Centre, forecourt at Victoria Station, London SW1 Open Easter-October daily 8-7, November-Easter Monday-Saturday, 8-6, Sundays 8.30-4. Waterloo international terminal, Arrivals hall, London SE1 7LT. Open 8.30-11.30. The **London Tourist Board** runs a hotel booking service. For a booking fee and a deposit they will book you into a London hotel immediately on request. **Telephone 0171 (020-7 from 4/2000) 932 2020 for the booking service. General accommodation advice, telephone 0839 (090 from 4/2000) 123 435.** Also LTB (now Expotel-run) offices at Heathrow Central station, London airport, Victoria and Liverpool Street stations. LTB also does theatre and tour bookings. Book a bed scheme for the rest of England. For London bookings enquire in person at Victoria or write at least 6 weeks in advance. Write to: **London Tourist Board, 6th floor, Glen House, Stag Place, London SW1E 5LT 0171 (020-7 from 4/2000) 932 2000. Visitor call service: (only while in Britain) 0839 (090 from 4/2000) 123 then add the following-General advice (hotels) 435, Theatre (how to book) 438, What's on 400/401, Travel (London) 430, River trips 432, What's on (children) 404. Millennium events 0891 (090 from 4/2000) 66 33 44 (only available within the UK). www.LondonTown.com for LTB website.**

Britain Visitor Centre, 1 Regent Street, Piccadilly Circus, London SW1Y 4NX. Central point for booking UK accommodation, buying guide books, maps and theatre tickets. **Scottish Tourist Board 020-7930 8661, Welsh Tourist Board 020-7808 3831, Northern Ireland 087555 250, Eire 020-7493 3201.**

City of London Information Centre, St Paul's Churchyard, London EC4. Telephone 0171 (020-7 from 4/2000) 606 3030. Open 9.30-5.

Daily Telegraph Information Bureau, Telephone 0171 (020-7 from 4/2000) 353 4242. Open 9.30-5.30. General information (not tourist information).

Information about Britain

National Tourist Information Centre, Victoria Station forecourt, London SW1. Telephone 0171 (020-7 from 4/2000) 730 3488.

Information for London and the rest of England.

Scottish Tourist Office, 19 Cockspur Street, London SW1. Telephone 0171 (020-7 from 4/2000) 930 8661. Also at Britain Visitor Centre, Regent Street.

Welsh Tourist Office, 020-7808 3831.

Northern Ireland Tourist Office, 087 555 250.

Travel in London

Buses. London Transport publishes free bus maps covering all London areas with details of bus routes. The bus states on the front where it is going (stating the obvious, but it's amazing how many tourists don't bother to look). It is wise to check first. If you are unsure about the exact amount for the fare ask the conductor and if necessary ask to be put off the bus at your destination. London conductors are often very friendly and full of useful information. Try and remember the British obsession with queues at bus stops, as people get very fraught if you jump queues.
Travelcards for the day (cheaper after 9.30am), week, month or year, are good value. Now there is the carnet system for 10 tickets and a weekend travelcard, so check what is best for you.

London sightseeing tours, start from Marble Arch, Piccadilly, outside the National Gallery and outside the Trocadero at Piccadilly Circus/Leicester Square, Victoria. It's really much cheaper to take the local buses and hop on and off where you want (hence the value of a travelcard). The bus routes 12 to the Houses of Parliament via Trafalgar Square, 24 from Trafalgar Square via Bloomsbury to South end Green Hampstead and 137 to Knightsbridge are some good ones to take and the 23 to the Tower of London via the city.
The Big Bus Company, 020-8944 7810. Victoria, Green Park or Marble Arch starting point for up to 30 stops to hop-on or off at across London.

Tube. If you arrive at Heathrow or Gatwick you will find that the fare to London is quite expensive. A push button machine at Heathrow will tell you how to reach your destination and the quickest route. After 9.30, a one-day travel pass is the best value, or a weekly or monthly travelcard and now carnet of tickets and weekend travelcard. Late night travel is difficult after 12 midnight but there are night buses. On New Year's Eve all travel is usually free, due to sponsorship.

Taxis. London cabbie/taxi drivers (black cabs) are world famous for their friendliness and charm. They are very knowledgeable about the city and have to take a test called "The Knowledge", to show that they know London well enough. Other radio car drivers do not take this test, so be careful and choose black cabs where possible. Radio cars at night time locally are cheaper however.

Cars. Hiring a car is expensive, but worth it for trips outside London. If you have a car, you may need a resident's parking permit or otherwise there are meters.

Holland Park, Japanese Gardens.

Bicycles. Definitely the quickest way to get around London and keeps you fit. There are cycleways in some parks, but since a whizz-kid roller-blader killed a cyclist in Hyde Park, no bicycles are allowed there except on the cycleway at the far end. Crazy logic as far as I am concerned! You can hire bikes or buy them secondhand for longer stays. See Yellow Pages phonebook for addresses and phone numbers.

Pickpockets! Beware, as London has groups of pickpockets from South America and Eastern Europe, that pray on Oxford Street in particular. A well-known trick is for two youths to stand, one in front and one behind, at a bus stop and one pickpockets while the other one draws attention away to something else. Always look streetwise!

Travel outside London

Buses
Green Line Buses, Eccleston Bridge, off Buckingham Palace Road, Victoria. Telephone 0171 (020-7 from 4/2000) 834 6563. Open 8.30-9.30pm. Take the bus to Hampton Court, Windsor, Surrey Hills, the zoo and various stately homes for the day.

National Travel, Victoria Coach station, Buckingham Palace Road, Victoria. Telephone 0171 (020-7 from 4/2000) 730 0202. Buses to most British towns, villages and cities.

Trains
All UK rail services, 0345 (084 from 4/2000) 48 49 50.
Virgin Trains, 03445 (084 from 4/2000) 222 333.
Charing Cross (southern region)
Victoria (southern region)
Waterloo (south west England)
Liverpool Street
St Pancras
Euston
Kings Cross (Scotland, York and northern England)
Paddington (Cornwall, Devon, South west England)
Check with the station for up-to-date fares and special inter-city reductions, bookable in advance.
Eurostar, 0345 (084 from 4/2000) 881 881.

Planes
Shuttle services to Scotland from Heathrow and Gatwick are better than before, due to fierce competition now with British Airways, British Midland, Air Uk and Easyjet all covering British

routes. Fare names and prices change so always ask for the cheapest one and insist on knowing that that definitely is the cheapest, unless of course you want to travel first-class.
British Airways, 0345 (084 from 4/2000) 222 111
British Midland, 0345 (084 from 4/2000) 554 455
Easyjet, 0870 6000000
AIR UK, 0345 (084 from 4/2000) 666 777

Travel Overseas

British Airways, 0345 (084 from 4/2000) 222 111.
Go, 0845 6054321.
Virgin, 01293 562000/01493 440239
Laker, 01923 775555
Debonair, 0541 500300

Time Out advertises cheap flights to most European cities and to the USA, Canada, Australia, New Zealand and worlwide. Also **The Evening Standard** does most days. They also often have last-minute cheap holidays to choose from.

Air Travel advisory bureau, Telephone 0171 (020-7 from 4/2000) 636 5000. Advice on the cheapest and best flights worldwide.

Europe
Eurostar 0345 (084 from 4/2000) 881 881.
Since Eurostar started this has definitely become the most pleasant way to travel to Paris or Brussels or even to the rest of Europe, by changing onto the TGV or other trains. Flying to other European cities is still the best way. Again Time Out and The Evening Standard have all the latest prices and offers. **Time Off** holidays are excellent value to most European cities.
Wasteels, Telephone 0171 (020-7 from 4/2000) 834 7066. Adjacent to Platform 2 at Victoria station. Excellent for Eastern Europe travel by train. Will help you work out the best way to travel between say Prague and Warsaw.

Overseas
Trailfinders, 42-48 Earls Court Road, London W.8. and 194 Kensington High Street, W.8. Telephone 0171 937 5400 for USA and Europe and Telephone 0171 938 3366 for long haul. This is one of the most professional and helpful travel agents in London, especially for long haul travel to Australia or Latin America. They can advise on round-the-world tickets or alternative routes with stopovers.

Useful Embassy Addresses

USA Embassy, Grosvenor Square, London W.1. Telephone 0171 (020-7 from 4/2000) 499 9000.

For UK artists about to visit the USA, also contact the **British American Arts Association,** Telephone 0171 (020-7 from 4/2000) 247 5385 for advance arts information. Visas not needed now for UK visitors to the USA.

Canadian High Commission, Grosvenor Square, London W1X Obb. Telephone 0171 (020-7 from 4/2000) 930 9741. Cultural Attaché: Diana Jervis-Read. UK citizens do not need a visa for Canada.

Dome, Galeries Lafayette, Paris.

Australia House, The Strand, London WC2. Telephone 0171 (020-7 from 4/2000) 438 8000
Visas needed for Australia. Australian artists wishing to exhibit in London should contact the Public Affairs department. Cultural Attaché: Rebecca Hossack. She also runs her own gallery in Windmill Street (see Galleries section). There are exhibitions at Australia House on a regular basis.

New Zealand House, Haymarket, London SW1. Telephone 0171 (020-7 from 4/2000) 930 8422.
Visas required by UK visitors to New Zealand. Gallery space at New Zealand House on the mezzanine floor for exhibitions of work by New Zealand professional artists. The Cultural Affairs department organises art exhbitions and other cultural events.

French Embassy, 58 Knightsbridge, London SW1. Telephone 0171 (020-7 from 4/2000) 235 8080. Cultural Affairs department is at 27 Wilton Crescent, London SW1. Ciné Lumiere at the Institut Français has excellent French films.

German Embassy, 23 Belgrave Square, London SW1. Telephone 0171 (020-7 from 4/2000) 235 5033.
See Cultural Centres section for the Goethe Institut which shows exhibitions of work by German artists.

Greek Embassy, 1A Holland Park, London W.11. Telephone 0171 (020-7 from 4/2000) 727 8040.
The Hellenic Insitute, in Paddington shows work by Greek artists as does Gallery K in Hampstead.

Italian Embassy, 39 Belgrave Square, London SW1. Telephone 0171 (020-7 from 4/2000) 235 8643.
The **Accademia Italiana,** shows work by Italian artists and holds conferences and receptions. See Galleries section.

Other Useful information

Bank Opening Hours. Monday-Friday 9.30-4.30. City of London 9.30-3. Hours vary at certain branches and some banks open on Saturday, but not many. Harrods bank is open on Saturday but you have to pay a £3 charge to cash a cheque. Bureaux de change or Thomas Cook are better value. **M&S Marble Arch branch does not charge commission on foreign currency.**

Shopping Hours. Generally 9.30/10-6, but often late on Thursdays until 7/8 in Oxford Street and Wednesday in

Knightsbridge. Locally a half-day on Thursdays at Portobello Road market. Sundays usually 11/12-5/6.

Medical. Hospitals operate a 24-hour casualty service for emergencies at Middlesex Hospital, Mortimer Street, London W.1.; St Mary's Hospital, Praed Street, London W.2.; Westminster Hospital, Horseferry Road, London SW1.

Chemists. Emergencies. Boots at Piccadilly Circus SW1 has a late-night service. John Bell, 52-54 Wigmore Street W.1 is open daily 8.30-10.

Lost Property. Buses/underground: 200 Baker Street Lost Property Office. Taxis: 15 Penton Street, London N.1. Trains: at main line stations. General: local police station near where you lost the item.

Travel enquiries. Telephone 0171 (020-7 from 4/2000) 222 1234 is a 24-hour service advising on travel within London, by tube or bus. London transport information offices at Oxford Circus, Piccadilly Circus, Victoria and Euston.

Licensing Hours. Now much longer hours, but vary from pub to pub. Sunday openings are far longer now.

Information by telephone:
London weather, 090 500 951
Directory enquiries, 192. International 153.
Emergencies (Ambulance, fire, police), 999
Post Office Hours, Monday-Friday 9-5.30. Saturday 8.30-12.

Green and Stone, art materials shop.

Hampstead heath in autumn.

Parks

Central London Parks

Central London has a vast selection of parks to visit, each one with its own particular character.

Battersea Park, London SW11. Tennis courts, boating on a pond, running track and the **Buddhist Temple**, which makes impressive viewing from the Chelsea side of the river Thames. Open air circuses, ballet and firework displays have all taken place in this park. More a local park really.

Hampstead Heath, London NW3. This park has 800 acres of fields and woodlands and is perhaps one of London's most famous parks. The views of London are superb and it has the good fortune to be surrounded by a good selection of typical old English pubs. **Spaniards Inn** and **Jack Straw's Castle** are on the top part of the heath, the former being where Dick Turpin the highwayman is supposed to have stayed. Hampstead village has numerous pubs, restaurants and tea rooms. **The Flask** and the **Nags Head** for real ale fans and **The Freemasons Arms** at the foot of the heath, nearer Keats House. Highgate on the other side of Hampstead heath is the home of Highgate Cemetery where Karl Marx is buried. Highgate also has numerous pubs and a village atmosphere. At the top of Hampstead heath visit **Kenwood House**, which has open-air concerts in summer on the lawn. The house itself has a Vermeer and Rembrandt and is a beautiful Robert Adam-designed building. The heath has three swimming pools (open-air), tennis courts and space for dog-walking and open-air games, kite-flying etc. Underground Hampstead Heath/Belsize Park or 24 bus.

Holland Park, London W.8. Behind Kensington High Street and runs up the hill to Notting Hill Gate. This park was once the private garden of Holland House and although this building was bombed during the war, it now houses a splendid Youth Hostel in a wonderful park setting. Open air theatre and opera in the summer, tennis courts, squash courts and a cricket pitch. The wildlife in this park is exotic, with peacocks strutting around the elegant Japanese garden, created by ten Japanese gardeners and has a waterfall, pond and rock sculpture, a legacy of the 1991 London Japan Festival. It is beautifully peaceful here, except on summer Sundays. In the wooded areas you will often be surprised by a fox staring at you or an escaped white pet bunny rabbit — never a dull moment for children. Squirrels are also very tame here. The orangerie has exhibitions and concerts occasionally and the murals are worth looking at, re-creating a sunny day in the park over 100 years ago. There are exhibitions in the Ice House also, often of craft, jewellery or photography. The park café is excellent and in summer an ice cream stand is recommended for hungry children. Underground Holland Park.

Hyde Park, London W.1. A royal park since 1536 and once highwaymen rode through it. More recently it has held rock concerts, charity walks and dancing displays, also agricultural events and even a fairground. You can swim in the man-made **Serpentine river** although it is run by a company that employs an aggressive Kray-brothers-lookalike who has no sense of humour. I once just leapt in along from the ducks in sheer frustration and to cool off one summer day, to the amazement of passing tourists. You can hire boats on the river and there is a riding school on the Bayswater side of the park. Speakers Corner is at the Marble Arch end of Hyde Park and here you can listen to obsessive fanatics, eccentrics, mavericks, nutters and join in if you like. There is also a cycle path round by the river. 340 acres of wonderful parkland. Underground Queensway, Marble Arch, Knightsbridge.

Kensington Gardens, London W.2. **Kensington Palace** is worth visiting, after renovations and to see the sunken garden. The Orangery restaurant and café is excellent and in an attractive setting. It is now a focal point for Diana worshippers and the gates to the Palace often have flowers beside them. There are plans for a new childrens playground and gardens at the north side of the gardens to commemorate Diana, Princess of Wales, who died in 1997 tragically young. **The Albert Memorial** has been renovated next to the **Albert Hall** on the Kensington Gore side of the gardens. Albert is now a shocking gold, but otherwise the renovations are long overdue. The brown gates and deer sculpture leading up to it though, look, to my taste, quite wrong. **The Round Pond** always has either remote-control boats on it or children feeding birds. The Peter Pan sculpture is worth visiting to show children and for adults, **The Serpentine Gallery** has been totally modernised and is now one of London's leading contemporary art spaces. Whatever is on, you can guarantee lively discussion afterwards. Underground Queensway, High Street Kensington or Notting Hill Gate.

Kew Gardens, Richmond, Surrey. Although out of London officially, it is well worth visiting these wonderful gardens to see the plants, Pagoda, **Queen Anne's House** near the Thames and the **Marianne North Gallery**. The Cacti houses also occasionally have orchid or other displays. This is an ideal place for a picnic with children or a large group of students and there are many shady trees for summertime and three cafés, with a reasonable restaurant at one. From the Thames side of the gardens you can see the magnificent gates of Sion House on the other side of the river and sometimes boats practising for the many races that take place on the River Thames. Take a bus or underground on the District line or catch a boat from Westminster Pier to Kew Gardens. Underground Kew Gardens

Regents Park, London NW1. This park is surrounded by some of the most beautiful London terraces in the Regency style, designed by Robert Nash. The park itself contains the famous **Zoo** and the **Open air Theatre**, which in summer holds plays by Shakespeare and other more 20th century playwrights. **Queen Mary's Rose Garden** is a favourite photo setting for overseas married couples, just after the wedding, so don't be surprised if you suddenly see a Malaysian or African bride amongst the blooming roses! The Japanese bridge and lake is also another attractive area near the Park Café. **The Knapp Gallery** in the Inner Circle holds regular contemporary art shows, next to the Baker Street side of the park. You can also reach the park by taking a barge from Little Venice to the zoo. Underground Baker Street.

Richmond Park, Surrey. Richmond Park could well be somewhere deep in the country or the estate of a stately home. Golf, riding, polo and football are all possible here and deer wander about freely across acres of parkland, 2500 acres to be precise. This is an ideal park for long walks in the fresher air, away from polluted London. Richmond the town is an attractive shopping centre, with a quaint village charm around the green where there are antique shops and an excellent theatre. Underground Richmond.

St James's Park, London SW1. This park contains a bird sanctuary and magnificent weeping willows next to an attractive lake. This is the setting for fictional spyland, as many civil servants work near here. It lies next to the Mall (which leads up to Buckingham Palace) and the **ICA (Institute of Contemporary Arts)** is directly opposite it. You can walk through this park from Admiralty Arch, Trafalgar Square, to Victoria. Underground St James's Park or Green Park.

Wimbledon Common, London SW19. This common is also quite countrified. You can walk from Putney or Wimbledon to **Roehampton village**. The latter has a lovely old pub and small cottages. On Wimbledon Common you can golf, ride or run for miles. The Windmill café is a favourite walkers' meeting place. Cannizaro Park and House nearby are also well worth a visit. Underground Wimbledon.

Markets

London markets vary enormously from the world-famous antique market **Portobello Road, Camden Market** for New Age and retro clothes and jewellery, to **Bermondsey** for jewellery and silverware.

Bermondsey and New Caledonian Market, London SE1. This is primarily a dealers' market for antiques and jewellery. Fridays only, starting early. This is the ideal place for buying antique jewellery, and also if you are looking for stolen jewellery from burglaries and have given up hope of ever finding it!
Underground London Bridge.

Berwick Street, Soho, London W.1. Monday-Saturday 8-7. Fruit and vegetables and plenty of **Soho** atmosphere. Cheap material also for sale here. If you are tired of shopping in Oxford Street or Regent Street, wander over to have a look. Soho is now a media and film area. Underground Leicester Square or Piccadilly Circus.

Brick Lane, London E.1. Sundays 7-2. This is the poor relation of Petticoat Lane and therefore more interesting. Worth visiting the extraordinary **Clifton Indian restaurant** with its exotic, bizarre murals of Indian women. It is very cheap to eat here. The market itself is very rock bottom in items for sale, but will show you another side of London — refugee and immigrant London. Underground Whitechapel.

Camden Passage, Islington High Street, London N.1. Wednesdays and Saturdays 9-6. Good selection of antiques and attractive shops in this olde worlde pedestrian precinct. Excellent 20s and 30s clothes shop. Good restaurants and the **Camden Head pub** has a pleasant atmosphere. Underground Angel.

Camden Lock, London NW6. This market is at the top end of the Regents Canal and you can in fact catch a boat to it from Little Venice. Mainly a craft market with retro clothes now as well. It is very fashionable, especially with Europeans, Russians, French and Germans in particular. Saturdays and Sundays 8-6. Good restaurants by the canal and New Age stalls. Underground Chalk Farm or Camden Town.

North End Road, Fulham, London SW6. The **Fulham** area is worth a visit as it is a close-knit community rather like the East end once was. Houses are in neat terraces off the North End Road. The market is friendly and mainly local, with cheap clothes, pots and pans and fruit and vegetables. Fulham Broadway has more upmarket shops and restaurants. Underground Fulham Broadway.

Portobello Road, London W.11. Open all week except Thursday afternoons for fruit and vegetables. Friday and Saturday 7-6 are the main days for antiques and old clothes and the market stretches for miles from W11 to W10. The top end near Notting Hill Gate specializes in expensive antiques but from the Westway bridge up to Golborne Road you can find amazing bargains in furniture and 20s, 30s, 40s and 70s clothes. As a student I used to buy and sell Hungarian blouses and 30s dresses, but the 80s consumer Thatcherite attitude towards designer clothes changed everything. Luckily the retro approach has come back into fashion and Portobello Road is having a field day. Good pubs in the area and two contemporary art galleries **East West** and the **Special Photographers Company**. **"Notting Hill",** the film, was made here with Hugh Grant and Julia Roberts. Underground Ladbroke Grove or Notting Hill Gate and walk down the hill.

Restaurants
Pubs & Bars

The London restaurant scene has changed dramatically in the last five years. London has now become a major international centre for cosmopolitan restaurants with some 12,000 restaurants and 60 different national cuisines. Many new large restaurants opened in the late 90s, such as **Quaglinos, The Atlantic Bar, Mezzo, L'Odéon** and **The Criterion**. What London excels in is small, ethnic restaurants in village areas: atmosphere, friendliness and good service are all-important in restaurants such as **Mon Plaisir** in Covent Garden, **The Khyber** on Westbourne Grove, **Costas** at Notting Hill Gate where there is an open-air courtyard in summer, **Prego** at Richmond and **Jason's** at Little Venice.

The restaurants are listed by area first, then under art eating places, cafés, theatre pubs and at the end of the section, I have categorised some Thai, Turkish, Indian, Japanese and French restaurants.

Soho

This area has changed quite substantially recently and now has trendy, smart shops, cafés, bars, restaurants, but the red-light aspect is still there in the background although it is better known recently as a gay bar centre. Publishers, film production studios and restaurants are neighbours with **Chinatown** across the road in Gerrard Street, where there are Chinese pagoda phone boxes. The Chinese New Year is the most lively time, usually in January or February, when there are processions and celebrations. The restaurants are excellent, especially **Harbour City**. **West Soho**, off Carnaby Street, near Liberty's, has small designer shops and local restaurants, but has become a fashionable area for creative people.

Mash, 19-21 Great Portland Street, London W.1. Telephone 0171 (020-7 from 4/2000) 637 5555.
A very cool place to be at the turn of the millennium. Space Age appearance and run by the fashionable Oliver Peyton. Clientele tend to be very fashion-conscious and aware of all the latest hip news. Asian and western food — crispy duck and wood-fired pizzas for example. Sadie Coles provided the paintings (Sadie Coles HQ gallery).

Rasa Sayang, 10 Frith Street, London W.1. Telephone 0171 (020-7 from 4/2000) 734 8720.
Delicious Indonesian food. Satay, nasi goreng and other dishes. Inexpensive and friendly and ideal for groups too. Open Monday-Saturday 12-3 and 6-11.30. Underground Leicester Square.

Criterion Brasserie, 222 Piccadilly, London W.1. Telephone 0171 (020-7 from 4/2000) 925 0909.
Spectacular interior and ceiling. Good atmosphere. Star-studded clientele. Expensive but beautiful décor and next to the Criterion Theatre for theatregoers. Underground Piccadilly Circus.

Blues Bistro and Bar, 42-43 Dean Street, London W.1. Telephone 0171 (020-7 from 4/2000) 494 1966.
Next door to the Groucho, the media club. Cool air-conditioning in summer. Smart restaurant and bar, but stylish atmosphere. Monday and Tuesday, £10 for dinner for 3 courses.

Kettners, Romilly Street, London W.1. Telephone 0171 (020 7 from 4/2000) 734 6112.
Several bar/restaurant outlets. No reservations taken. Publishing and film and arts people mainly. Reasonable prices.

Soho Soho, 11-13 Frith Street, London W.1. Telephone 0171 (020-7 from 4/2000) 494 3491.
Expensive restaurant upstairs and downstairs the rôtisserie and café bar with open-air eating in the summer months on the pavement. Favourite film and media-world eating place for lunchtime. Mediterranean cooking. Open 8am-2am, Sunday 11-11pm.

Bar Italia, 22 Frith Street, London W.1. Telephone 0171 (020-7 from 4/2000) 437 4520.
Very Soho; good espresso and cappuccino for coffee addicts. Bar atmosphere.

The French House, 49 Dean Street, London W.1. Telephone 0171 (020-7 from 4/2000) 437 2799.
The pub is downstairs, the original French meeting place in London, but now frequented by various heavy drinking journalists and writers. Upstairs the restaurant serves old-fashioned but excellent food with a more English menu.

Mezzo, 100 Wardour Street, London W.1. Telephone 0171 (020-7 from 4/2000) 314 4000.
Murals by Allen Jones the artist (see photo at beginning section of guide). Europe's largest restaurant with international modern cuisine. Sometimes feeds 2500 people a day. Ideal for groups.

Harbour City, 46 Gerrard Street, London W.1. Telephone 0171 (020-7 from 4/2000) 439 7859.
Cantonese food, especially dim sum at lunchtime. One of the best restaurants in Chinatown. Good service. Reasonable prices.

Bloomsbury/Fitzrovia

Traditionally this area is connected with the **Bloomsbury Group** (Virginia Woolf, Duncan Grant, Vanessa Bell), but around Charlotte Street there are many restaurants worth visiting. Windmill Street galleries are nearby.

St Christopher's Place, off Oxford Street, in summer.

Chez Gerard, 8 Charlotte Street, London W.1
Excellent menu with French steak and frites and other French dishes. Now has a more modern interior. Reasonably expensive.

Museum Street Café, 47 Museum Street, London WC1. Telephone 0171 (020-7 from 4/2000) 405 3211.
Near the British Museum. Bring your own wine and no smoking. Closed at weekends and no credit cards. If you still want to visit after that, the food is very southern, with sun-dried tomatoes, fresh fish and delicious puddings.

Wagamama, 4 Strathen Street, London WC1. Telephone 0171 (020-7 from 4/2000) 323 9223.
Noodle bar, healthy food, modern décor. Japanese beers and saké. Very reasonable prices. Branches elsewhere.

West End

This covers other restaurants not in Soho or Bloomsbury /Fitzrovia.

Hard Rock Café, 150 Old Park Lane, London W.1. Telephone 0171 (020-7 from 4/2000) 629 0382.
It's been around for 25 years now, but still serves the best hamburgers and sundaes in London. Very American and attracts tourists. Loud music. Children love it!

Café Fish, 39 Panton Street, London SW1. Telephone 0171 (020-7 from 4/2000) 930 3999.
Near West end theatres and cinemas. Every variation on fish and reasonable prices. The wine bar downstairs is cheaper and just as good.

Café Royal, 68 Regent Street, London W.1. Telephone 0171 (020-7 from 4/2000) 437 9090.
The Brasserie is more accessible price-wise, but don't miss seeing the Grill Room with its exotic interior, paintings and mirrors. Oscar Wilde used to dine here with friends, also Whistler, Anna Pavlova, Garibaldi and others. I was taken here once after the theatre and remember being disconcerted by the fact that your reflection could be seen about 7 times while you ate! Now run by Marco Pierre White the famous restaurateur.

Zen Central, 20-22 Queen Street, London W.1. Telephone 0171 (020-7 from 4/2000) 629 8103.
Unusual décor. Designed by Rick Mather. Crisp modern Chinese food matches the crisp glamorous interior. More expensive than Chinatown but more pzazz.

L'Odéon, 65 Regent Street, London W.1. Telephone 0171 (020-7 from 4/000) 287 1400.
Seating for 200. Run by Bruno Loubet. Mixture ot cuisines and pricier than smaller restaurants, but stylish and central. Near Piccadilly Circus.

Covent Garden

This area has become a stylish fashion area with remnants of the specialist shops that once used to dominate the backstreets. The market area is very touristy, but still operates during the week selling old clothes, jewellery and craft and at weekends more touristy junk. It still has its charm as an area, especially up the quaint backstreets. The restaurants have improved enormously.

Bertorelli's, 44 A Floral Street, London WC2. Telephone 01717 (020-7 from 4/2000) 836 3969.
Expensive restaurant upstairs and a terrific one downstairs, which usually has a lively clientele in the evening. I took two Australian friends, geologists, there and they loved it. They thought Covent Garden, and the restaurant, were both full of pzazz and that was in October, not even in summer.

Mon Plaisir, 21 Monmouth Street, London WC2. Telephone 0171 (020-7 from 4/2000) 836 7243.
One of London's most charming French restaurants. French atmosphere, French waiters and relaxing village ambiance. Good food as well. Reservations essential for dinner.

Porters, Henrietta Street, London WC2. Telephone 0171 (020-7 from 4/2000) 836 6466.
Home-made English game, chicken and vegetable pies. Syllabub and English puddings. Spacious. Ideal family or group eating place. Recently refurbished and expanded.

The Opera Terrace (Chez Gerard), The Piazza, The Market, London WC2. Telephone 0171 (020-7 from 4/2000) 379 0666.
Wonderful setting, high up in the market, with open-air seating, looking down on the cobbled streets. £15 for 3 courses. Open 12-3 and 5.30-11.30, Sundays -10.30pm. Bar with snacks also during the day. Chez Gerard French menu but the setting is one of the best open-air venues in London.

Belgo Centraal, 50 Earlham Street, London WC2. Telephone 0171 (020-7 from 4/2000) 813 2233.
Moules (mussels) frites and Belgian beers. Very cheap. Designed by Ron Arad. 400 seats. Various special offers.

Rules, 35 Maiden Lane, London WC2. Telephone 0171 (020-7 from 4/2000) 836 5314.

This restaurant was 200 years old in1998 and has a history of serving actors, lawyers and writers. Traditional English food but served to perfection. Pre-theatre meals are good value, otherwise more expensive. It has a real sense of history.

The India Club, 143 The Strand, London WC 2. Telephone 0171 (020-7 from 4/2000) 836 0650.

This unpretentious Indian restaurant above a hotel (£29 a double room for interest) serves basic, good Indian food. Drinks can be bought downstairs. Ideal for a cheap night out, but definitely not a glamorous one! A group of us used to eat here after The Australian Film Society at Australia House (£5 a year-best film price in London).

Christopher's Café, 18 Wellington Street, London WC2. Telephone 0171 (020-7 from 4/2000) 240 4222.

Cartoons of Christopher Gilmour's family (the owner) by Andrea Cunningham. American-style cuisine. More expensive restaurant upstairs.

Notting Hill Gate

This lively area falls into two; up the hill near the tube and Holland Park and down the hill near Portobello Road market, where there are many restaurants on Kensington Park Road, near East West gallery and the Special Photographers Company. This area is a mixture of poorer people, often Portuguese and Spanish up near Golborne Road and more trendy "trustafarians" (wealthy trust fund people in their 20s and 30s) nearer the middle of the market. The mixture is heady, with small local Spanish delicatessens and trendy media people, actors and film stars at the Kensington Park Road bars. The film **"Notting Hill"** ('99) was made here with Julia Roberts and Hugh Grant. Once an art area, there are now only 3 contemporary galleries, whereas in the late 80s there were some 15. Up the hill the restaurants are more demure, but Uxbridge Street and surrounds are still charming.

Top of the hill (near Notting Hill Gate station)

The Pharmacy restaurant and bar, 150 Notting Hill Gate, London W.11. Telephone 01717 (020-7 from 4/2000) 221 2442.

So much has been written about this restaurant, partly due to all the fuss about the name. Complaints from the Pharmacy Society meant name changes weekly, such as Army Chap and Achy Ramp! Damien Hirst, the fashionable artist, is part owner which has attracted a star-studded crowd including famous fashion designers visiting London, rock celebrities, artists and locals who just wanted to see the décor — empty pill packets and metal limbs. Not for quiet suburban couples! Worth visiting once!

Kensington Place, 205 Kensington Church Street, London W.8. Telephone 0171 (020-7 from 4/2000) 727 3184.
Mural of a table by a lily pond by Mark Wickham on the far wall. Modern brasserie; popular with successful BBC journalists, actors, actresses, film producers and wealthy locals. Excellent food. Reasonably expensive.

Novelli's, 122 Palace Gardens Terrace, London W.8. Telephone 0171 (020-7 from 4/2000) 229 4024. In summer it has a pretty open-air courtyard for several tables. Inside it serves excellent food. Owned by Jean-Christophe Novelli, the famous French chef and restaurateur.

Off shore, 148 Holland Park Avenue, London W.11. Telephone 01717 (020-7 from 4/2000) 221 6090.
This new Mauritian seafood restaurant has become very popular with a set-price two course £14 lunch and evening £33 dégustation menu which includes lobster. Recommended.

Costas, 14 Hillgate Street, London W.8. Telephone 0171 (020-7 from 4/2000) 229 3794.
This restaurants is run by a friendly Greek-Cypriot family. The interior is not spectacular, but the welcome is, and the prices are very reasonable. Try the Cyprus wine for a change from Greek wine. The open-air courtyard at the back is usually heavily-booked in summer on good days, so reservations essential for open-air eating. Usual meze, moussaka, souvlakia and Greek dishes.

Geales, 2 Farmer Street, London W.8. Telephone 0171 (020-7 from 4/2000) 727 7979.
Old-fashioned, unpretentious fish restaurant. An ideal family eating place and very reasonable prices.

Down the hill (near Portobello Road market)

Dakota, 127 Ledbury Road, London W.11. Telephone 0171 (020-7 from 4/2000) 792 9191.
Southwestern American food in a fashionable setting. Ledbury Road has several small stylish shops for fashion and accessories. Madonna has eaten here and other passing-through celebrities.

192, 192 Kensington Park Road, London W.11. Telephone 0171 (020-7 from 4/2000) 229 0482.
Fashionable small restaurant, favoured by the trendy locals, actors, comedians, rock stars and media people who live in the area.

The Market Bar, 240 Portobello Road, London W.11. Telephone 0171 (020-7 from 4/2000) 229 6472.
Bohemian, local bar with lively atmosphere. The upstairs restaurant has Thai food in an amazing setting with Indian arches and screens. The pub/bar downstairs has a mixture of local media types and some strange locals as well as passing tourists on Saturdays.

Osteria Basilico, 29 Kensington Park Road, London W.11. Telephone 0171 (020-7 from 4/2000) 727 9322.
Recommended by local art dealers. Attractive restaurant with atmosphere, where Monsieur Thompson's used to be.

Café Med, 184 Kensington Park Road, London W.11. Telephone 0171 (020-7 from 4/2000) 221 1150,
Open-air tables in summer. Fashionable and good atmosphere. Bar and restaurant.

Café Rouge, 31 Kensington Park Road, London W.11. Telephone 0171 (020-7 from 4/2000) 221 4449.
There are branches of this Café all over London. Fashionable locals and media people eat and drink here.

Further down the hill

Mas Café, 6/8 All Saints Road, London W.10. Telephone 0171 (020-7 from 4/2000) 243 0969.
Now that All Saint's Road is fashionable, this is a café/bar for the locals. The road used to be a drug-dealing area and could still be, so be careful late at night.

Woz, 46 Golborne Road, London W.10. Telephone 0181 (020-8 from 4/2000) 968 2200
Chic and friendly. Set up by Antony Worrall-Thompson as a back-to-basics small local restaurant.

Westbourne Grove/Bayswater

Westbourne Grove is full of Indian, Malaysian and Chinese restaurants. Take your pick but I'd recommend **The Khyber** and **Kalamaras.**

Palio, 175 Westbourne Grove, London W.2. Telephone 0171 (020-7 from 4/2000) 221 6624.
Mediterranean restaurant with live jazz on Sundays and brunch.

The Khyber, 56 Westbourne Grove, London W.2. Telephone 0171 (020-7 from 4/2000) 727 4383.
Charming, friendly staff and very good Indian food. More relaxing than Khan's Indian restaurant nearby.

Khan's, 13/15 Westbourne Grove, London W.2. Telephone 0171 (020-7 from 4/2000) 727 5420.
Popular but very poor service, as it's so busy.

Kalamaras, 66 Inverness Mews, London W.2. Telephone 0171 (020-7 from 4/2000) 727 5082.
I hadn't been here for years, but returned recently with friends. It was still as warm and friendly as ever. Cheap Greek restaurant, in a back mews off Queensway.

The Cow, 89 Westbourne Park Road, London W.2. Telephone 0171 (020-7 from 4/2000) 221 0021.
Back to "trustafarian" territory. Run by Tom Conran, Terence's younger son. Trendy but lively nevertheless. Ideal if you are 20-28 and want to meet other temporary residents, i.e. not the real locals.

Chelsea

Chelsea was traditionally an art area in London in the 19th century. Nowadays it is a fashionable area for clothes shops and the Kings Road. The backstreets have some beautiful squares, with elegant houses and pretty gardens. In summer the window boxes are lush with richly-coloured flowers outside white Georgian houses. The **Chelsea Arts Club** is in Old Church Street, but only open to members. The restaurants vary enormously, but Kings Road, especially at the World's End part, has some excellent French and Italian bistros. **Chelsea Harbour** is really outside the traditional Chelsea but is still worth a visit, for attractive open-air settings by the River Thames. They also usually have open-air sculpture shows at Chelsea Harbour in the summer.

Café Milan, 312-314 Kings Road, London SW3. Telephone 01717 (020-7 from 4/2000) 351 0101.
This stylish new café, shop and restaurant opened in early '99. A contemporary Milanese restaurant with wood-burning oven, so delicious Italian modern food and the interior is unusual, with alcoves displaying modern glass. Good atmosphere and friendly staff.

Bluebird Café, Kings Road, Chelsea.

Charco's, 1 Bray Place, London SW3. Telephone 0171 (020-7 from 4/2000) 584 0765
A very Chelsea place, full of wealthy Chelsea hooray Henrys and Henriettas, or their current equivalent. Bar/restaurant.

Blushes, 52 Kings Road, London SW3. Telephone 0171 (020-7 from 4/2000) 584 2138.
Good food and atmosphere. Open lunchtime and in the evenings. Open-air seating in summer.

Daphne's, 112 Draycott Avenue, London SW3. Telephone 0171 (020-7 from 4/2000) 584 4257.
A very glamorous and fashionable restaurant, where you are likely to see media stars, successful actresses and wealthy locals. Ideal for star-spotting, if you can afford the bill!

Bucci, 386 Kings Road, London SW3. Telephone 0171 (020-7 from 4/2000) 351 9997.
I went here with my cousin and her 10-year-old son and they made a real fuss of him. The food was also delicious. Italian modern cuisine. Friendly staff.

Thierry's, 342 Kings Road, London SW3. Telephone 0171 (020-7 from 4/2000) 352 3365.
French cuisine, French owner and good local atmosphere.

The Brasserie, 272 Brompton Road, London SW3. Telephone 0171(020-7 from 4/2000) 584 1668.
Opposite the beautiful Michelin building at South Kensington. Typical French brasserie in this French area.

Bibendum, 81 Fulham Road, London SW3. Telephone 0171 (020-7 from 4/2000) 581 5817.
Magnificent Michelin building interior. The restaurant is owned by Terence Conran. Stylish, popular with publishing editors (Hamlyn/Octopus offices upstairs) actors, media people. Worth visiting even just once to see the stained-glass windows. Reservations essential. Expensive.

Ziani, 45 Radnor Walk, London SW3. Telephone 0171 (020-7 from 4/2000) 351 5297.
A small, smart Italian restaurant in a pretty Chelsea sidestreet. Friends of mine used to live above the restaurant, until their marriage broke up. It wasn't Ziani's cooking to blame but the smells used to be enticing. Reasonable prices for the area.

Hampstead

Hampstead village lies adjacent to Hampstead Heath, where actors and actresses such as Emma Thompson, Jeremy Irons and Tom Conti live. DH Lawrence the writer once lived here too and Dickens visited Jack Straw's Castle pub, often on horseback. Other notable pubs are **The Flask, Freemason's Arms** and **The Spaniard's Inn**. Louis' tearoom is also worth a visit. See Hidden Backstreets of Village London for further Hampstead corners to visit.

Dôme, 38-39 Hampstead High Street, London NW3. Telephone 0171 (020-7 from 4/2000) 431 3052.
French café/brasserie atmosphere. Designed by Lubin and Myers. Young literati and local 20s and 30s meeting place. Newspapers to read while waiting for friends.

Kenwood House café.

Café Rouge, 19 Hampstead High Street, London NW3. Telephone 0171 (020-7 from 4/2000) 433 3404.
One of a chain of restaurants, but still a relaxed café atmosphere.

Zen, 83-84 Hampstead High, Street London NW3. Telephone 0171 (020-7 from 4/2000) 794 7863.
Healthy Chinese food in a stylish setting. Architect Rick Mather who also designed Zen in central London. Floor-to-ceiling windows, ideal for Hampstead people-watching!

La Cage Imaginaire, Flask Walk, London NW3.
In a quiet cul-de-sac opposite Duncan Miller Fine Art gallery. French restaurant.

Hoxton

Hoxton has become a fashionable, lively area in recent years. If you do not already know it, it covers the area between Old Street, Curtain Road and Kingsland Road in north London, but bordering on east London. **The Blue Note** jazz club is a magnet for people from all over London and is part gallery, part club and part bar and meeting place. The **Lux Arts Centre** opens next to the club with a cinema, café and studios for artists, with multi-media facilities. Hoxton Square is right at the heart of this hip area. Local meeting places include the following bars, restaurants and pubs. There's even a Circus skills training centre here, for a change of lifestyle!?

Hoxton Square Bar and Kitchen, 2-4 Hoxton Square, London N.1. Telephone 01717 (020-7 from 4/2000) 613 0709.
Stylish bar atmosphere. Art for sale on the walls.

Shoreditch Electricity Showrooms, 39A Hoxton Square. See Art eating places for details. Unusual interior.

Blue Note, 1 Hoxton Square, London N.1. Telephone 0171 (020-7 from 4/2000) 729 8440.
Art exhibitions here, also jazz venue and bar.

Sole, 7 Chapel Place, London N.1. Telephone 01717 (020-7 from 4/2000) 739 4002.
Lebanese restaurant.

Canteloupe, 35-42 Charlotte Road, London EC2. Telephone 01717 (020-7 from 4/2000) 613 4411.
Bar and restaurant.

Gabriel's Wharf, South Bank SE1.

Theatre Pubs

The Gate Theatre, Pembridge Road, London W.11. Telephone 0171 (020-7 from 4/2000) 229 0706.
Above the Prince Albert pub, which has hysterically funny notices in the window about all the people that it won't allow in! Membership and reasonable entrance fees to the Gate theatre and some excellent new plays.

Bush Theatre, Shepherds Bush Green, London W.12. Telephone 0171 (020-7 from 4/2000) 743 5030.
Well-worth a visit. Good selection of new plays by travelling companies.

Kings Head, 115 Upper Street, London N.1. Telephone 0171 226 1916.
Nice pub atmosphere. The Theatre offers a variety of interesting plays. You can have a meal in the theatre itself before the play starts. Also lunchtime plays.

The Orange Tree, 45 Kew Road, Richmond. Telephone 0181 (020-8 from 4/2000) 940 3633.
Beautiful pub with ornate mirrors. Tiny stage but good plays. Underground to Richmond.

Time Out gives up-to-date details of more theatre pubs and current plays. **Leicester Square booth** sells tickets for most West end performances that day. Queue at 12-2 for matineé performances that day or 2.30-6.30 for evening performances. Do not confuse the one near the tube with the real one which is in the square!

260

Some other interesting London Pubs

The Dove, 19 Upper Mall, Hammersmith.
16th-century pub overlooking the Thames.

Bulls Head, Strand on the Green, Chiswick.
Waterfront pub in a picturesque area near Kew Gardens.

Prospect of Whitby, 57 Wapping Wall, London E.1. 020-7481 1095.
660 year-old pub in an area that many artists and designers now live in. Overlooks the Thames.

Nell Gwynne Tavern, 2 Bull Inn Court, London WC2. 020-7 240 5579.
Up a tiny alleyway near the Adelphi Theatre on the Strand. Dates from 1623. Voted one of London's top 10 pubs.

Jack Straw's Castle pub, Hampstead Heath.

Hollands, Exmouth Street, London E.1.

Princess Louise, 208 High Holborn, London WC1. Telephone 0171 405 8816.
Central London pub. Many publishing people go there.

Anglesea Arms, 16 Selwood Terrace, London SW7.
Open-air setting in summer, next to attractive leafy streets with wisteria.

The Warwick Castle, Warwick Place, London W.9.
Little Venice pub, next to the canal, in a sidestreet. Peaceful setting.

Art Eating Places

The following restaurants/bars/cafés are either in or near museums or galleries in central London, or places where art-world people meet.

Delfina Studio Café, 50 Bermondsey Street, London SE1. Telephone 0171 (020-7 from 4/2000) 357 0244.
Open Monday-Friday 10-3pm - lunch only. Artist-run studios next door, but also open to the visitors to the gallery. Excellent lunch fare such as blinis or char-grilled dishes.

Bradley's Spanish Bar, 42-44 Hanway Street, London W.1. Telephone 0171 (020-7 from 4/2000) 636 0359.
Hilariously unfashionable bar, with attempts at a Spanish atmosphere, exotic food and European beer. Art historians, curators and art critics often come here to this tiny bar, near Tottenham Court Road.

Poetry Café, 22 Betterton Street, London WC2. Telephone 0171 (020-7 from 4/2000) 240 5081.
An alternative arts café and restaurant with char-grilled fish, crunchy vegetables and tasty cakes, below the Poetry Society in Covent Garden. Art for sale on the walls and an interesting mix of people.

Shoreditch Electricity Showrooms, 39A Hoxton Square, London N.1. Telephone 01717 (020-7 from 4/2000) 739 6934.
Bars on the ground floor and basement and uncomfortable seating with white melamine tables. It is extraordinarily popular with artists, style victims and trendy 20s and 30s. Hoxton is a buzzy area now with bars, jazz club, galleries and design shops.

Archduke Wine bar, Concert Hall approach, London SE1.Telephone 0171 (020-7 from 4/2000) 928 9370.
Successful wine bar with restaurant. Open-air seating at the courtyard in the back. Near the Hayward Gallery and South Bank Centre.

Museum Street Café, 47 Museum Street, London WC1. Telephone 0171 (020-7 from 4/2000) 405 3211.
Near the British Museum. Home-made food. You have to bring your own wine.

The Pharmacy restaurant and bar, 50 Notting Hill Gate, London W.11. Telephone 0171 (020-7 from 4/2000) 221 2442. Part-owned by Damien Hirst the fashionable artist. The inside has pill packets, metal limbs and is furnished in a cool (in every way) manner. If you are into fashionable young, hip bars and restaurants, then this is your place. Make sure you wear black and the season's latest fashionable black. You might meet Miuccia Prada the Italian designer, Madonna or some artists, locals or rock celebrities. Always heavily booked and worth a visit once. Hilarious history of fight over the name due to complaints. Achy ramp and Army Chap are now at peace!

Tate café, Millbank.

Sotheby's: The Café, 34 New Bond Street, London W.1. Telephone 0171 (020-7 from 4/2000) 408 5077.
Expensive, but fascinating to see the customers who are mainly Sotheby's clients and local Bond Street art world.

The Globe Theatre restaurant, Shakespeare's Globe, New Globe Walk, Bankside, London SE1. Telephone 0171 (020-7 from 4/2000) 928 9444.
Next to the Tate Bankside, new Modern Art Gallery. Recommended. Sunday jazz brunches at the café. Popular with theatregoers and will be popular with Tate visitors from 2000.

Barbican Waterside Café, Barbican Arts Centre, Silk St, London EC1. Surprisingly good food here as well as cappuccino and cake fare. Open-air eating by the lake in summer.

St John, 26 St John St, London EC1. Telephone 01717 (020-7 from 4/2000) 251 0848.
An elegant restaurant in a converted smokehouse. British food and its own bakery. Near the Barbican Arts Centre.

National Gallery, Trafalgar Square, London SW1.
In the Sainsbury wing, the murals are by artist Paula Rego. Stylish restaurant with brasserie food and good cappuccinos. In the main part of the museum the Prêt a Manger café is in the basement.

Royal Academy restaurant, Burlington House, Piccadilly London W.1. Telephone 0171 (020-7 from 4/2000) 439 7438.
Excellent daily creations both hot and cold, in this basement self-service restaurant.

Most artists tend to meet at pubs in areas such as Hoxton, Spitalfields or at other people's houses in the East end, but the Alternative Art Spaces are also good meeting places (see section). **Private views** in London tend to be from 6-8 most evenings. It really depends on the gallery, as to whether you are likely to meet new faces and go on to pubs/bars or restaurants. The Windmill Street and Cork Street parties are annual events in September and summer respectively.

Other interesting restaurants

Afghan
Caravanserai, 50 Paddington Street, London W.1. Telephone 0171 (020-7 from 4/2000) 935 1208/224 0954.
Afghan restaurant with tandoori dishes. Recommended.

French
Maison Novelli, 29-30 Clerkenwell Green, London EC1. Telephone 01717 (020-7 from 4/2000) 251 6606.
Jean-Christophe Novelli owns several restaurants in London, but this is the best. Good on fish dishes.

L'Escargot, 48 Greek Street, London W.1. Telephone 01717 (020-7 from 4/2000) 437 2679.
Once a famous London restaurant, but now under new ownership a traditional French restaurant. More expensive on the first floor.

Mon Plaisir, 21 Monmouth Street, London WC2. Telephone 01717 (020-7 from 4/2000) 836 7243.
For me the best French restaurant, with a relaxed atmosphere and no trendy customers in sight.

Thai
Tawana, 3 Westbourne Grove, London W.2. Telephone 0171 (020-7 from 4/2000) 229 3785.

Churchill Arms, 119 Kensington Church Street, London W.8. Telephone 0171 (020 7 from 4/2000) 727 4242.
At the back of the Churchill Arms pub there is an excellent Thai food restaurant. It is very unpretentious and very good. It is also popular with the locals, so go early.

Thai Gardens, 249 Globe Road, London E.2. Telephone 0181 (020-8 from 4/2000) 981 5748.

Bangkok Restaurant, 9 Bute Street, London SW7. Telephone 0171 (020-7 from 4/2000)584 8529.

Iranian
Alounak 2, 44 Westbourne Grove, London W.2. Telephone 0171 (020-7 from 4/2000) 229 4158.
Similar menu to the other Alounak. Fountain in the middle of the room and more gracious surroundings than the other one though.

Javad's Restaurant, 45 Cricklewood Broadway, London NW2. Telephone 0181 (020-8 from 4/2000) 452 9226.
Vegetarian menu.

Open-air

Costas, (See Notting Hill Gate)

Opera Roof Terrace (Chez Gerard), (See Covent Garden)

Novelli's, (See Notting Hill Gate)

Café Pasta, Wimbledon Village London SW19

Café Rouge and Café Med, Portobello Road area, Kensington Park Road

Soho Soho, (See Soho)

Maison Blanc patisserie, Holland Park..

Cafés

A selection of some of London's cafés. The following range from typical English to delicious French patisserie or Eastern European. **Prêt a Manger**, **Starbucks** and the **Seattle Coffee Company** have all revolutionised the café scene in London and brought far more variations than there ever used to be.

W.1
(Central London near Oxford and Regent Street, also in Soho)

Patisserie Valerie, 44 Old Compton Street, London W.1. Telephone 0171 (020-7 from 4/2000) 437 3466.
Deliciously freshly-made patisserie, croissants, strawberry tarts, with tea or coffee. This is one of London's best-known continental patisseries. The décor is very plain, but the atmosphere and people very Soho. Open Monday-Saturday 8.30-7. Underground Leicester Square. Also a branch now at Knightsbridge on Old Brompton Road and Regent Street.

Maison Sagne, 105 Marylebone High Street, London W.1. Telephone 0171 (020-7 from 4/2000) 935 6240.
Swiss patisserie and bakery serving a wide range of freshly-baked cakes. Tea and coffee. Monday-Friday 2.30-4.45. Underground Bond Street/Baker Street.

Maison Bertaux, 28 Greek Street, London W.1. Telephone 0171 (020-7 from 4/2000) 437 6007.
French patisserie with an amazing variety of cakes. Open Tuesday-Saturday 9-6. Underground Leicester Square.

Fortnum and Mason, Piccadilly, London W.1.
This store has the most amazing displays of English fresh and preserved food in the most beautiful tins and wrapping. Variety of restaurants and English tea and cakes downstairs. Expensive but wonderful setting. Don't miss the chiming clock outside the front door, as it is spectacular.

The Ritz, Piccadilly, London W.1. Telephone 0171 (020-7 from 4/2000) 493 8181.
Scene of the famous Palm Court Orchestra. Afternoon tea 3.30-5.30. Booking essential as it is apparently so popular now! Expensive, but what a setting!

W.2

Maison Bouquillon, 45 Moscow Road, London W.2.
Croissants, brioches, petits pains chocolats and other delights.
Open seven days a week 9-11.30pm. Underground Bayswater.

Pierre Péchon, 127 Queensway, London W.2. Telephone 0171
(020-7 from 4/2000) 229 0746. Also a bakery branch at
Pembridge Villas nearby. Family-run cake shop with original
recipes for their cakes. Open seven days a week 9-5.
Underground Bayswater.

W.8

Muffin Man, 12 Wrights Lane, London W.8. Telephone 0171
(020-7 from 4/2000) 937 6652.
Devon cream teas, delicious freshly-baked cakes and an English
country town atmosphere (well, a bit more Eastern European
due to new ownership) to match, right in the heart of
Kensington, just off the high street. Open 8.45-5.45, Monday-
Saturday. Underground High Street Kensington.

W.11

Cullens Patisserie, 108 Holland Park Avenue, London W.11.
Telephone 0171 (020-7 from 4/2000) 221 3598.
A relaxed and friendly Holland Park patisserie, open daily including Sundays. Reasonable prices for lunch, coffee or afternoon
tea. Near Holland Park and the beautiful Japanese Gardens,
both worth a visit.

Maison Blanc, 102 Holland Park Avenue, London W11.
Telephone 0171 (020-7 from 4/2000) 221 2494.
No seating area here, but the window displays are true to French
style. They also operate a catering service for weddings, parties
and picnics.

NW3

Louis' tearoom, 32 Heath Street, London NW3. Telephone
0171 (020-7 from 4/2000) 435 9908.
Visit this patisserie and tearoom after a walk on Hampstead
Heath. Hungarian patisserie with freshly-baked cakes and fresh
tea, no tea bags! Open seven days a week, 9.30-6.
Underground Hampstead.

Richmond and Kew

Newens Maids of Honour, Kew. Telephone 0181 (020-8 from 4/2000) 940 2752.
Next to Kew Gardens, but sadly not open on Sunday. Perhaps the most English tea place in London. Dates back to Henry VIII, with original recipes. Waitresses are dressed in old-fashioned country-girl dresses. Good atmosphere and many English families come here after a walk in Kew Gardens.

Wimbledon

Cannizaro House, Wimbledon Common West side. Telephone 0181 (020-8 from 4/2000) 879 1464.
This wonderful old Georgian house has beautiful grounds with a lake and gardens, also an aviary. Wimbledon art school sometimes shows sculpture here. Afternoon tea is expensive but what a setting in spring or summer! They also have live jazz and theatre in the gardens In summer.

Music Places

Classical

English National Opera, London Coliseum, St Martin's Lane, London WC2. Telephone 0171 (020-7 from 4/2000) 836 3161/240 5258.

South Bank Arts Centre-Royal Festival Hall, Queen Elizabeth Hall, Purcell Room. The South Bank houses the National Theatre, the National Film Theatre and the Hayward Gallery. The three main concert halls mentioned above, offer a variety of classical music, ranging from quartets to full-scale orchestral concerts.

Royal Albert Hall, London SW7.
Home of the annual Proms (promenade concerts) from July-September. Also other events and rock concerts.

Wigmore Hall, 36 Wigmore Street, London W.1. Telephone 0171 (020-7 from 4/2000) 935 2141. Where Jacqueline du Pré famously played her last concert.

Royal Opera House, Covent Garden.
Box office in Floral Street. Opera and ballet. Tickets are expensive but cheaper if bought on the day of the performance.

Barbican Hall, Barbican Arts Centre, Silk Street, London EC2. Telephone 0171 (020-7 from 4/2000) 628 8795 for reservations. Variety of concerts in this beautifully-designed hall.

Jazz

Jazz Café, 5 Parkway Camden Town, London NW1. 020-7344 0044. Stylish venue in trendy Camden Town. Also has occasional art shows by contemporary artists.

Pizza on the Park, 11 Knightsbridge, London SW3. 020-7235 5273. This is a stylish, but more conventional and mainstream venue.

Ronnie Scotts, Frith Street, London W.1. 020-7439 0747. Right in the heart of Soho. London's main jazz club. Expensive but worth a visit.

The 100 Club, Oxford Street, London W.1. Live jazz.

The Vortex, 139-141 Stoke Newington Church St, London N16. 020-7254 6516. British jazz a speciality. See Time Out for other jazz venues in London.

Rock

The Britpop explosion and beyond has made London a centre again for rock music internationally. There are now so many venues that it would be best to buy **Time Out magazine** weekly to check the places. Here are a few.

The Ministry of Sound, 103 Gaunt Street, London SE1. 020-7378 6528. £15 entrance fee, but the club for most people.

The Blue Note, 1 Hoxton Square, London N.1. 020-7729 8440. Hoxton is a lively area with many restaurants, galleries and bars.

The Rock Garden, 6-7 The Piazza, Covent Garden, London WC2. Telephone 020-7836 4052. Bar and live rock music. Groups change each night.

Subterania, 12 Acklam Road Ladbroke Grove, London W.10. Telephone 020-8960 4590.
Run by Vince Power who seems to own half of London's clubs. Like the Ministry of Sound,a must.

Homeless W10, the other side of London.

Sport

A variety of sports facilities feature below; tennis, swimming, football, cycling, horse-riding, fishing and boating. See under Parks for specific facilities in each London park. Boating in Battersea and Hyde Park for example.

Cricket

Visit Lords Cricket Grounds and the Oval in South London to see first class cricket.

Tennis

You can only play for an hour at a time at most London parks. Parks are listed in the telephone directory. The Lawn tennis Association, Barons Court, London W.14., will give a list of tennis clubs in London if you send an sae. Wimbledon is the big event in tennis at the end of June and beginning of July annually.

Football

The season runs from August until April. Some London teams are Chelsea, QPR, West Ham United and Tottenham. Football Association, Lancaster Gate, London W.2. for further details.

Rugby

Rugby Football Union, Twickenham for all information about rugby. There is also a Rugby museum at Twickenham now.

Skating

Queens, 17 Queensway, London W.2. Open daytime and evenings. Prices vary according to the time you visit. **Broadgate Centre**, has an open-air skating rink, next to Liverpool Street station, in winter.

Swimming

Indoor public pools are usully approximately £2 entry fee. Central London pools at Marshall Street, West Soho, Porchester Baths W.2., Oasis, Endell St Covent Garden, Seymour Place W.1. Open-air pools at Hampstead (three), Richmond 020-8940 0561, Serpentine, Hyde Park, Victoria Park, Brockwell Lido 020-7 274 3088, Finchley Lido 020-8343 9830, Oasis, Covent Garden WC2 020-7831 1804, Gospel Oak NW5 020-7485 3873, Tooting Bec Lido 020-8871 7198.

Sports Centres

YMCA, Great Russell Street, London WC1. Telephone 0171 (020-7 from 4/2000) 637 8131.
Squash, swimming, dancing, mountaineering, badminton, keep-fit. Excellent sports shop here.

Crystal Palace, National Recreation Centre, Norwood, London SE19. Telephone 0181 (020-8 from 4/2000) 778 0131.
One of the best sports centres in London. British Rail from Victoria.

Swiss Cottage Centre, Adelaide Road, London NW3. Telephone 0171 (020-7 from 4/2000) 278 4444.
Squash, swimming, badminton.

Sobell Centre, Hornsey Road, London N.7. Telephone 0181 (020-8 from 4/2000) 607 1632.
Squash, badminton, mountaineering.

Health Clubs

Ring each club to find out about classes and facilities. Some local swimming pools do provide gym, solarium and other facilities for as little as £2. Health clubs are rather elitist and local sports centres often provide the same facilities. Health clubs are, however, usually free of children whereas sports centres thrive on them — take your pick! These are just a selection.

The Sanctuary, 11-14 Floral Street, London WC2. Telephone 0171 (020-7 from 4/2000) 240 2744. Magnificent swimming pool and very relaxing club. You can visit just for the day, but it's not cheap!

Dance Works, 16 Balderton Street, London W.1. Telephone 0171 (020-7 from 4/2000) 629 6183.
Ideal for dance fanatics.

The Hogarth Club, 1A Airedale Avenue, London W.4. Telephone 0171 (020-7 from 4/2000) 995 4600.
Smart club in Chiswick with gym and other facilities.

Holmes Place, 188 Fulham Road, London SW10. Telephone 0171 (020-7 from 4/2000) 352 9452.
Swimming pool, gym, classes and steam room.

Holmes Place at the Barbican, Barbican, London EC2. Telephone 0171 (020-7 from 4/2000) 374 0091.
Largest health club in Europe. Pool, 3 gyms, circuit training, jacuzzi, steam and sauna, classes and crêche for children. Holmes Place now has branches at 23 venues throughout London and the South East. www.holmesplace.co.uk website for details and numbers.

Reclining figure, Henry Moore, Kenwood House estate.

Heather Waddell

Heather Waddell was born and brought up in Scotland. She has written for the following papers and magazines; The Independent, Independent on Sunday, The Times, The Glasgow Herald, Vie des Arts (London correspondent 1979-89), The European (Arts Events editor '90-'91), Chic magazine (Visual arts editor '94-'98), Artline, The Artist, Artists Newsletter, Artnews USA and many others. Her books include this guide, The Artist's Directory, Henri Goetz: 50 years of Painting and she has contributed to L'Ecosse; lumière, granit et vent (1988) and Londres ('97 & 2000), Editions Autrement, Paris; MacMillan's Encyclopaedia of London and the Blue Guide to Spain, Australian Arts Guide and the Glasgow Arts Guide. In 1981 she set up Art Guide Publications, publishing art guides to Paris, New York, Amsterdam, Berlin, Madrid, Glasgow, Australia, Great Britain and London, which was the first guide.

She has five art world photo-portraits in the National Portrait Gallery 20th-century Archives and Camera Press sells her photos. In 2000, her photos of The London Art World '79-'99 will be shown in an exhibition and a book.

1. Coronet cinema
   Gate cinema
   Costas Greek restaurant (open air)
   Italian restaurants
2. Geales fish restaurant
3. Kensington Place restaurant
4. Calzone Pizzas
5. Sun in Splandour pub.
7. Wine bar
8 Paul Smith store
11. Special Photographers Company
   Café Rouge, Caffè Med
12. Blenheim Crescent
   Travel Bookshop
13. Blenheim Gellery
   East West Gallery
14. Books for Cooks
17. Portobello Green craft/jewellery/design
23. Police Station
24. Julies restaurant and wine bar
25. Holland wine bar
27. Themes and Variations
28. Lalbag Indian restaurant
29. Antique Galleries and Led bury Rd fashionshops
30. Todd Gallery
   England and Company, Needham Rd.
31. Khyber restaurant
33. Khans Indian restaurant
34. Le Montmartre French restaurant
35. Pharmacy restaurant-bar
36. All Bar one

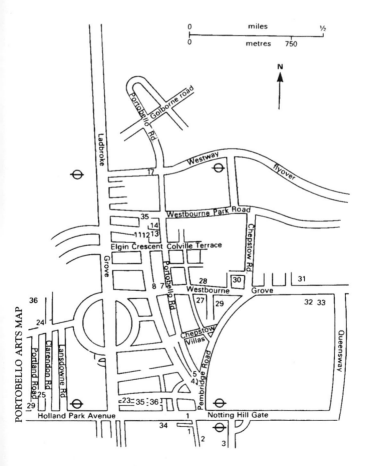

PORTOBELLO ARTS MAP

0 ——— miles ——— ½

0 ——— metres ——— 750

N

276

CITY AND EAST LONDON ARTS MAP

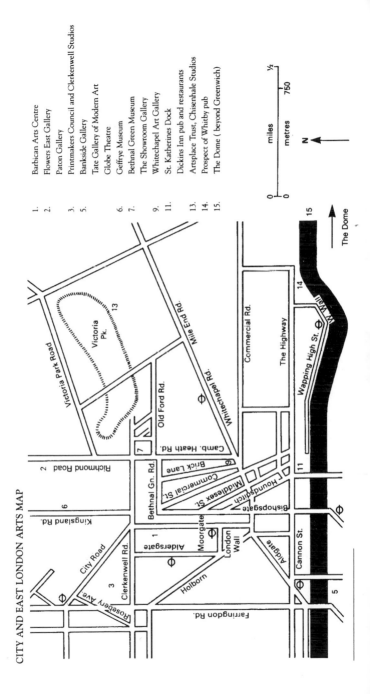

1. Barbican Arts Centre
2. Flowers East Gallery
   Paton Gallery
3. Printmakers Council and Clerkenwell Studios
5. Bankside Gallery
   Tate Gallery of Modern Art
6. Globe Theatre
   Geffrye Museum
7. Bethnal Green Museum
9. The Showroom Gallery
   Whitechapel Art Gallery
11. St. Katherines Dock
13. Dickins Inn pub and restaurants
    Artsplace Trust, Chisenhale Studios
14. Prospect of Whitby pub
15. The Dome (beyond Greenwich)

NORTH LONDON ARTS MAP 4

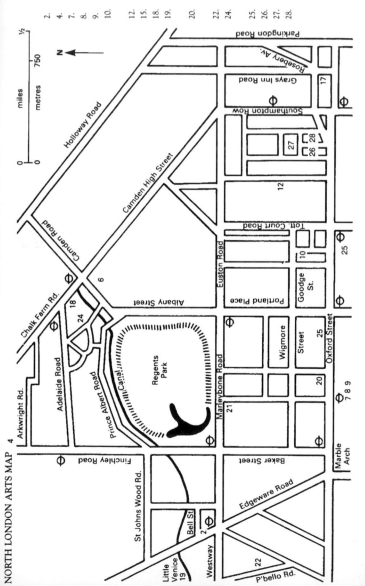

2. Lisson Gallery
4. Camden Arts Centre
7. Anthony Reynolds
8. Annely Juda
9. Anthony D'Offay Gallery
10. Curwen Gallery
12. Rebecca Hossack Gallery
15. Architectural Assoc ation
18. Cockpit Theatre Gallery
19. Camden Lock Market
20. Little Venice (barge trips to Regens Park and Camden Lock)
    Barbara Hepworth sculpture (open air)
22. Portobello Road Market
24. London Film Makers Cooperative
    London Musicians Collective
25. Jason Rhodes gallery
26. Focus gallery
27. British museum
28. Austin Desmondfine art